PAN-AFRICANISM
AND EAST AFRICAN
INTEGRATION

Written under the auspices of
The Center for International Affairs
Harvard University

PAN-AFRICANISM AND EAST AFRICAN INTEGRATION

Joseph S. Nye, Jr.

HARVARD UNIVERSITY PRESS

Cambridge, Massachusetts

1967

This book of John
is for M.H.N.

PREFACE

One of the most interesting developments in international politics since the end of the Second World War has been the attempt to integrate the sovereign states of Europe into some form of larger unity. It is not surprising that both scholars and statesmen from other areas of the world have begun to make generalizations about regional integration based largely on the European experience.

Thus far we have too few cases of regional integration to develop a satisfactory comparative study. We are not sure how the process of becoming more interdependent in social and economic affairs relates to unification, the process of forming a larger political union. We do not know whether there is enough similarity between regional integration among industrial states and among developing countries to allow us to explain the process in both contexts with the same theory. For example, current theory regarding European integration assigns ideology a minimal role. Yet most Africans who are interested in regional integration of their continent are committed to Pan-Africanism, an ideology of unity.

This book is not about Pan-Africanism in the sense that it is concerned with its lengthy history or varying content in different parts of Africa. It is rather an attempt to evaluate the impact of a system of ideas that East Africans call Pan-Africanism upon a particular case of integration and attempted unification. Can we understand regional integration in Africa on the basis of our "European theories," or must we adapt those theories to take ideological rhetoric into account?

Preface

East Africa—the formerly British and now independent countries of Tanzania, Uganda, and Kenya—was a perfect place to study the problems of African regional integration in 1963. Vast in size—the area between the great lakes and the Indian Ocean is equivalent to Western Europe, or to the United States east of the Mississippi—the East African states nonetheless came to independence with more social, political and economic integration among them than did any of the other new states in Africa. Moreover, the political leaders of the three countries all expressed a commitment to Pan-Africanism. The attempt of these leaders to form a federation in 1963—unsuccessful, as it turned out—provided a rare opportunity to study the interplay of Pan-Africanism with political and economic factors in African integration. Early in 1964 a coup on the small islands of Zanzibar off the Tanganyika coast, was followed by mutinies in the armies of the three East African countries. But by 1964 the attempt to create an East African federation had already clearly failed.

The conclusions to be drawn from a single case with respect to African integration must of necessity be limited, as we shall see in the final chapter. Nonetheless, since that case represents a failure of Pan-Africanist leaders working under the relatively favorable conditions of 1963, it is of considerable importance to anyone interested in problems of African integration. Moreover, both as a case study and as a qualification of the existing "European" theory, the East African failure to federate in 1963 is important for anyone interested in comparative problems of regional integration.

My main concern is with the effect of ideology upon integration among states, and I have focused on the period between mid-1960 and January 1964. The reader should not look here for details of constitutional development or local government in Kenya, Uganda, or Tanganyika; nor for material on Zanzibar except insofar as that country affected the federal negotiations of 1963.

Finally, I have not been entirely consistent on prefixes to African names. For "the Ganda" I retain the prefixes "Ba" (plural), "Mu" (singular), "Bu" (place), "Lu" (language), but have dropped the adjective "Ki". For most other groups —for example, the Luo, Kikuyu, and Sukuma—I have dropped prefixes.

A scholar builds on the ideas of others, and he tries to acknowledge this in his footnotes. But some people provide more than just ideas. I am deeply grateful to Colin Leys of Makerere College, who read the entire manuscript, for his stimulus, patience, friendship, and, of course, sense of humor. At Harvard, Rupert Emerson and Robert Rotberg also read the manuscript and were extremely generous and patient in their help and criticism. For reading parts of the manuscript as well as for helping in a number of other ways, I am indebted to Okot p'Bitek, Dharam Ghai, and Ali Mazrui of Makerere; Cherry Gertzel of University College, Nairobi; Roger Leys and John Nottingham of the College of Social Studies, Kikuyu; Carl Rosberg and Michael Lofchie of the University of California at Berkeley and Los Angeles, respectively; Stanley Hoffmann of Harvard; Donald Rothchild of Colby College; Jane Banfield of Loyola College; Clyde Sanger of the *Manchester Guardian;* Jo W. Saxe of the Organization for Economic Cooperation and Development; Werner Muller; B. L. Jacobs of the Uganda Government; Erisa Kironde of the Uganda Electricity Board; and and a number of others in East Africa who have asked to remain anonymous. I am grateful to the great number of people who gave their time in interviews and discussions.

Preface

I am grateful also to the staffs of the East African Institute of Social Research, Kampala, and Kivukoni College, Dar es Salaam, for their assistance; and to the Ford Foundation and the Harvard University Center for International Affairs for the funds which made this work possible. Of course all conclusions, opinions, and other statements are my responsibility and not necessarily those of the Ford Foundation or any other persons mentioned.

My greatest debt is to my wife, and I dedicate this book to her.

J. S. NYE, JR.

Cambridge, Massachusetts
February 1965

CONTENTS

MAPS

TABLES

PAN-AFRICANISM
AND EAST AFRICAN
INTEGRATION

ABBREVIATIONS

ASP	Afro-Shirazi Party (Zanzibar)
CLA	Central Legislative Assembly
EACSO	East African Common Services Organization
EAHC	East African High Commission
ECA	Economic Commission for Africa
EEC	European Economic Community
IBRD	International Bank for Reconstruction and Development
KADU	Kenya African Democratic Union
KANU	Kenya African National Union
KAU	Kenya African Union
KCA	Kikuyu Central Association
KFL	Kenya Federation of Labour
OAU	Organization of African Unity
PAFMECA	Pan-African Freedom Movement of East and Central Africa
PAFMECSA	Pan-African Freedom Movement of East, Central, and Southern Africa
TAA	Tanganyika African Association
TANU	Tanganyika African National Union
TFL	Tanganyika Federation of Labour
TRAU	Tanganyika Railway African Union
TUC	Trade Union Council (Uganda)
UAM	*Union Africaine et Malgache*
UNC	Uganda National Congress
UPC	Uganda People's Congress
UPU	Uganda People's Union
ZNP	Zanzibar Nationalist Party
ZNPP	Zanzibar and Pemba People's Party

Part One

PAN-AFRICANISM

Africa. (East Africa is shown in bold outline.)

I

Nationalism, Pan-Africanism,

and Integration

It appears to be the tendency of all people in the world to try to come together. In the past this has been because of danger. Now common markets are used as a second best form of achieving unity. We must not miss our chance.

A Tanganyika Cabinet Minister,
February, 1963

Uhuru na umoja—freedom and unity! is a popular slogan in East Africa. There, as in much of modern Africa, most politically minded people profess belief in Pan-Africanism, an ideology of integration.

"Poppycock," say some observers, and they predict the failure of all efforts toward greater unity. Others, particularly participants, predict unity because of the ideology. In the words of a prominent politician: "The political philosophies of the three ruling parties [in Kenya, Tanganyika, and Uganda] are identical and it is for this reason that, when the time comes, we shall gladly surrender our territorial sovereignty . . ."[1] Both views are too simple, as East Africa's experience in 1963 helps to show.

On June 5, 1963, the President of Tanganyika and the Prime Ministers of Kenya and Uganda announced their intention of forming a federation by the end of that year. In their words, "our meeting today is motivated by the spirit of Pan-Africanism . . . We believe that the East African Federation can be a practical step towards the goal of Pan-African unity."[2]

They failed in their stated intention. "It was," said President Nyerere of Tanganyika, "the biggest disappointment of the year."[3] Even if a federation is some day formed, years must pass before its success can be judged. In West Africa the Mali Federation, which was important "because it gave tangible expression to the Pan-African idealism that has such compelling attraction for the younger generation of African intellectuals and political leaders," lasted only a few months and left relations between its members worse than if nothing had happened.[4]

Unity is a short word for a long process. For more than sixty years, long before Pan-Africanism became a force on the African continent, various men with varying motives tried to shape a single political unit from that part of Africa between the great lakes, Indian Ocean, and Ethiopian desert —an area equal in size to Western Europe. These early efforts are important, but they will not concern us here except insofar as they set the stage for the nationalist actors. Our concern will be to determine the importance of the Pan-Africanist dialogue. Was it superfluous rhetoric or an integral part of the action? And what does this mean for our theories about how states integrate?

It is difficult to study the role of ideas or ideology within a short period. Modern political analysis tends to leave out time, and seeks to chart empirical reality at a given moment. Only with the longer time span of the historian is the role of ideas easily, perhaps too easily, described.[5] In the case of success, ideas will have been sufficient, in the case of failure, insufficient, to bring about change. But this tells us very little. It says nothing of how ideas and interests interact in successful or unsuccessful attempts to integrate states.

Moreover, both politicians and theorists are busy forming generalizations without waiting for the verdict of history. Because the actual relationship of ideas and interest is complex, these theories often place too much or too little emphasis on ideology. This inadequacy of existing theory justifies a description of an integration process before documents are accessible or perspective is possible.

Sincerity is another problem in trying to appraise the role of ideas in relations between states. Since Marx and Freud, there has been a tendency to see ideology as mere rationalization of prior conscious or unconscious interests. This shifts the focus of study from the content of ideas to their origin—away from their creative impact. Some observers argue that Pan-Africanism is merely the symptom of a racial inferiority complex. The more sophisticated leaders do not really believe in Pan-Africanism, say the skeptics, they just use it.

But what is important is that Pan-Africanism *is used,* not the motives for its use. One must beware of too lightly attributing insincere motives. The motives of people who make political decisions are at least as complex as our own; every man blends interest and ideal. Rarely does one find a case in international politics where clear and weighty interest has been sacrificed for an ideal. But in cases where the scales of interest are more nearly balanced, ideas play a subtle part that renders inadequate interpretations of motive that are based solely on interest. This, as we shall see, was the case in East Africa in 1963.

AFRICAN NATIONALISM AND PAN-AFRICANISM

Few people doubt the importance of nationalism in the history of international relations. If anything, "forces of nationalism" has become too facile an explanation, disguising rather than distinguishing the variety of factors involved. This is especially true of Africa. Strictly speaking, nationalism in the sense that it was known in Europe in the last century scarcely exists in Africa.[6]

One way in which we use the word "nation" is roughly synonymous with "community." Benjamin Disraeli spoke of the two nations, rich and poor, in Britain of the last century. More recently a New York State Social Welfare Board endorsed a program on the grounds that "we cannot tolerate the development of a separate nation of the poor, unskilled, the jobless, living within another nation of the well-off, the trained and employed."[7] Community is the vital condition of political life in which men accept mutual obligation and interest. In contrast to "society," which involves arrangements for filling specific needs and is open to all on a basis of achievement, "community" is characterized as "particular" (only some are members), "ascriptive" (I am a member because of who I am, not what I have done), and "diffuse" (it fills a wide variety of needs). Where political community exists, men will obey without coercion; sometimes even die for the group.

During the early days of nation-building in Europe, community and legitimacy were based mainly on religion and dynasty.[8] After the disruption of these principles by the Reformation and French Revolution, men searched for something else on which to build community. It came to be assumed that there was some natural community called the "nation," and gradually, in the post-Napoleonic period, the

6

nation became the only form of community which could legitimize the state. Where states did not conform to it, the nation was supposed to reconstruct the state. In other words, the nation-state became the superior form of community, the terminal focus of loyalty.

This history has left us with another common meaning for "nation" which is based on an ideal of a single people in a well-defined territory, speaking the same language, acknowledging a distinctive culture, and with long-shared historical experience.[9] In this classic sense of nationalism, the nation makes (and justifies) the state. Ireland, Italy, and Germany are the prominent examples. Nationalism means an existing popular sentiment that defines and legitimizes boundaries.

In this sense nationalism does not exist in Africa. Nor were its assumptions of a natural form of community realistic even in Europe. In the post-World War I period, the anarchy in the classic definition of nationalism and its normative corollary, national self-determination, became apparent. People began to realize what a study of the medieval formation of France or a careful appraisal of Bismark's Germany might have told them earlier; that power and community are intertwined, that there is no "natural" form of community, and that power considerations set the limits to the process of self-determination.[10]

Nationalism became a hollow shell, but a useful one. Most descriptive content vanished from the concept of nation as it was asserted and applied more widely, but this did not detract from its normative value. It became primarily a strategic concept used by elites to gain power. Whether the elites were ruling dynasties, threatened middle classes, East European nobles, or educated Africans, nationalism helped to generalize their particular interests and gain them wider acceptance; it allowed them to use concepts of legitimacy which had become an accepted part of world history; and permitted them to wield power more easily by asserting that a community and its obligations existed.

In Africa, European states had formed sub-states with an apparatus of power—police, armies, broadcasting stations, budgets, and civil services. (Colonies were more obviously sub-states in British practice than in French.) Less intentionally, Europeans had also created a disadvantaged and humiliated elite of educated Africans who asserted the existence of a nation in order to use prevailing international concepts of legitimacy to seize the sub-state. The African elites were able to do this before they had gone very far in creating a feeling of community. Once in control of the state, they began to use it to create a nation that would make their exercise of power more efficient.

This is not to deny that there were proto-nationalist feelings, sometimes quite widespread among the populace— what Lord Hailey writing in 1956 referred to as "Africanism." Thomas Hodgkin has ably described the role of various tribal and welfare associations, separatist churches, prophetic movements, and labor unions in preparing the way for nation states.[11] Nor was African nationalism unique in involving a number of strands. Yet it seems important to lift the label of nationalism and distinguish the various things hiding under it: a sense of loyalty or patriotism to some group; an anti-feeling, or xenophobia; a feeling of cultural unity; a movement toward statehood in the international state system; and the assertion of the uniqueness or superiority of a given national community. Because of the importance of international power considerations in determining which nations are successfully asserted, it seems best to use the terms "anticolonialism" and "culturalism" for most of the strands in the bundle and to reserve "nationalism" for movement toward statehood.

In Africa, as elsewhere, control of the state which makes the nation depended partly on acceptance by the international state system. Such acceptance often depended on how much pressure a group could put on the system. For instance, in 1960 Buganda, the central kingdom in Uganda, was rebuffed in its efforts to achieve recognition as a state, while Cyprus, with less than a third of Buganda's population and less internal homogeneity, but with an island suitable for guerilla harassment, was accepted as part of the system. Once it had failed, the nationalism of Buganda became stigmatized as tribalism. Similarly, because the Yoruba people are part of a larger recognized state, Nigeria, their feelings of ethnicity are labeled tribalism, although there are ten times as many Yoruba as there are inhabitants, for example, of the independent state of Gabon.

In Africa, tribe and race constituted two primary forces for "natural community." The choice between them—between tribalism and Pan-Africanism—was not made by any popular plebiscite, but by the educated elite, who have generally opted for Pan-Africanism because of their views about size and power in world politics. They believe that tribal nations would be divided and ruled from outside, whereas a Pan-African nation would mean world power and dignity. According to President Julius Nyerere of Tanzania:

> It was . . . the tribe to which a man felt traditional loyalty, not the nation. Yet once the tribal unit has been rejected as not being sensible in Africa, then there can be no stopping short of Africa itself as the political grouping. For what else is there? "Nations" in any real sense of the word do not at present exist in Africa.[12]

But because power was built on individual colonies, the nationalists had to focus on their separate states. Thus most of them call themselves "Pan-African nationalists." This caused no problems (indeed it helped) in the struggle for control of the colonies. After independence, however, as we shall see, some of the incipient conflicts in "Pan-African nationalism" began to unfold.

Pan-Africanism is more than just a sentiment of nationalism. Nonetheless, it represents a weaker sense of community than tribe, and because its more enlightened proponents refuse to identify it entirely by race, it is frequently weaker even than new feelings of loyalty to the nation-state. To engender commitment, Pan-Africanists must rely on a structure of ideas and a view of the world rather than rest on sentiment alone.

If Pan-Africanism is the same thing as nationalism, then the attempted unification of East Africa in 1963 was simply another case of nationalism. But there was more to it than this. The three countries—Kenya, Tanganyika, and Uganda —had already developed a certain territorial identity. The struggles for independence were waged within the separate power frameworks of each territory. Tanganyika had had nearly two years of sovereignty and Uganda nearly one before the federation issue came to a head. Both had attempted to build a nation in those intervals. For Tanganyika, with less to gain economically and something to lose politically, it is questionable whether mere sentiment unsupported by related propositions would have been sufficient to account for its leaders' actions.

Pan-Africanism differs from nationalism by incorporating more propositions about the world.[13] The difference, of course, is one of degree. All nationalisms involve a few propositions, and some of them, like the integral nationalism of Charles Maurras and Maurice Barrès in France at the turn of the century, were rudimentary ideologies.

Nationalism, Pan-Africanism, and Integration

Pan-Africanism, despite a number of similarities, involves more ideas than most "pan" movements have had. Pan-Arabism or Pan-Germanism resembled nationalist movements and could rely more on the sentiments of ethnically and linguistically homogeneous populations. Pan-Africanism has been aptly compared with Pan-Slavism in its concern for political unity based on racial affinity rather than racial identity; in its desire for independence from cultural imitation; and in its concern with size. But Pan-Africanism has so far escaped three problems that confronted Pan-Slavism: no independent African state holds the disproportionate place that Russia did in the Pan-Slav movement; the Pan-African movement commands far greater and wider organizational support; and Pan-Africanism involves a more functional set of ideas.[14]

Finally, Pan-Africanism is something like, but something more than, "modernizing nationalism"—the name given to a body of ideas that seem to be common to a large number of the intellectuals who control governments in underdeveloped countries.[15] Several of these ideas—socialism, belief in neocolonialism, preference for strong government with single or dominant parties, faith in industrialization, and a moralistic view of world politics—were also part of Pan-Africanism in 1963. Others, like a Leninist theory of imperialism, and an elitist concept of democracy, were not. But most important, Pan-Africanism was concerned with forming larger states. Most Pan-Africanists tended to argue that the bigger the scope of African union, the better the prospects of achieving "real" economic independence, a voice in world affairs, and "dignity."

Africa is not alone in its unification movement. Such movements are one of the outstanding characteristics of current world politics. Among Pan-Africanists, at least, this reflects less a disillusionment with the nation-state which some people see in postwar Europe, than a popular belief that only large states can carry out their essential functions efficiently. In the face of modern military technology, small states seem ill-equipped to cope with the essential function of defense. One of the goals of Pan-Africanists is to equip themselves more effectively to defend their independence.

A second major function of the state is the provision of welfare for a restricted group of people, and the Pan-Africanists are convinced that larger states do this better. Many economists, however, would deny that there is an optimal size of state. Large populations and markets make it possible to establish a greater number of industries, but economic advantages may easily be offset by political disadvantages. Cohesive small states may be better at providing welfare than large states incorporating antagonistic populations.[16] For this reason it is impossible to argue about the advantages of enlargement without relating them to integration or creation of a sense of community. Reallocation of wealth in French West Africa, in the absence of a sense of community, left a deep sense of grievance in the Ivory Coast and eventually helped cause the breakup of French West Africa.[17] Nonetheless, Pan-Africanists stress the dangers of "Balkanization," with its connotations of poverty and dependence, never the possibilities of "Scandinavianization," with its implied prosperity and independence.

Closely related to a sense of community is a third major function of the state, the provision of a source of identification, of grandeur, of pooled self-esteem. This provides another motive for enlargement when it is accompanied by a sense of community which allows members to identify themselves with the larger unit. In the broad sense the major goals were not a matter of dispute among Pan-Africanists. The real area of dispute, at the time of the federal negotiations in East Africa, was over means.

When we consider the obstacles to African unity it is not surprising that there are disputes over the way in which that unity is to be achieved. A continent of eleven and a half million square miles, Africa is nearly four times the size of the continental United States. Its 250 million or more people speak more than a thousand African, and seven foreign, languages. Not one power, but seven colonized Africa. The modern economies and communications superimposed by the colonial powers incline African countries not toward each other, but toward the former colonial powers. At the time of the 1963 Addis Ababa conference—which founded the Organization of African Unity (OAU)—there were thirty-three independent African states with perhaps half again as many more to come. When these states were departing from their heritage of separate colonial institutions, they were replacing them with single parties and heroic leaders. One hero held in common among several states makes unification easier, but too many heroes spoil the broth.

Faced with the enormity of the task of uniting Africa, Pan-Africanists tend to divide on two concepts—functionalism and regionalism. Functionalism is sometimes called "horizontal slicing of sovereignty." It shifts attention away from "vertical divisions of human society which are symbolized by the sovereignty of states, toward the various strata of social needs cutting across national dividing lines."[18]

The African debate on functionalism vs. federalism echoes an earlier one in Europe. In 1949 some advocates of European unity insisted on "forming a federation before the post-war momentum had been lost—even if the federation should have very limited powers," while others wished to provide "institutions one by one as the problems to be solved might dictate."[19]

In Africa, Ghana's President Kwame Nkrumah, though he at times resorted to functionalist devices, has been the strongest proponent of the outright federalist approach. Nkrumah fears that if newly independent African states do not sacrifice their sovereignty while it is new, they will grow increasingly reluctant to do so. Though for diplomatic reasons he speaks of preserving state sovereignty, in 1963 he urged the African summit conference to establish one government with "overall economic planning on a continental basis; unified military and defense strategy; and unified foreign policy and diplomacy."[20] Anything less, he feared, would allow outside powers to play on African weakness and keep the continent divided. One effect of his beliefs was that Ghana, upon gaining independence in 1957, severed her cooperative ties with the rest of British West Africa—a policy that Tanganyikan leaders regarded as mistaken when faced with a similar decision four years later.[21]

Other African leaders, such as President Leopold Senghor of Senegal, President Nnamdi Azikiwe of Nigeria, and Emperor Haile Selassie of Ethiopia, have urged a functional approach to unity. In the Emperor's words, "the foundations must be laid first." According to Azikiwe, "economic integration . . . is destined to crystallize a spirit of oneness and thus quicken the pace towards political integration."[22]

In practice, only two successful instances of functional cooperation between states existed in Africa in 1963—the East African Common Services Organization (EACSO), and the *Union Africaine et Malgache* (UAM).[23] The achievements of the UAM formed by twelve former French states, were modest. A combination of internal dissension and external pressure brought about its dissolution and its replacement by an even more limited *Union africaine et malgache de cooperation economique* in 1964. Functional cooperation in East Africa has been impressive, as we shall see in Chapter V. Nonetheless, it represented a colonial legacy which was not entirely secure after independence.

Closely related to the problem of functionalism was the dispute over regionalism. At one time there was no such dispute. George Padmore, author of a classic work on Pan-Africanism, urged regionalism as the path to unity; and the first All Africa Peoples' Conference which met in Accra in 1958 planned to build Africa through five regional units—Northern, Western, Eastern, Central and Southern.[24] Nkrumah's first efforts, such as the Ghana-Guinea Union of 1958, which was expanded to include Mali and renamed the Union of African States in 1961, were regional, even if they were designed (in Nkrumah's words) to "form the nucleus of the United States of Africa."

But the formation of the UAM (sometimes also called the Brazzaville Group), led to the creation of the "Casablanca Bloc" of more radical states (Morocco, which joined for special reasons was an exception) "convinced that political unity should come first."[25] This in turn led to creation of the "Monrovia Bloc." Meanwhile, in East and Central Africa, the Pan-African Freedom Movement of East and Central Africa (Pafmeca) was expanding to include new areas. In February 1962 a Ghanaian observer at the Pafmeca conference in Addis Ababa expressed his concern over the growth of regionalism. By the time of the African Summit

Conference in May 1963, a large number of African leaders, in addition to Nkrumah, were concerned about the development of regional blocs. As a result, the Casablanca and Monrovia blocs were declared dissolved, and after the conference Julius Nyerere announced the impending termination of Pafmeca.

The question of what, if anything, was a legitimate regional grouping was left unresolved. Since functional cooperation is more easily established at the regional level, attitudes on the two questions tended to be parallel. Nonetheless, the coincidence was not complete. Even functionalist-oriented Nigeria joined Guinea in attacking the UAM at the meeting of the foreign ministers of the Organization of African Unity in Dakar in August 1963, and UAM members disagreed among themselves about the legitimacy of their organization.[26]

Nkrumah went further and opposed the formation not only of blocs, but also of regional federations in Africa. While most East Africans argued that their proposed federation was different, since it meant surrender of sovereignty to a larger unit and thus set a good example for African unity, Ghana opposed the federation as divisive. *The Spark,* a publication of the Ghana Government's Bureau of African Affairs, labeled East African federation a "regional grouping which is not in accord with the Addis Ababa concept of one Africa." In Nkrumah's words, "Regional federations are a form of balkanization on a grand scale . . . Whereas it may be inexpedient geographically and otherwise for Ghana to join an East African Federation, there would be no difficulty for Tanganyika, let us say, joining a political union of Africa."[27]

The basis of the Ghanaian position was a fear that larger regional states might feel sufficiently strong to go it alone and forget about African unity. Only if all states remained weak was there hope that they would realize their plight and come together once and for all, much as the American colonies had done in 1787. Cynics might say that Nkrumah's sole concern was his inability to join and thus dominate an East African federation. Whatever the truth of that accusation, there was more to the Ghanaian position than that alone. A political scientist has suggested that there is a self-limiting tendency in the growth of states whose populations are rapidly increasing their participation in political and social life.[28] If this is true, then Nkrumah's opposition to federations was not dictated entirely by self-interest.

In any case, most East Africans (the exceptions will become clear below) were convinced that a regional and functional approach was correct. By this means, Kenya's Minister for Justice and Constitutional Affairs, Tom Mboya, expected to see a United States of Africa in his lifetime. "Look how fast things move," he said, "but we must have cooperation first before a United States of Africa is possible. We must work together in areas and federations first. I feel that to encourage regional cooperation first is bound to lead to wider cooperation and politics."[29]

THEORIES OF INTEGRATION

How do you integrate a number of states? For much of man's history, force was the answer. More recently, Europe has captured the imagination with new methods of integration. Journalists, theorists, and African leaders have all generalized from the European experience. Jean Monnet, President of the Action Committee for a United States of Europe, argues that Europe's "new institutional method" is "permanently modifying relations between nations and men."[30] But the heavy coat of European theory needs alteration before it can be worn in African climates.

By doing some injustice to the complexity of various writers, we can abstract a "European theory" that goes something like this: Economic agreements and customs unions of various kinds increase trade and transactions so much that the increased flows across borders create problems which are difficult to solve by separate state machinery. A supranational bureaucracy is created to deal with these problems. Industrial groups (particularly labor and business) organize on a supranational level to put pressure on the new bureaucracy, which itself acts as a pressure group for further integration. Gradually, loyalties follow economic interests and become focused on the new center, and a new political union comes into existence.

Time, the theory suggests, is on the side of this gradual process of integration. "Because the modern 'industrial-political' actor fears that his way of life cannot be safeguarded without structural adaptations, he turns to integration . . ." Ideology, including the weak sentiment of "Europeanism," is unimportant except as a background condition.[31] The politics of supranational integration are the politics of interest, of "upgrading the common interest." They occur in a "post-ideological" period and reflect the style of industrial bargaining.[32] As Dr. Hallstein, President of the EEC Commission, described the process: "The ground on which we work is common sense rather than emotion, our strength reasoned conviction rather than myths, our tactic discussion rather than the sway of passion." Or, in the words of two British writers: "The steady and irreversible progress of economic integration will go on linking the destinies of the member countries more and more closely."[33]

18

Nationalism, Pan-Africanism, and Integration

Whether this theory is adequate to explain the complexities of the European integration that it is based on is a good question. An unresolved problem is how the masses are brought into what has been a group- and elite-centered process.[34] Related to this is the question of final goals. Is Europe seeking to create a larger nation-state into which individuals will pool their self-esteem, or is it creating something new? Are supranational institutions a new and stable form of government? Does the theory pay sufficient attention to the role of ideas, considering the Catholic background of many of its proponents and the considerable impact that General de Gaulle has had on it? Whatever the judgment, our purpose here is to point out the difficulties in applying the theory to East Africa. To be fair, some theorists are fully aware of the limitations.[35] Others, including some Africans leaders, are not.

Among the propositions which seemed questionable in the East African situation is the idea that increased transactions across borders create new institutions to cope with them.[36] Monnet, for instance, sees the disequilibrium created by integration of one sector as an important force pushing the integration process forward. But this theory assumes a situation in which governments are able (and willing) to establish the new institutions. However, when problems of increased re-exports to the Congo overtaxed the East African customs administration in 1963, the governments prohibited such re-exports in the future.

Not only may there be this "spillback" instead of "spillover," but it is also not clear that the economy will provide the most favorable sector for spillover into increased integration. The East African governments were deeply dissatisfied with their underdeveloped economies and were in a great hurry to change them. In practice this involved government action most easily (though not most farsightedly) carried out at the national level—as we shall see in Chapter V. For the same reasons, the whole strategy of "gradualism" which, as one of its proponents admits, "serves best when the political structure itself is stable," assumes a patience and immunity from pressures from below which did not exist in East Africa in 1963.[37]

Yet of all the qualifications which have to be made about the "European theory" with respect to Africa, the most important is the different role of interest groups in an industrial-pluralist European setting from that in the pre-industrial, partially unitarist setting in East Africa. Groups are a key part of the European theory. Along with the supranational institutions, they are the motors which drive the integration process forward. A writer in the London *Economist* once remarked that the success of the European Economic Community had been assumed "because the business community is so committed . . ."[38] In East Africa, also, the business community was committed to the East African common market, but no one would have dared predict the future of the market because of it. Another writer supports his belief that economic union, rather than military cooperation or tariff negotiations, is most likely to spill over into political union on the grounds that the latter two affect only a few groups like defense contractors or importers and exporters, while economic union "affects all societal groups— consumers, producers, management, labor, farmers, small business—and therefore tends to have extensive political repercussions."[39] But this conclusion is obviously based on the assumption that societal groups (rather than the government or the political elite, for example) are the critical factors in bringing about further integration. This was not the case in East Africa.

GROUP THEORY AND EAST AFRICA

Despite criticism and reservations, group theory remains a characteristic feature of American political analysis. It assumes that the dynamic element in the relationship between government and society comes from within the society. Yet in many underdeveloped countries governmental systems are foreign imports little related to their societies. Initiative tends to come from educated elites controlling this foreign machinery as much as, if not more than, from the needs in the society.[40] The African elite inherited an authoritarian structure which was democratized only partially and at a late date.

A second limitation of group analysis in East Africa in 1963 was the existence of a unitarist ideology. Unlike pluralist Western societies, groups in East Africa were left with the burden of proof of their own legitimacy. Since anything which appeared to disrupt unity was regarded with suspicion, a considerable restraint was placed upon their actions. Third, the existence of what we think of as pressure groups tends to be somewhat ephemeral in pre-industrial society. Poor agricultural economies do not generate the spectrum of interests which exists in Western society. Perhaps more important, such economies lack the middle-level managerial skills to organize what interests do exist. In such situations, political decision-makers are deprived of a source of information from which they derive their sense of direction. As a result, they have to rely more on their party or government bureaucracy and, where that is weak, on ideology, to fill in gaps in information.

This is not to say that groups did not exist in East Africa in 1963. Thousands of societies were registered in each country. But many were little more than a name, most were preindustrial, and few had much interest in integration. While it would be possible to analyze the politics of Tanganyika in terms of groups of a sort, it would be difficult to relate them to the integration process.

There were four strong "groups" in East Africa in 1963 other than those based upon tribe or tradition. They were racial, religious, business, and labor organizations. For example, Muslims in Tanganyika represented a group which had to be conciliated, but their legitimacy as a group was questioned when their pressure became too great. In the words of one Member of Parliament, people who persist in promoting religious dissension "should be shot." In October 1963 at least twenty speeches were made warning religious leaders not to mix in politics.[41] Actions matched words. As early as 1958 Nyerere expelled from the Tanganyika African National Union (Tanu) a Muslim leader who complained about Muslim representation. In 1963 several religious leaders were rusticated or deported.

In Uganda, Roman Catholics constituted the strongest religious group. The structure of the Democratic Party originally coincided to a considerable extent with the administration of Catholic mission schools. Yet this has hurt the party at the hustings. And in 1963, when Catholic parents acted as a group to try to limit government control over their schools, they were not successful.

Racial minority pressure groups, if they can be called that, were groups more by the fact of their presence than by organization. Certain influential Europeans and Asians had access to the African elite because of political contributions and may occasionally have put in quiet words for their communities. But their right to participate as groups in the political process was denied. Thus these two societal groups with important cross-territorial ties were denied effectiveness as a lobby for integration.

Most large businesses were staffed and owned mainly by non-Africans, and were strongly in favor of federation.[42] Yet their support did not have the importance that business support had in Europe where national industrial pressure groups united in representation at Brussels. There were a loosely structured Association of Chambers of Commerce and Industry of Eastern Africa, and an Association for the Promotion of Industry in East Africa, both located in Nairobi where the Common Services Organization had its headquarters. But the interaction of bureaucracy and pressure group did not provide an engine for integration, partly because the bureaucracy had few executive powers, and partly because open pressure politics were of questionable legitimacy.

For years these business associations lobbied unsuccessfully for a common commercial legislation for East Africa. In 1961 an important African politician successfully pleaded with the Association of Chambers of Commerce to shelve a resolution supporting federation because their advocacy might prove a hindrance.[43] Power, of course, remained with the separate territories—as indicated by the decentralization of the Association of Chambers of Commerce in 1963. Yet even within territories, Chamber officers were wary of passing resolutions concerning interterritorial affairs.[44]

African traders were more effective at exerting pressure, but rather as a racial group than as business per se. The governments of the three countries responded in a number of ways to their demands for assistance in their competition with Asian retailers. But small traders had little effective organization. In 1960 the Tanganyika African Traders Union and its counterparts in Kenya and Uganda announced plans for an interterritorial grouping.[45] Nothing came of it.

Trade unions were the other major industrial organization. In Tanganyika where the Federation of Labor (TFL) had

200,000 members in 1961 and in Kenya where the Federation of Labor (KFL) represented 165,000 workers (but not in Uganda where a weaker Trade Union Congress [TUC] had only 43,000 members), unions were the only interest groups with organization, funds, and membership of the right color to effectively challenge the government. Yet they did not.

Unions were able to ensure passage of minimum wage laws in all three countries, but in Tanganyika they were unable to maintain their independence of government control. In Kenya, when a number of union leaders ran for election to Parliament in 1963, they were overwhelmingly defeated. Indeed, the government was able to get "its man" elected Secretary-General of the KFL. In Uganda the TUC successfully staved off a challenge by a government-supported rival organization, but most of the labor leaders' energies were concentrated on maintaining their independence rather than putting pressure on the government for federation.

On several occasions representatives of the three labor movements met in efforts to establish an East African labor organization. Existing legislation on registration made the task difficult but the unions put little pressure on their governments to remove the legislation. As one union leader stated the problem: "If the governments cannot agree on federation, what will happen to us if we seem to be pushing for it?" Or, in the words of another, "Federation is a good thing, but it is a matter for governments to decide on."[46]

Other groups, such as university students, passed resolutions in favor of federation. It was hard to find any significant group (other than tribal) which was opposed.[47] Yet the political leaders failed to achieve their avowed intention of federation in 1963. It is necessary to look for other explanations of that failure.

Nationalism, Pan-Africanism, and Integration

THE ROLE OF IDEOLOGY AND THE ELITE

To study integration in areas like East Africa, less attention should be paid to groups, or to supranational bureaucracy, or to the growth of trade than would be necessary in an industrial setting. On the other hand, more attention should be given to ideology. In "European theory," groups are one of the independent variables, or moving forces, and ideology a controlled variable, or background factor. In East Africa the roles should be reversed; ideology is not everything, and groups nothing, but one must nevertheless shift his focus of attention.

This is not to contrast supposed European rationality with African irrationality. Many foreigners shake their heads in dismay at the dominance of politics over economics in new African states. Two things must be said about this: first, it is simply not true that all African leaders are unaware of economics. Among the top decision-makers in all three East African countries in 1963 were a number trained in economics and a larger number aware of the economic costs of their policies. Second, and more fundamentally, paying primary attention to economic interests when making decisions makes sense only when the ideological and political framework within which interests interact can be taken for granted. When this framework cannot be taken for granted, politics is a necessary first consideration. Most African states are still involved in determining—and changing—the structure within which interests work.

Ideology is an interdependent set of value- or action-oriented ideas. It is not just a shared set of values or a vague nationalist sentiment of solidarity. The value and sentiment part is important, and sometimes leads to sacrifice, but the ideas are equally important, for they determine how the world appears to the people making decisions. For instance, an outsider—say an anthropologist—might see the structures of East African tribes as very different from one another; the Pan-Africanist might see only their similarities. The same can be said about differences in inherited colonial constitutions, which the outsider might argue made integration difficult. From inside the ideology, however, these differences might appear insignificant.

We shall explore these problems of ideology at greater length in the next chapter. One more thing, however, must be said at the outset. We cannot assume that ideology is always favorable to integration; it may exacerbate divisions by accentuating differences. Indeed, at times this was its role in East Africa. The effects of ideology were sometimes ambiguous but one had to pay attention to them nonetheless.

As important as ideology is the structure of political power. As Stanley Hoffmann points out about the "European theory," "too 'deep' an explanation may explain nothing at all; to put the spotlight on values and social structure may be necessary, but to put it on the specialized political sector (who governs?) may well be sufficient."[48]

In East Africa one must focus on the political elites which control the state machinery and the one political institution which they created—the major nationalist party in each country.

There have been attempts to apply sampling techniques to East Africa, but the results have been somewhat questionable. In 1960 the Market Research Company of East Africa began a series of polls on (among other things) federation. When they used an inadequate sample which was supposedly representative of the whole population they discovered that the federation was favored by 84 per cent of

Africans in Tanganyika, 82 per cent in Kenya, and 71 per cent in Uganda. Later, when they polled "thought leaders" (defined as those earning more than 500 shillings a month), the figures came out 93 per cent for Tanganyika, 92 per cent for Kenya, and only 36 per cent for Uganda. This second set of figures corresponds more closely with a poll of 150 students in 1963, and with a poll of 200 Ugandans in the early 1950's.[49] Local party officials and anthropologists confirm that the level of knowledge of federation among the majority of the population (still mainly engaged in subsistence agriculture) is very slight. In the words of one anthropologist (whose view is corroborated by others working in different areas):

> I can say without any reservation at all that the very existence of anything deserving the name of "public opinion" on the issue of federation is extremely doubtful in rural areas. There are no "trends" and there is no awareness of the issue below the "elite" level, whether that is judged by social position or by education (amounting to about the same thing.[50]

Most African leaders admit this. According to a Tanganyikan cabinet minister, "The man in the field knows about growing coffee, not federation. But we have sold him on the idea from the political platform and there is no other leadership."[51] In this sense it might be possible to obtain a widespread favorable response to a questionnaire about federation. African political rallies are educational affairs in which participation by the audience in the form of repeating attitudes may take up almost a quarter of the time of the rally.[52] Thus the common man (or the man common enough to have gone to mass political rallies) may have learned that federation is a good thing, but essentially he is a passive factor.

27

Passive factors cannot be ignored however. Politics is about people and it is important to describe the relationship between the elite and the masses. Another important passive, or background, feature is the social integration of East Africa. Karl Deutsch's important contribution to the study of integration has been to remind theorists that political events do not occur in a vacuum. We will inspect briefly the growth and problems of "transnational" society in Chapter III. In Chapter IV we will study the political background and the important institution, the party, with which the elite worked. In Chapter V, we will look at the economic forces which were important in creating change—though the direction of the change was not necessarily in the direction of integration.

But primarily we will focus on the elites and their ideology. In Chapter II we will inspect the ideology, and in Chapters VI and VII, once the setting has been filled in, we will study the complex way in which ideology interacted with the interests of the elite in particular decisions. These data are based on interviews with 115 people and informal conversations with many others. The interviews included at least two thirds of the cabinet of each country, focusing on those ministers who held important positions in the party. Lesser party officials, civil servants, and members of Parliament were also included. The interviews were designed to seek information as well as to probe attitudes. One difficulty is that these results cannot be quantified. But the search for numbers must take second place to the search for significance. In 1963, as the new African elite tried to accomplish what others had failed to achieve before in East Africa, the most significant new factor, for better or worse, was the ideology of Pan-Africanism.

II

Pan-Africanism in East Africa

> Whether they discuss things in an explicitly Pan-Africanist vocabulary or not depends on the context. But their Pan-Africanism is explicit, not just an unspoken assumption—very explicit.
>
> (A non-African cabinet member describing his colleagues)

East Africa's leaders, according to some critics, are pragmatic to a fault. How then could they have an ideology? In part, the answer depends on how the term is used. Ideology is not, unfortunately, a neat concept with a single meaning. It is sometimes used to stigmatize, sometimes to define. Even when we limit ourselves to the latter use, we find two main types of definition—by function and by structure. The functional definition of ideology—an example is Marx's view of ideology as a "superstructure" of thought which reflects and protects underlying economic interests —tends to prejudge analysis of the causal effect of an ideology and to shift the focus of interest away from ideas to their social origins.[1]

Here we will define ideology in terms of the structure of the thought. Ideology is a set of value-related beliefs which are at least partly systematized. The three necessary components of an ideology are beliefs, values, and system (interdependence). Values account for action orientation and commitment associated with ideology.[2] System gives the ideas resilience so that when facts are used to attack one part of the ideology, related beliefs support the part attacked. The ideas need not be logical or logically related, but they must hang together in the minds of those who believe them—as did the ideas of the East African leaders.

Whether there was an ideology in East Africa in 1963 can be more easily determined if we think of different types of value-related beliefs ranging along a spectrum from unsystematic to its opposite. We can think of the ideas of Pan-Africanism as somewhat more developed and systematized than those of nationalism, but much less systematized than those of Marxism or of a religion like Islam. We will call highly developed ideologies "specific," and those that are less developed "diffuse." The important point is that diffuse ideologies, or "world-views," can have as important an impact on the integration of states as specific ones. Neither type of ideology provides a detailed program for action; both predispose people to perceive interests and actions in certain ways.

Naturally, not every value-related set of ideas is important in causing events. This is where the functional aspect comes in. To be effective, an ideology must have the backing of powerful persons or groups. Many ideas are offered but fail to attract support. Pan-African ideas generated by Negro intellectuals of the Western Hemisphere date back to before the turn of the century, but it was not until after the independence of Ghana in 1957 and the convening of two conferences in Accra in 1958 that states and organizations rather than individual exiles became involved, and that Pan-African ideas became a significant social force.[3] This chapter is concerned with the extent to which Pan-Africanist ideas existed among, and what they meant to, the East African political elite in 1963.

Pan-Africanism in East Africa

Little was heard of Pan-Africanism in East Africa before 1958. Although Jomo Kenyatta was one of the organizers of the Manchester Pan-Africanist conference in 1945, and his resolution calling for complete independence of Kenya, Uganda, Tanganyika, Nyasaland, and Somaliland was reported in the East African press, he focused the attention of his colleagues primarily on Kenyan problems after he returned home in 1946.[4] James Gichuru, former president of the Kenya African Union and later Finance Minister in Kenya, has said that Pan-Africanism first appeared in East Africa while he himself was in detention, between 1955 and 1960. Tom Mboya, Minister for Economic Planning and Development in Kenya, has said that his feeling of African unity received its greatest impetus from the first All African Peoples' Conference (AAPC) in Accra in 1958 (of which he was elected chairman).

Roland Mwanjisi, a junior minister in Tanganyika who graduated from Makerere College in Uganda as recently as 1957, reported that there was little campus concern with Pan-Africanism at that time, and that he was "a nationalist at Makerere, but a Pan-Africanist after the first AAPC in 1958." President Julius Nyerere of Tanganyika became interested in Pan-Africanism during the process of building his political party in the middle 1950's.[5] Indeed, African unity as such did not figure prominently in the first meeting of the Pan-African Freedom Movement of East and Central Africa in September 1958.

Within four years, however, Pan-Africanism had become sufficiently important in East Africa that a large majority of students, civil servants, and politicians paid at least lip service to it. In 1962, when African students at Makerere

College were polled, two thirds considered themselves Pan-Africanists, a quarter did not, and the remainder had no opinion. Students from the kingdom of Buganda were the significant deviants with only two fifths professing to be Pan-Africanists. Fourteen per cent of all the students felt they owed their first loyalty to "Africa," only five per cent to East Africa, ten per cent to their group or tribe, and ten per cent were equally divided in their loyalties. The rest—slightly over half—felt their first loyalty to their country. About the meaning of Pan-Africanism, the students agreed less, and the rate of abstentions rose.[6]

The most significant opinions about Pan-Africanism were, of course, those of the cabinet and top party members who actually made the decisions affecting unification. As one non-Pan-Africanist Makerere student said, "Pan-Africanism will be an important point in the creation of this federation for the simple reason that the prime movers of [the federation] at present are Pan-Africanist to the core."

What were these leaders like? Of the seventeen Tanganyika cabinet ministers in mid-1963, fifteen were African, one Asian and one European. In age, six were in their early forties, six in their late thirties, and four between thirty and thirty-five. All the most populous tribes and all regions were represented, but only one tribe had more than one representative. In religion, eleven were Christian, five Moslem. Five were sons of farmers, three of chiefs, or headmen, three of clergymen, two of teachers, and two of businessmen or traders. In their previous occupations, four had been teachers, four local or central government employees, three came from cooperative movements and two from labor; two were farmers and one a businessman. Six cabinet members had bachelors' degrees, five of them from overseas. Three had attended a cooperative college, one had a theological degree, and six had only secondary school (Tabora), and five had been to Makerere.

Of sixteen Kenya cabinet ministers in mid-1963, fifteen were Africans and one a European. They included a number of considerably older members than in Tanganyika or Uganda. Six were over fifty, three in their forties, five in their late thirties and two were between thirty and thirty-five. Eight had been officeholders in KAU, the first real party in East Africa. Again, unlike Tanganyika (but like Uganda, where a disproportionately large and well-educated tribe exists), there were two predominant tribes in the Kenya cabinet. There were five Kikuyu members and four Luo. The six other Africans came from six tribes. By occupation, nine were teachers at one time or another; three came from the civil service, two had been farmers, one a doctor and one a trade unionist. Their level of education was somewhat higher than in Tanganyika. Only three members had no education beyond secondary, and of seven with bachelor's degrees, three also had higher degrees. Nine had attended the same secondary school (Alliance High School) and five Makerere College.

The sixteen members of the Uganda cabinet were all Africans in June 1963. Five were Baganda, two, including the Prime Minister, were Langi (from the North) and the remaining nine represented different tribes. One member was over fifty, and seven were in their forties; seven were in their late thirties and one in his early thirties. Four had been teachers, and three were lawyers. Three came from business (two of them employees, one self-employed), three from cooperatives. One had been a veterinary officer, one a doctor, and one had been a Buganda government minister. Only three had no more than a secondary education. Of seven with bachelor's degrees, four had higher degrees. Ten cabinet members had been to Makerere and seven to the same secondary school (King's College, Budo).

Nearly all the Tanganyika cabinet members called themselves Pan-Africanists, although one or two may have meant little by it. A similar situation existed in Kenya. The Uganda cabinet was less thoroughly Pan-Africanist, although one Uganda cabinet minister claimed, "We are all Pan-Africanists." Nonetheless, one or two ministers refused the label upon questioning, and another minister (who said he was a Pan-Africanist) felt that only one third of the cabinet was *committed* to Pan-Africanism. The political ideas of this third were very similar to those of the Kenyans and Tanganyikans, and it is to these ideas that we now turn.

THE DOMINANT POLITICAL IDEAS IN EAST AFRICA[7]

East African leaders who called themselves Pan-Africanist shared at least ten major ideas and attitudes from which were derived a dozen or more corollaries. Some leaders disagreed with others on certain points and some saw connections between ideas where others did not, but there was a large enough consensus to allow the ideas to be set forth in a somewhat idealized form.

A View of History

The East Africans saw history as relative, not as a predetermined pattern. Few disagreed with Julius Nyerere that "particular patterns or traditions grow up in different countries because of the historical circumstances during the period of growth."[8]

Two facts dominated the East African's view of history. Recent African history was a tale of oppression. "Foreign rule has played havoc for 60 years," said Prime Minister

Obote of Uganda. Similarly, Kenyatta lamented that "we have been trodden down for so long,"[9] and Nyerere saw Pan-Africanism growing out of African history because "we were all oppressed."

The second fact was that this alien oppression had been maintained by a policy of "divide and rule." The fault was with the small societies of traditional Africa which had been too easily set against each other by colonial rulers. Moreover, history might repeat itself. "In the first Scramble for Africa," wrote Nyerere, "one tribe was divided against another tribe to make the division of Africa easier . . . In the Second Scramble for Africa one nation is going to be divided against another nation to make it easier to control Africa . . ."[10]

Even on rare occasions when a Pan-Africanist like Uganda's Minister of State, Grace Ibingira, would admit that "rather than divide us, on the contrary, the British have united us! . . . the fault lies within ourselves," the point of the statement was to read the same conclusion from African history—the importance of unity.[11]

The Dominance of the Value of Unity

"Unity is strength" declares the Pafmeca motto, and according to the former Pafmeca Secretary, Mbiyu Koinange, "the common element in Pan-Africanism is the spirit of unity." "Without unity in Africa," said Uganda's Attorney-General, Godfrey Binaisa, "we will never be politically and economically free, but always at the mercy of outside powers."

So strong an emphasis on unity cast suspicion on anything which appeared to disrupt it, not only between states but within them. While interest groups in Western society can rely on pluralist theory for justification and protection, in East Africa groups had to contend with the belief that unity is strength. In the words of Milton Obote, "Unity is essential . . . the Europeans have changed tactics and try to support one party or group against another." And the Youth League of the Uganda People's Congress (UPC) resolved that the state should be strengthened because "educational institutions, trade unions, newspapers, etc., were often used by colonialists as a means of retaining their control."[12]

Words were louder than actions. Groups existed, and freedom of the press still had some meaning in East Africa in 1963. Likewise, academic freedom existed in all three countries, and trade unions preserved a considerable degree of autonomy in Kenya and Uganda. In Tanganyika, however, trade unions were largely controlled by the government on the ground that "if a government is a socialist government, representing the working people of the country, then it must be acknowledged and treated as such, not only by the capitalists, but by the workers themselves."[13]

Although the leaders of the opposition in Kenya and Uganda regarded themselves as Pan-Africanists and naturally saw no need for single-party systems, most of the Pan-Africanists linked the need for unity with single parties. "There is a danger of a two-party system in Africa," said Obote; "outsiders can use two parties to cause trouble or buy one of them." In Nyerere's view, "Where there is one party, and that party is identified with the nation as a whole, the foundations of democracy are firmer than they can ever be where you have two or more parties, each representing only a section of the community."[14] Roland Mwanjisi of Tanganyika argued that "one party and strong government are part of Pan-Africanism because it was our traditional system to have a strong chief. . ."

Pan-Africanism in East Africa

In 1963 Tanganyika began discussion of legislation making more than one party illegal, and although Kenya and Uganda had not gone this far, Obote and Kenyatta did not hide the fact that they hoped the opposition parties would disintegrate. In practice, politicians helped the process of disintegration along by threats that a district would not prosper if it became an island of opposition.

Commitment to "Democracy"

Despite the strength of unitary feeling, East African Pan-Africanists were strongly committed to "democracy" and seldom hinted at elitism or suggested that mass movements must be "led and guided by a vanguard political party."[15] East Africans admitted the need for leadership, but refrained from elevating this into a conscious Leninist elitism. "The common man understands unity; we can explain things to him in terms of unity," argued Tanganyikan Vice-President Kawawa. Similarly, Foreign Minister Oscar Kambona felt that "the masses understand Pan-Africanism because they feel the need for dignity even if they have not read books like the intellectuals." And in Nyerere's view: "In a One-Party system, party membership must be open to everybody and freedom of expression allowed to every individual."[16]

An Ambivalent View of the Small Traditional Polity

Thus the Pan-Africanists affirmed a belief in democracy at the same time that they rejected the institutions identified with democracy in Western thought. They avoided the apparent contradiction by appealing to traditional African polity. "We have our own form of democracy that has a strong man at the top with final say after discussion is over," explained Kenya's Minister of Health and Housing, J. D.

37

Otiende. "Party is unknown to Africans," Obote asserted. "Elders would gather and discuss. Differences came up, but they would adjourn and discuss them and then meet again and find a majority."

At the same time that the Pan-Africanists extolled the consensual decision-making that a small community such as the tribe made possible, they deplored the use of the small community (tribe) as a basis for political support because it endangered unity and the process of "nation-building." "Tribalism" was the antithesis of Pan-Africanism, and it was rare to hear a statement about the loyalties of Africans such as that made by Chief Abdullah Fundikira, a Tanganyika cabinet minister from 1961 to 1963, when he said: "Their tribal areas have always been, and I believe always will be, their homeland."[17]

The appeal to tradition was a two-edged spear which required cautious handling. Particularly in Uganda, with its four hereditary monarchies, politicians solved the problem in different ways. Abu Mayanja, who had been mentioned in the foreword of George Padmore's book, *Pan-Africanism or Communism,* and who still considered himself a Pan-Africanist of sorts, was frequently attacked as a tribalist because he had accepted a ministry in the Buganda government. John Babiiha, Chairman of the Uganda People's Congress, regarded the Baganda as tribalistic but not his own Toro people. The Baganda, he said, "see themselves as a state." Other important Uganda politicians, among them Grace Ibingira of Ankole and George Magezi of Bunyoro, argued that the existence of monarchs was compatible with Pan-Africanism only if the monarchs did not oppose African socialism and if they did not "insist on living in the feudal eighteenth century."

Belief in the Efficacy of Size

Another central tenet of Pan-Africanism in East Africa was a belief that only large states could achieve power, wealth, and dignity in the world. As we noted in the last chapter, the Pan-Africanists thought in terms of "Balkanization," not "Scandinavianization." Not only Africans argued this way; in 1945, Kenya settlers wanted a (white) Pan-African conference. And not all Africans argued this way. Former Uganda Minister of Commerce J. S. Mayanja-Nkangi, who once called Pan-Africanism "political megalomania" argued that "the larger a state becomes, the more difficult it is to administer."[18]

For Pan-Africanists, however, the arguments for size were compelling. "Small states can't do much in this world . . . ," said Tanganyika's George Kahama, then Minister of Commerce and Industry. And Obote explained at the time of Buganda's attempted secession in 1960: "African nationalism hates small states because this is an emergent Africa. It wants to compete with Europe, with America, Russia, and Asia, and it will not tolerate Buganda making agreements with these countries—it will crush Buganda."[19]

This belief in size caused ambivalence toward the principle of self-determination and the alteration of boundaries —even though the boundaries had originally been drawn to suit the balance of power in Europe rather than to fit ethnographic realities in Africa. It was ironic that the materials for better defining frontiers were now becoming available, for Pan-Africanists had no interest in realigning boundaries.[20] On the contrary, the sanctity of existing boundaries, of the sub-state whose machinery they were using to build the nation, was a necessity.

39

Pan-Africanism and East African Integration

The only legitimate boundary changes (and federations) were those which united, not those which divided. In the words of the Kenya delegation to the Heads of State conference in Addis Ababa in May 1963: "The principle of self-determination has relevance where FOREIGN DOMINATION is the issue. It has no relevance where the issue is territorial disintegration by dissident citizens."[21]

In 1963 few East Africans had worked out the incipient contradictions of "Pan-Africanist nationalism." Tribal ties across borders which might be an integrative factor were denied legitimacy. The unitarist approach to nation-building not only hindered the formation of groups across national borders, but it also ignored the role of modern interest groups in nation-building and thus increased the importance of national symbols, statues, and heroes which might prove a greater obstacle to African unity than tribalism.[22]

These problems were covered over by statements like Obote's, that "we are building our young countries as integral parts not only of an East African body, but of a bigger body of all Africa"; or Nyerere's, that "African nationalism is meaningless, is anachronistic, and is dangerous, if it is not at the same time Pan-Africanism."[23]

The Unity of Africa as Utopia

The belief in size was related to the central myth or Utopia of the Pan-African movement—in Obote's words, "the unity of Mother Africa."[24] The Pan-Africanist leaders differed only on *when* they expected to see Africa united, not on whether Africa would be united. Some East Africans, including Kenyatta and Mboya, said they expected to see unity in their lifetimes. In 1963 few trade union and party officials at the Tanganyika African National Union's adult education college felt they would see Africa united in five

40

years, but nearly all expected unity within thirty years.[25]

Other politicians like Oscar Kambona in Tanganyika, Grace Ibingira in Uganda, Julius Kiano and Joseph Murumbi in Kenya, felt that unity would take a long time—though when Murumbi said it might take centuries he was severely criticized by younger politicians.

The nature of the unity to be achieved was not particularly clear. In Kenya, parliamentary secretary Fred Kubai felt it would mean a common market with political cooperation, while Tanganyika's Minister of Education, Solomon Eliufoo, aspired to a federation of Africa. Uganda Minister of Housing and Labour, George Magezi, felt that success depended on "quick acceptance of a timetable for joining states," a sentiment with which Obote agreed in his speech to the Heads of State at Addis Ababa.

At the beginning of 1963 most East African Pan-Africanists agreed that the regional-functional path was the best way to approach their ambiguous ideal of African unity. As parliamentary secretary Mwai Kibaki wrote of Kenya's position on "the debate now raging as to how best to approach our common goal of Pan-African unity" early in 1963: "There are areas where it is best to start out planning with all Africa as the unit . . . But it looks equally obvious to us that in promoting the 'political unification' of Africa, the regional federation approach is the most practical."[26]

East Africans were careful to stress that regional federation was only a means and not an end. In 1962 Nyerere warned a regional youth conference to avoid creating "even a block of friendly neighbors,"[27] and, in the June 1963 declaration of intent to federate, the three East African leaders emphasized that "our meeting today is motivated by the spirit of Pan-Africanism and not by mere selfish Regional interests. We are nationalists and reject tribalism, racialism or inward looking policies."[28] During the summer of 1963 this ideological harmony was threatened in East Africa. Nonetheless, as we shall see in Chapter VI, the dispute was not over the desirability of Utopia, but over the road to Utopia.

"Anti-racial Racialism"

Related to the view of history as colonial oppression were Pan-Africanist propositions rejecting racial justifications of colonialism and asserting the value of things African. East Africans did not develop a poetic concept of negritude as Senegal's Leopold Senghor did, but they shared what he called "anti-racial racialism," or what Colin Legum more accurately but less colorfully termed "anti-racial race consciousness."[29] Race was the mother of Pan-Africanism. A search for identity in a world where the white man made the rules led Western Hemisphere Negro—and later African —intellectuals, to develop the ideas of Pan-Africanism. But the origins of ideas are less important than their current meaning, and in 1963 Pan-Africanist ideas in East Africa were not racialist.

East Africans asserted racial equality, not racial superiority. Racialism asserts inequality.[30] East Africans had no "chosen people" mentality. On the contrary, most leaders were consciously opposed to racialism. The East Africans had thrashed out this issue in the first Pafmeca meeting and had decided to phrase their arguments in egalitarian rather than xenophobic or racial terms.

This is not to say that Pan-Africanism could not become racialist or to deny that racialism often existed in practice in East Africa. Race was an easy way to gain political support, and racial issues played a major part in the disturbances which shook East Africa early in 1964. But the existence of racialism in East Africa merely proved that Pan-Africanists had failings like the rest of us. More important was the fact that men like Julius Nyerere felt that "the leaders must safeguard against it by identifying Pan-Africanism with social justice and human rights. We must tell the people that we have been through the furnace of racialism and want no more of it."

The Myth of a Common African Culture

"We have one culture," claimed the Pan-Africanists. Julius Nyerere spoke of "the African," and Kenya Vice President Oginga Odinga argued that "ethnically Africa is one."

North Africa was generally included. Achieng Oneko, Minister of Information in Kenya, defended the idea of a common culture with North Africa on the grounds that "we have Arab influence and religion in much of African life." Jacob Namfua of Tanganyika argued that social systems were the same all over the continent; "They have the horizontal family structure and no one need go hungry when a neighbor has enough." Godfrey Binaisa was more cautious: "Our culture is different from that of the Arabs," he said, "but they fit in."

The dissimilarity of culture between North and South was not the only problem. Among African tribes within a few miles of each other there were often significant differences in cultural patterns. But the differences which the anthropologist would perceive were less important to the Pan-Africanists than the moral imperative of asserting brotherhood and so stressing similarities. As Kenya's Minister of Commerce and Industry, Julius Kiano, explained; "We believe that we have basically the same social forms—that 'Africans do things this way.' We assert it despite the fact, for instance, that the Baganda and Kikuyu were ruled in very different ways. It is almost an intellectual refusal because of faith. Similarly we assert the brotherhood of the Arabs even though we know they are different."

In other words, an "African culture" was more a normative than a descriptive concept. "African" was an adjective which was applied to imported concepts like socialism, democracy, and personality to "nationalize" them and to sanction departures from the restraints of their Western definitions. Nonetheless, as a shrewd observer warns, the concept of a single African culture may become a self-fulfilling myth. If a "youthful generation" finds it hard to remember that a fiction is a fiction, for how long will it remain so?[31]

Outsiders must distinguish between political myth and social fact. In 1963 tribe was still a basic form of community for most of the East African population, and an important source of political support. For instance, three fourths of the Tanganyika members of parliament represented their tribal districts, as did an even higher proportion in Kenya and Uganda. In the words of a Uganda cabinet minister: "Most of these M.P.'s are here for tribal merit." Problems of tribal affiliation complicated efforts to build party organization, as we shall see in Chapter IV.

But ideology is not a mirror image of facts; it is a highly selective portrait, and one which helps to determine the facts for the next generation. The very assertion of a common culture may be as important as whether it exists or not. There is the possibility, of course, that when a myth includes such a large synthetic element various social forces can tear it apart and prevent it from becoming self-fulfilling. It is too early to tell whether this will happen to the assertion of a single African culture, but the nature of the struggle be-

44

tween the sense of community already existing and the ideal community of the ideology can be seen in Kenya's rebuttal of Somali claims to Kenya's Northern Frontier District:

> Pan-Somalism is essentially a tribalistic doctrine based on the ethnic homogeneity of the Somalis . . . The Kenya leaders point out that seeking to create new African nations on a basis of tribal or religious identities is a sin against Pan-Africa and a most dangerous weapon for destroying African solidarity. The Somalis are Africans. Those who live in Kenya are KENYA AFRICANS. The Somalis are Africans. Those who live with us in Kenya, they are perfectly free to leave us and our territory . . . This is the only way they can legally exercise their right of self-determination.[32]

African Socialism

Most East African Pan-Africanists were also "African socialists." Although the notion of "socialism" was often ambiguous, almost everyone regarded it as a good thing or as word of praise, in much the same way as "capitalism" or "free enterprise" is used in America. Similarly, a taint of suspicion attached to the word "capitalist." In Nyerere's view, a capitalist was a person who used wealth to dominate his fellow men, and the wrong of capitalism was in having divorced wealth from its true purpose—the satisfaction of basic human needs.[33] Obote argued that capitalism was not possible in Africa: "We have no giant companies like Britain and America and would have to rely on them from outside. But we want economic independence, not control, so we must develop our own way."

Not everyone saw a connection between Pan-Africanism and African socialism, but most did. Nyerere saw the connection in the oppression of colonial history: "The positive effort to build an African dignity or personality most often turns to socialism. It is the egalitarian nature of socialism which links it to Pan-Africanism."

45

Although there was no full agreement on the meaning of African socialism, most East Africans emphasized an egalitarian distribution of wealth rather than a Marxist class control of the major means of production. African socialism was "an attitude of mind, of familyhood," in Nyerere's view. African socialists appealed to tradition. "Socialism is natural to us; we have never had capitalists who employ others," said Tanganyika's Vice-President Kawawa. "We all had communal societies," said Koinange, and Mwanjisi believed that "we are trying to build a Pan-African socialist economy that was once common to us all."

Murumbi dissented on the grounds that "African socialists base their ideas on the idea of communal life—a pure and simple socialist life. But this must be adjusted for the complex world of today." Others, like Kenya's Ambassador to the United Nations, Burudi Nabwera, argued that "there is no such thing as African socialism . . . the principles of socialism are universal." But on another occasion, when he was seeking to prove the unity of East Africa, Nabwera pointed to the consensus on African socialism.[34] Oginga Odinga also argued that the principles of socialism were universal, but he emphasized that "we have no class struggle because our social system will not allow it. My family and relatives are quick to eat up my salary."

The notion of African socialism was primarily an abstract point of consensus on economic affairs, a handy label for people to agree on. The label left considerable leeway for practical programs. In reality, East African countries with their inexperienced bureaucrats, small budgets, and peasant economies were socialist in only a broad sense. Moreover, one might question whether socialist forms and incentives were best suited to solve East Africa's major economic problems of expanding the money economy, when the scarcest resource was trained middle-level manpower. But East Africans like Oscar Kambona argued that while they might have been influenced by European socialism, African socialism was "a reality of African psychology" which allowed them to stress their ideological neutrality: "Pan-Africanism gives leaders the advantage of explaining socialism as an African thing and in stressing that we must go our own way."

Neocolonialism and Positive Neutralism

Finally, Pan-Africanists all agreed on the evil of imperialism and suspected that developed countries, particularly in the West, sought to impose a neocolonialism. "Imperialism" was such a common term of abuse in East Africa that in August 1962 Oginga Odinga, a supporter of Kenya African National Union (Kanu), was calling a Luo movement within Kanu "an imperialist attempt to make a mountain out of a molehill" at about the same time that Daniel arap Moi of the Kenya African Democratic Union (Kadu) was calling a nonpartisan but predominantly Kanu-oriented public conference "an imperialist projection."[35]

East Africans viewed imperialism more broadly than Lenin did. "The principal driving force that motivated our ex-colonisers in their colonial adventure was economic and political power," said Obote. "The predominant consideration in their present attempt to maintain their influence in Africa is still the same."[36] And Julius Nyerere warned that "the socialist countries themselves, considered as individuals in the larger society of nations, are now committing the same crimes as were committed by the capitalist before . . . Karl Marx's doctrine that there is an inevitable clash between the rich and the poor is just as applicable internationally as it is within national boundaries."[37]

47

The practical policy derived from this view was positive neutralism—a policy of nonalignment that had an ideology of its own and so did not hesitate to take moralistic and critical positions on a wide number of world issues. In Mboya's words, "We intend to decide every international issue on its merits."[38] According to Jacob Namfua, "If we come together, we can be a force in the world situation and help stabilize or balance groupings who think differently." An added benefit from this position was that it allowed Pan-Africanists to be unabashedly eclectic in using outside ideas and institutions without suffering from a feeling of loss of independence in the process.

SYSTEM IN EAST AFRICAN IDEAS

East African leaders who called themselves Pan-Africanists shared a similar set of ideas which other East Africans did not. Through personal connections and through their ideas, East African Pan-Africanists considered themselves part of an All-Africa movement. With slight differences, the East African ideas paralleled those of the Pan-African movement as set forth in the writings of Padmore and Nkrumah, and in the resolutions of the first All African Peoples' Conference in 1958.[39] Both in origin and content the dominant East African political ideas could be called Pan-Africanist.

But, as we stated earlier, to be an ideology a set of ideas must be interdependent, must hang together in the minds of the believers. Did the basic tenets of the East African Pan-Africanists bear sufficient relation to each other to warrant calling them an ideology rather than a random set of ideas? System becomes apparent if we start with the view of the past as oppression under alien rule. The view of

48

the past, of imperialism, is the common point of departure for a number of ideas. For instance, the historical association between imperialism and racialism breeds anti-racialism, which in turn stresses equality as a value. This leads into egalitarian socialism. Socialism can also derive from reaction to the association of imperialism with capitalism and foreign companies.

Another aspect of imperialism and the colonial experience was a denigration of indigenous African culture (with a few exceptions, particularly in Buganda). Imperialism meant the imposition of foreign standards which the new elite had to assimilate, in part at least, to achieve status in the new system. Reaction against this had led to ambivalence toward the new standards and to attempts to assert the value and dignity of traditional ways. It has tended also to create a romanticized view of African culture, including traditional forms of rule. This view is used to support single parties, personalized leadership, and some form of communal social-ism. It also leads to the assertion of a common culture which can be used as a normative concept to legitimize new ideas accepted into the system.

The view of African history as oppression, because Afri-cans have been divided and ruled, leads to the axiom that unity is strength. The internal ramifications of this elevation of the principle of unity are antipluralism and single parties. In foreign affairs the emphasis on unity induces belief in the efficacy of large states and an ambivalence toward self-determination. It accounts for the widespread acceptance of the Utopia of African unity and the ability to sustain the belief in a common African culture.

Finally, the view of history as oppression by foreign powers breeds strong anti-imperialism. This anti-imperialism supports a belief in the existence of neocolonialism whose dangers reinforce the importance of the premise that unity is strength and the belief in the efficacy of size. The consequences we have just traced above.

These ideas, then, were more than a random set of attitudes; they were more than simple anticolonialism. The view of history as oppression was the core of the ideological system, but their particular form was the result of a number of contingent forces, including other twentieth-century ideas and some much older African ones. After all, the result of anticolonialism among the American elite in the eighteenth century was just the opposite—a distrust of centralized power and a belief in pluralism which remain effective to this day.

The Baganda, most of whose leaders were not Pan-Africanists, were the exception that helps demonstrate the validity of this description of a system in East African ideas. The Baganda were treated as a privileged group by the British colonizers, and the full impact of alien rule upon the individual was blunted by the resilient traditional institutions. As one historian has asserted, it is not surprising that in the "torrent of change" in current Africa, people turn to Pan-Africanism in their profound concern about their personal and collective identity. "For many, very many, Baganda, however, the problem hardly arises: their identity lies with their age-old constantly reinvigorated kingdom."[40]

E. M. K. Mulira, a Ganda politician who read a paper on Pan-Africanism to the first Pafmeca conference in 1958, later revised his ideas "because in order to build you must start with something and what purpose is served by further destruction? The Baganda are not Pan-Africanist because we have an identity and do not have to search for one."[41] In the words of another eminent Ganda, "We all have felt race when we have been excluded but we don't build a philosophy upon it here."

Godfrey Binaisa, one of the few important Baganda politicians who considered himself a Pan-Africanist, gave two reasons why Baganda were not more interested in Pan-Africanism: "First, Buganda was guarded by the British like a sentry and insulated. There was no real encounter with the British because we had our own government and could focus on it. Second, the Kabaka and his government stopped the leaders from teaching the people Pan-Africanism."[42]

In short, the impact of imperialism was blunted in Buganda. Baganda did not see history as alien racial oppression—the key to system in East African Pan-Africanist ideas. In the words of Achieng Oneko, a Kenya Pan-Africanist; "The difficulty with Buganda was that they felt free."[43]

PAN-AFRICANISM AND CAUSATION

Many outsiders were troubled by the amount of consciously created myth in Pan-Africanism. Sometimes Pan-Africanist statements seemed to have so few empirical referents that the normative element stood virtually alone. For instance, it was difficult to see what pre-existing characteristics—as distinguished from an idealized view of the past —determined African personality or African socialism. Because of this, some observers felt that Pan-Africanism had no causal significance but was merely a gloss of words painted on by politicians after they had acted for totally different reasons.

To what degree is sincerity relevant in determining social forces? If an idea is cynically propounded by a leader but widely believed by his followers, sincerity may be irrelevant.

A cynical leader may have to act in terms of his idea in order to keep his following. A cynically generated myth may become self-fulfilling.

Nonetheless, it is useful to distinguish cases in which an ideology is merely accepted as a means of expression, and cases where the values in the ideology engender commitment on the part of the believers. In the latter case we would expect decision-makers to be more willing to sacrifice personal and national interests for the sake of African unity. But we would be mistaken to expect African leaders, any more than other people always to act in accord with ideals rather than interests.

Whether propounded merely by acceptance or by commitment, or by a combination of the two, ideology influences actions by affecting perceptions. The way of thinking implicit in the ideology has an impact of its own. For example, defectors from the Soviet Union after World War II still continued to see things in terms of the dialectic.[44] Ideology predisposes the actors in certain directions. It is mainly in marginal cases, where the advantages to be gained in two courses of action are nearly balanced, that ideology may become apparent when predictions made solely in terms of interest are discovered to be incorrect. But even when there are no sacrifices or surprises, ideology sets certain bounds to discourse and explains the manner in which the elite approach a problem. We shall return to this in Chapter VI when we evaluate the role of Pan-Africanism in the failure to federate in 1963.

Ideas are generated by exceptional individuals (according to Weber), but then they become associated with interests which select those features of an idea with which they have an affinity.[45] What interests did Pan-Africanism serve in East Africa? If we look for the answer to the usual economic groups, we are likely to be misled. Some businesses favored the idea in hopes of tapping a larger market, but others feared competition and preferred the protection of the home market. Similarly with labor; some unions saw themselves as stronger if allied with unions in neighboring countries, while others preferred the job protection inherent in national labor markets. African traders may have found the racial aspect of the ideology to their economic interest, but they were not a significant group.

The group which accepted and promoted the ideology of Pan-Africanism was the political elite—a radical intelligentsia competing for wealth, power, and dignity through participation in world politics. This acceptance can be explained by the social situation immediately prior to independence. As we saw in Chapter I, the intelligentsia wished to assert "nationalist" rights of "self-determination" in order to gain control of colonial states. Since no nation corresponded with states, and tribal community was too small for their purposes, they asserted Pan-Africanism and nationalism simultaneously. The Pan-African element represented community based primarily on race, thus demonstrating the alien nature of colonial government. The nationalist element represented the need to focus political movements on capturing the power structure of colonial states.

After independence (we may speculate), the ideology, subject to certain changes, remained useful to the political elites. It provided a Utopia as a focus of hope; it provided a scapegoat in the form of neocolonialism, and diversion from domestic problems in the form of anticolonialism. It also provided normative concepts to help reconcile conflict over domestic problems by "Africanizing" them. It fostered an attitude toward the impact of technology which did not entail rejection of the African past. From a "vulgar Marxist" point of view its unitarist implications protected the disproportionately large salaries and perquisites of office which the political elites enjoyed. Less cynically, these unitarist implications gave the elites power to promote their strategies for economic development.

Yet it was probably in foreign affairs and world politics that Pan-Africanism was most useful to the leaders. Certainly this seems to have been the area in which East Africans most often applied it. Continued dependence on European technicians, businesses, and administrators on the part of African elites which had rejected alien standards and rule was bound to create anxiety and to result in emotional reactions, particularly in foreign policy. The ideas of Pan-Africanism expressed this ambivalence at the same time that they provided the elites with a weapon and a policy.

How the interests of the political elite will influence the future of Pan-Africanism is an interesting question. Already in the past few years we have noted such changes as the downgrading of the doctrine of nonviolence and equivocation about self-determination. In 1963 the problem of sovereignty remained only partially solved. Domestically, it is interesting to note that with accession to power, Nyerere's views changed from advocacy of free trade unions to government control; and Obote's from belief in the necessity of a political opposition to a desire that the opposition fade away. In 1963, however, all these changes in the ideology had taken place within the cosmology and ethics of "Western civilization" (in a broad non-Cold War sense), and the ideology remained sufficiently diffuse that communication between those believing in it and those outside it remained possible.

Interesting as these speculations may be, the important point is that during the period of discussion of East African unification in the early sixties, a widely accepted diffuse ideology expressed the interests of the political elites in the three countries. Much of its system and many of its incipient contradictions had not been worked out, but Pan-Africanism provided the framework of ideas within which East African unification was approached and discussed.

Part Two

EAST AFRICAN
INTEGRATION

III

Social Integration

> The present stage of economic development, par-
> ticularly in regard to communications, is such that it
> still imposes serious obstacles to the effective operation
> of any new authority with executive functions through-
> out the whole of so large an area.
>
> (Joint Select Committee on Closer
> Union in East Africa, 1931)

There is more to the integration of states than elites and ideology. In 1963 members of the East African elite spoke their words on a well-set stage. It was not always thus, as the various commissions which studied the unification problem in the 1920's noted. In 1925 Lord Delamere, a Kenya settler leader, arranged a conference of settlers at Tukuyu, Tanganyika, to discuss unification. To reach the meeting place, the settlers had to bump along some 450 miles of the "Great North Road, a track partially cleared of tree stumps." Delamere had had to send gasoline supplies ahead by truck.[1]

Compare this with the June 1963 meeting at which the East African leaders announced their intention to federate by the end of the year. Several Kenyan cabinet ministers flew to Tanganyika for a few hours on a Saturday afternoon to greet a visiting West African head of state. In the course of conversation with Tanganyikan leaders, they hit on the idea of a meeting to announce their intention to federate.

The missing Ugandan leader was reached by telephone. He agreed. On the following Wednesday the Ugandans and Tanganyikans flew to Nairobi and, with Kenya, agreed to federate. Their decision was announced to reporters, who quickly wired it to all three capitals.

Political integration, the process which leads to the formation of a political community, is generally preceded by social integration, which is the growth of communications and transactions across borders—the development of what might be called "transnational society." There is no simple one-to-one relation between these two forms of integration, between the growth of communications and the growth of community. But it is hard to conceive of community without communications.

The various physical and social factors affecting communications—geography, language, economic development, racial and other differences—set the limits within which the leaders had to work, and determined their capacity to respond to each other's demands. By contrasting the growth of transnational society between the three East African states with that between them and their non-East African neighbors, we can see to what extent East Africa was socially integrated and how much greater the obstacles would have been to unification of a larger area. By contrasting the growth of communications and contacts at the East African level with their growth *within* the separate states, we get an idea of the problems which the leaders had to overcome; and, to some extent, the trends of changes which were occurring outside the arena of conscious political decisions.

One aspect of social change which probably affected unification adversely, was "social mobilization," a concept which refers to a number of changes—of residence, of occupation, of face-to-face associations, of roles—which go together at certain stages of economic development.[2] On the one hand, social mobilization made people susceptible to new loyalties and, through processes like interterritorial migration, increased the number of those participating in transnational society. But, on the other hand, increased participation in national society by people who had previously been relatively dormant presented leaders with national problems which demanded their attention and were most easily handled through the existing machinery of the nation-state. In other words, while some social changes increased transnational social integration and made possible a coordination that had been beyond the reach of those who had tried to unify East Africa in the 1920's, other social changes were strengthening the importance of the territorial states.

GEOGRAPHICAL BACKGROUND

Geography, a constant factor which is basic to the development of communications, does not deserve undue attention; but comments are sometimes made that East Africa "has obvious geographical unity."[3] It is obvious only on a map. The only major geographical feature that the three countries have in common is Lake Victoria.[4] Otherwise, Kenya and Tanganyika share the coastal strip and the Masai plain, but the borders between Uganda and the other two have no particular geographical logic.

Northern Uganda is more like the southern Sudan than like southern Uganda, Kenya, or Tanganyika.[5] The same can be said about the similarity of northern Kenya to southern Ethiopia and Somalia, or of southern Tanganyika to Mozambique. In their natural features there seems no reason to believe that any of three levels—the individual countries, East Africa, Greater East Africa—is more a natural unit than

61

another. The "obvious unity" of East Africa is man-made.

In size, Tanganyika's 362,000 square miles account for 53 per cent of the 679,000 square miles of East Africa, while Uganda's 92,000 square miles (equivalent to Britain, Ghana, or Illinois) account for only 13 per cent of the total. Kenya makes up the remaining third. Tiny Zanzibar—two islands off the Tanganyika coast which were to join Tanganyika in 1964—was only 1,000 square miles, or 1/679th of East Africa.

So far as was known at the time of the federal negotiations in 1963, nature had not blessed East Africa with any outstanding natural resources which could serve as an impetus for rapid economic growth and social change. Diamonds from Tanganyika and copper from Uganda were less than 10 per cent of East African exports in 1962. East Africa had nothing like the copper of Zambia or the oil of the Middle East. And although its wealth is agricultural, half of East Africa (including two thirds of Kenya and a third of Tanganyika) is too arid for regular cultivation. Only a quarter of the area receives more than 30 inches of rainfall a year, and two fifths is infested with tsetse fly which prevents livestock-raising.[6] In 1963 the "frontier" in East Africa was not a rich one.

POPULATION STRUCTURE

In 1962 an estimated 26 million people lived in East Africa. Table 1 gives the territorial breakdown.

By African standards, East Africa is quite populous. For instance, in 1963 it had three times the population of the former Central African Federation. Population was growing at about 2.4 per cent a year—a rate which would double it in 30 years. In 1962 nearly 50 per cent of East Africans were

Social Integration

Table 1
East African Population (Millions)

	1931	1948	1962	% of total
Tanganyika	5.6	7.5	9.6	38
Kenya	4.0	5.4	8.7	34
Uganda	4.0	4.9	7.0	27
Zanzibar		.26	.3	1
East Africa	13.6	18.1	25.6	100

Sources: EACSO, *Economic and Statistical Review*, June 1963, p. 4: East Africa High Commission, *Economic and Statistical Bulletin*, September 1948, Table A 2.

under the age of 16.[7] This population structure is a good example of a social problem which deflects attention from unification and increases the importance of existing state machinery. Education is one of the most pressing demands that citizens make upon their governments in East Africa; yet even if Kenya succeeds in its plan to double the number of Africans attending secondary school by 1966, the per cent of primary school students who are able to go on to secondary school will still decline from its 1962 level of 12.9 per cent to only 3.3 per cent.[8]

In 1963 East Africa's population was very unevenly distributed, with Tanganyika sparsely settled (28 persons per square mile) and Uganda more highly settled (90 per square mile). The intermediate figure of 40 for Kenya is misleading, however, for only a thirtieth of her population lived in the arid northern half of the country. In some Kikuyu and Maragoli areas there was a heavy pressure of population on land, which was accentuated by the reluctance of other tribal groups to share sparsely settled but tribally owned land. The Pan-African belief that "we are all Africans" does not seem to work at this bread-and-butter level. In any case, Kenya was a net exporter of persons in East Africa. Uganda, with only a quarter of East Africa's people, was well aware of these population problems when she disagreed about common citizenship and free movement of populations during the negotiations of 1963.

Only two per cent of the people in East Africa were not Africans, but because of their role in social change their uneven distribution was important. Nearly two fifths of the non-Africans lived in Kenya. The number of non-Africans in Tanganyika and Uganda was not greatly affected by independence, but the population in Kenya declined by approximately 20 per cent in the year following independence.[9]

Table 2
Non-African Population

	European	Asian	Arab
Kenya 1931	16,000	39,600	12,200
1961	66,000	178,000	39,000
Tanganyika 1931	8,200	23,400	7,100
1961	22,700	90,500	27,600
Uganda 1931	2,000	13,000	500
1961	11,600	77,400	2,100

Sources: *Economic and Statistical Review,* June 1963, Table B 3; *Economic and Statistical Bulletin,* September 1948, Table A 2.

"Tribe" is not a precise term, but it is "a convenient shorthand for differences of language, culture, and traditional economy," and it is politically meaningful.[10] Although there is no precision in the numbers, there are 120 major tribes in Tanganyika, 48 in Kenya, and 28 in Uganda.[11] Along the Coast, Islam and the Swahili language make "tribe" a less important category.

In the past, East African tribes were grouped in several categories, sometimes referred to as racial but largely based on linguistic similarity—Bantu, Nilotic, Hamitic, Nilo-Hamitic, and some small groups. Although these categories are

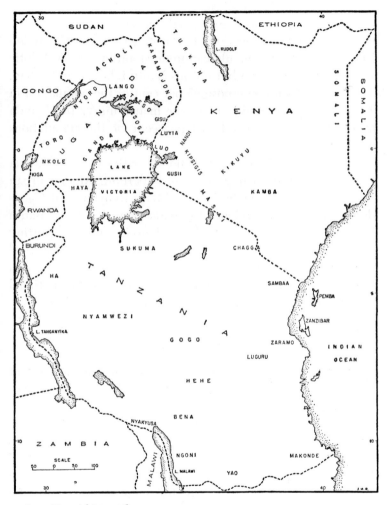

Some East African tribes.

not very satisfactory for anthropological purposes, they have become part of the political vocabulary in East Africa, and the fact that they are based partly on language means that they affect communication. For instance, a Nilotic Acholi from the North of Uganda can understand his fellow Nilotic Luo in western Kenya but not his Bantu fellow-countryman. That Bantu groups compose 95 per cent of the population in Tanganyika is a significant factor in her unity. In Uganda and Kenya approximately 70 per cent of the populations are Bantu.

In urban situations, new economic patterns and a lingua franca make these categories less important. Among urban workers in Uganda (who included both Kenyans and Ugandans) there was a tendency to divide along Nilotic or Bantu lines for social gatherings, but when it came to putting pressure on the state to promote economic and political interests, they tended to divide along Ugandan-Kenyan lines. Thus, though social cleavages cut across national boundaries, this was imperfectly reflected in politics.[12]

LANGUAGE

Language is such a basic aspect of communication that students of nationalism have long treated it as almost synonymous with community.

English was the official government language in all three East African countries in 1963, although Tanganyika introduced Swahili as an official language in Parliament and began to translate laws into Swahili. English was an elite language, restricted mainly to the small proportion of the population with more than a few years of education.

Swahili is the closest thing to a common language in East Africa. A Bantu language that has been considerably influenced by Arabic, it is believed to have developed along the East African Coast and been carried inland as far as the Congo along trade routes which ran primarily through Tanganyika.

No tribe in Tanganyika was large enough to impose its language on the others, and Swahili was strengthened chiefly by the German administration which used Swahili-speaking Africans from the Coast. As a result, Tanganyika is one of the few African countries with an indigenous national language. This important social factor made a great difference to African leaders when they were building a strong political organization, as we shall see in the next chapter. According to Julius Nyerere, "In eight years, I needed an interpreter only twice."[13]

In Uganda, trade routes had not developed to the same extent that they had in Tanganyika; but an even more important reason for the weakness of Swahili was the existence of a large and powerful tribe able to press the claims of its own language. Nearly a third of the population of the country live in the central Buganda kingdom and speak its language, Luganda. Moreover, a number of other peoples, particularly in the Eastern Region, understand Luganda, partly because Baganda administrators were used in this area in the early days of British rule, and partly because the first vernacular books were in Luganda.

In 1963 a large number of people in Uganda understood enough Swahili to carry out market transactions; a smaller number could speak the language more fluently. Trade unions and political parties used English at meetings and offered Luganda and Swahili translations. The Baganda, however, opposed extension of Swahili. It was taught in Uganda schools during the period of the closer union movement only to be dropped again in the 1930's.

Despite a 1962 resolution of the governing Uganda People's Congress urging greater use of Swahili for the sake of unity, Uganda government policy perpetuated linguistic diversity by using tribal languages rather than Swahili for radio broadcasts.[14] The elite was split on the language issue. In a 1960 debate, Cuthbert Obwangor, Mathias Ngobi, and Grace Ibingira (all of whom later became cabinet ministers) supported greater use of Swahili. In Ngobi's view, it would be impossible to address a mass meeting in English for twenty years. On the other hand, Serwano Kalubya, who later became Deputy-Speaker and W. W. Nadiope, later Vice President, strongly opposed Swahili.[15] More recently, in 1963, the Prime Minister, Milton Obote, advocated greater use of Swahili; but UPC Chairman John Babiiha was cool to it and Attorney-General Godfrey Binaisa claimed that Buganda would never accept Swahili.[16]

In Kenya, according to the Minister of Information (and strong Swahili proponent), Achieng Oneko, approximately half the population understood Swahili in 1963. This was the major restraint on greater use of Swahili.[17] But rather than promote linguistic diversity, the Kenya Government limited the languages on national radio programs and as qualifications for citizenship to English and Swahili. Unlike Uganda, Kenya had "native" speakers of Swahili at the Coast, and a corrupt version had long been used between employers and employees. The language had also withstood the colonial government's efforts gradually to eliminate it.[18]

Newspaper circulations, shown in Table 3, provide a rough index of the extent to which the various languages were used to express ideas and opinions, rather than just to carry out market transactions. The figures confirm the pattern of Swahili as a national language in Tanganyika, a major language in Kenya, and limited in use in Uganda. This linguis-

Social Integration

Table 3
Per Cent of Newspaper Circulation in Various Languages, 1962

	% Swahili	% English	% Vernacular
Tanganyika daily	70	30	—
weekly	72	27	2
Kenya daily	36	64	—
weekly	46	41	13
Uganda daily	—	49	51 (Luganda)
weekly	—	7	93

Sources: Tanganyika Information Service, *Tanganyika Press Directory*, May 1962: Uganda Ministry of Information, Broadcasting and Tourism, *Press Directory of Uganda*, December 1962; (Kenya Government), *Newspapers and Periodicals Published and Sold in Kenya*, October 1962.

tic similarity between Kenya and Tanganyika helps explain the vague feeling expressed by a number of politicians in 1963, that somehow Kenyans and Tanganyikans were closer to each other than to Ugandans.

MIGRATION

There were few restrictions on the movement of the African population between the East African territories, a notable exception being Kenya's Kikuyu, Embu, and Meru people during the "Mau Mau" Emergency in the 1950's. In 1963 the only important restriction (and one which caused some bitterness when it was imposed in 1961) was on the movement of certain Kenyan tribes into the crowded Northern Province of Tanganyika. The Tanganyika government compensated for this restriction by giving land in western Tanganyika to Kenyans for a resettlement scheme.

Only a small proportion of the African population moved between the three territories in any given year. Kampala proved a considerable attraction for Luo and Luhya, who constituted the largest part of the 18,000 Kenyans employed in Uganda. Some 33,000 Tanganyikans crossed from the Lake Province into Uganda and back each year, but only 2,500 Tanganyikans were permanently employed in Uganda. The influx of Ugandans and Tanganyikans into Kenya was not so great as the flow of Kenyans in the other direction. Only 13,000 non-Kenyan Africans (three per cent of the adult male labor force) worked in Kenya in 1960.[19]

In terms of migration East Africa was not a significantly integrated unit. As many migrant laborers came from outside East Africa as moved between the territories. More than a quarter of the Uganda labor force in 1951 and 1961 were outsiders; but at both times the largest number came from Rwanda and Burundi.[20] In Tanganyika some ten per cent of the labor force came from outside the country, but of these, fewer than one in seven came from Kenya or Uganda. Mozambique provided nearly half the total.[21] At the same time, some 20,000 Tanganyians worked outside East Africa, more than worked in Kenya and Uganda combined.[22]

In addition to migration there was considerable coming and going where tribes were divided by the unpatrolled borders. Masai, for instance, crossed frequently between Kenya and Tanganyika, as did Samia between Kenya and Uganda. At least one member of Uganda's Parliament was probably born on the Kenya side of the border; another had a brother in the Kenya Parliament.

ECONOMIC GROWTH AND STRUCTURE

One need not accept all Marx's conclusions to see the truth of his general premise that economic change precedes social change. As the Joint Select Committee on Closer Union stated in 1931, "The present stage of economic development, particularly in regard to communications . . . imposes serious obstacles."[23]

Even in the 1960's, East Africa's low level of economic development imposed limits on both social and political change. With a 1961 Gross Domestic Product (GDP) of £557 million (see Table 4), of which £155 was produced

Table 4
Gross Domestic Product (GDP) of East Africa, 1961 (£ million)

Primary industries (including £155 nonmonetary)	302
Trade and transport	93
Manufacturing and construction	61
Government	49
Services	36
Rents	16
TOTAL	557

Source: *Economic and Statistical Review,* June 1963, Table K 1.

outside the modern monetary sector, the East African economy was about the size of that of Cambridge, Massachusetts, or equal to the 1963 earnings of the General Motors Corporation. Moreover, it was highly dependent on agriculture (nearly three-fifths of its total product) and exports (35 per cent of GDP in 1962)—particularly coffee, cotton, and sisal. From 1954 to 1962, the prices received for these exports declined by 24 per cent.[24] Earnings from these exports, which the East Africans could not control, were a vital source of social change. Such a small and dependent economy could not generate or support the large cities or middle classes that are often associated with rapid social change, nor the strong industrial groups which generate political change according to the "European theory" of integration.

Although East Africa's gross capital formation was quite respectable for a poor area (21 per cent of monetary product in 1960), the growth of total product between 1957 and 1961 was not sufficient to outstrip the population increase and per capita income fluctuated around a constant level of £23.[25] Table 5 shows the territorial variations.

Table 5
Per Capita Income

		Total GDP (£ million)	Population estimate (million)	Income per capita (£)
1957	Kenya	206	6.7	30.9
	Tanganyika	162	8.9	18.8
	Uganda	147	6.2	23.7
	East Africa	505	21.6	23.3
1961	Kenya	225	7.3	30.8
	Tanganyika	187	9.4	19.9
	Uganda	156	6.9	22.8
	East Africa	557	23.5	23.7

Source: *Economic and Statistical Review,* June 1963, Table K 3.

Some of the differences between the economies of the three East African countries go back to decisions made early in the colonial period. Uganda, regarded as unsuitable for European settlement, developed through cultivation by peasants (who accounted for 90 per cent of monetary agricultural production in 1960) of cotton and coffee (79 per cent of her exports in 1961).[26] After World War II, the colonial government tried to diversify the pattern by constructing a hydroelectric scheme on the Nile, and starting a Uganda Development Corporation, but with high transport costs to the sea and low incomes in the Lake Victoria market area, Uganda did not prove to be a particularly attractive location for industry. In 1960 the Nile dam remained under-utilized, and manufacturing accounted for only four per cent of GDP.[27]

Social Integration

In Tanganyika the Germans had relied largely on plantation agriculture. African agriculture, especially around Mount Kilimanjaro and Lake Victoria, was encouraged by the British after World War I and accounted for 40 per cent of agricultural product by 1945.[28] In 1961 sisal grown mainly on plantations, and coffee and cotton grown mainly by African peasants, each accounted for about 30 per cent of Tanganyika's exports.[29] Industry developed slowly, accounting for only 3.9 per cent of GDP and employing only 18,000 Africans in 1960.[30]

European agriculture was the early source of growth in Kenya. By 1927 Europeans produced £2.4 million of £2.8 million total exports.[31] More recently, two important changes have occurred. The Swynnerton plan, adopted in 1954, encouraged African agriculture, and a politically motivated scheme has resettled Africans on more than a million acres of formerly alienated land. In 1962 marketed farm produce from outside the "White Highlands" accounted for 30 per cent of gross farm revenue.[32] This began to reduce some of the economic differences between Kenya and her neighbors.

Even more important was the growth of light industry in Kenya during the 1950's. By 1960 manufacturing accounted for ten per cent of both GDP and employment in Kenya.[33] Moreover, many of these manufactured products were sold in Uganda and Tanganyika.[34] Even during the slump of the early 1960's, export of manufactures to Uganda and Tanganyika was one sector of the Kenya economy which remained buoyant.[35] As we shall see in Chapter V, this interterritorial trade was one of the most important forms of contact between the countries. Moreover, East Africa was a significantly integrated unit. In 1961 interterritorial trade was about three times the value of exports (including re-exports) to eleven neighboring countries of Greater East Africa.[36]

73

URBANIZATION

These differences in the economies of the three countries resulted in differences in the social forces within them. One of the most important social changes, the sociologists assure us, is the growth of cities.[37] Here, old loyalties and ways of life are gradually eroded by new economic and social pressures. Unlike parts of West Africa, East African cities are new and small. In 1962 a million persons (a quarter of them non-African), or only four per cent of the population, lived in urban areas (defined as cities of 10,000 or more). As Table 6 shows, eight per cent of Kenyans, three and a half

Table 6
Urbanization in East Africa

	Towns over 10,000	Population in towns (thousands)	Total population (millions)
Kenya			
1948	4	233	5.4
1962	7	650	8.7
Tanganyika			
1948	5	136	7.5
1957	11	292	8.8
Uganda			
1948	1	22	5.0
1959	4	101	6.5

Sources: *Economic and Statistical Review,* June 1963, Table B 5; Tanganyika, *Statistical Abstract,* 1962 (Dar es Salaam, 1962), Table C 6; *East Africa Statistical Bulletin,* September 1951.

per cent of Tanganyikans, and less than two per cent of Ugandans were "urbanized."[38]

The great majority of East Africans had not experienced the changes which go with urbanization. This is one reason why it is important to focus on the actions and opinions of the elite rather than on "public opinion" in the study of East African unification.

Wage-earning and regular employment may also change peoples' outlook and habits. In 1960, slightly over four per cent of the African population were wage-earners—8.5 per cent in Kenya, 3.7 per cent in Tanganyika, 3.1 per cent in Uganda. (By comparison, 43 per cent of Britain's population were wage-earners that year).[39]

Unemployment is as important in its social effects as employment. In East Africa it is one of those problems accompanying "social mobilization" which diverts attention from interterritorial integration and creates pressure for action by national states. Unemployment was difficult to measure; to some extent its effects were alleviated by the ability of many Africans to return to live with relatives on family land. Nonetheless, it was a problem for each of the East African countries. In 1959, a Kenya government study estimated that 120,000 adult males, 7.5 per cent of the adult male population of Central and Nyanza Provinces, were surplus to their agricultural economies. Nearly 40,000 of these people were in towns.[40] Again in 1963, the Kenya Government estimated that between 30,000 and 40,000 people had been thrown out of work during the second half of 1962.[41] Tribal differences helped prevent the unemployed from becoming an active revolutionary force, but even so, African leaders were aware of the social problem that the unemployed represented for each of their states.

TRANSPORTATION

Trade, migration of labor, and the interterritorial personal contacts of all sorts which make up "transnational society"

75

assume the existence of transportation. Yet transportation cannot always be assumed in East Africa. Even in 1962 a former governor described Tanganyika's communication network as "an endless drain, a sort of running sore . . ."[42]

Railways were the backbone of the East African transportation system. The completion of a 582-mile rail line between Mombasa and Lake Victoria in 1901 reduced the cost of moving goods to the Coast from six shillings a ton-mile by head porterage to one-fifth of a shilling in the 1950's (when costs had risen considerably).[43] In 1930, at the time when the Joint Select Committee was concluding that transportation facilities were inadequate to permit unification of East Africa, there were 2825 miles of track; in 1960, there were 4075 miles.[44]

Not until 1963 did a new 120-mile extension link the Kenya-Uganda rail system with the Tanganyika central system; and there was still no rail line to the southern part of Tanganyika or (more understandably) to the northern half of Kenya. Nor were there any rail links between East Africa and her neighbors (except with the Congo by ferry across Lake Tanganyika), despite periodic overtures toward Northern Rhodesia. Whatever the limitations of its rail system, East Africa compared with Greater East Africa, was an integrated unit in its rail system.

The same could be said about road communications. There were no paved roads between East Africa and her outside neighbors in 1963. There were no completely paved roads between the three East African countries either, but the roads were partly paved and in good condition. Internally, the road systems of the countries differed greatly. In 1961 Kenya and Uganda each had about 700 miles of paved roads and twice as much road mileage in proportion to area as Tanganyika.[45]

Social Integration

According to the first Tanganyika Development Plan, "the present main road system looks outwards, particularly in the north, and facilitates the flow of purchasing power from the rich provinces in the north to Kenya and Uganda rather than inwards to Tanganyika."[46] Though Tanganyika's road system integrated her northern provinces into the rest of East Africa in 1961, this was one thing the planners hoped to change. In other words, the pressures of national planning cut down this proportionately greater orientation toward interterritorial communication.

Air transportation, although limited almost entirely to the elite and expatriates, was a new factor compared with the communications of the 1920's. In 1961, Nairobi Airport handled some 11,300 commercial aircraft movements, Dar es Salaam, 6,700 and Entebbe (Uganda), 6,100.[47]

POSTAL FACILITIES AND TELECOMMUNICATIONS

To what extent did East Africans communicate with each other? In 1925, when the postal and telecommunications administrations of Kenya and Uganda were amalgamated, there were only 1200 telephones in Kenya and 450 in Uganda.[48] In 1933, when the Tanganyika service was brought under the same administration, and Nairobi and Dar es Salaam were first linked by phone, there were 4,500 telephones in the three territories, 10.6 million pieces of internal mail and half a million inland telegrams. There were fewer than a thousand licensed radios, and the only radio station was in Kenya.[49] In other words, postal and telecommunications were little developed at the time of the 1920's Closer Union Movement.

Compare this with the situation in 1960 as outlined in Table 7 on the following page.

Table 7

Postal Facilities and Telecommunications in East Africa

	1938	1945	1960
Total mail, except parcels (million pieces)	27	64	125
Telephones	7,500	12,000	73,000
Telephone calls (millions)	6.7	16.3	73
Radios licensed	4,000	7,600 (K)	61,000 (K&T)
Inland telegrams (millions)	.8	1.5	.95

Sources: *Economic and Statistical Review,* Table E 6; East African Postal and Telecommunications Administration, *Annual Reports* (Nairobi).

Between 1951 and 1960, the amount of mail increased 64 per cent; the number of post offices 41 per cent; the number of telephones 185 per cent, and telephone calls 140 per cent. The decline in internal telegrams was more than offset by the rise in telephone calls. Not only did total mail increase, but internal East African mail also increased slightly as a proportion of total mail: from 60 per cent in 1936 and 61 per cent in 1945 to 65 per cent in 1955. Kenya's importance as an entrepôt was reflected in its proportion of total East African mail—nearly three fourths in 1955.

NEWS MEDIA

It is sometimes said that the transistor radio revolutionized politics in the Middle East. Such a statement would be too strong to make about East Africa, but the expansion of broadcasting was certainly one of the most important changes after World War II.

In 1960 Radio Uganda broadcast 56 hours a week in English and six vernacular languages (not Swahili) to some 630,000 people daily—about ten per cent of the population.[50] The Tanganyika Broadcasting Corporation transmitted 105 hours a week in English and Swahili to some 500,000 people, or about five per cent of the population.[51] The Kenya Broadcasting Corporation (K.B.C.) broadcast 85 hours in English, 110 hours in Swahili, and 90 hours a week in Hindustani on nation-wide programs. In addition, three regional stations each broadcast 45 hours a week in 16 vernacular languages. Officials of K.B.C. estimated that close to two million Kenyans (a quarter of the population), listened daily. In addition, in 1962 K.B.C. commenced 31 hours a week of television broadcasting to an estimated 100,000 viewers (at the end of 1963).[52] In October 1963 Uganda also started television broadcasting.

Unfortunately, there was no way of discovering the extent to which listeners in one country tuned in the neighboring country on a short-wave set, but since Tanganyika and Uganda estimated their total number of sets at under 100,000 each, it was presumably not a large part of the population.

Figures on interterritorial newspaper circulation were obtainable (see Table 8). There were two major groups of newspapers with a paper in more than one territory, and these related papers used each other's news services. Nairobi had a clear dominance in circulation of papers to other territories. Very few Uganda or Tanganyika papers were sold in Kenya.

If we use the *East African Standard's* estimates of four readers per English paper and ten readers (or listeners) per Swahili paper, more than 110,000 Tanganyikans and about 90,000 Ugandans read Kenya papers weekly—about two per cent of the population in each case. Using the same figures, 180,000 Tanganyikans and 61,000 Ugandans were reading Kenya papers in 1957. Margaret Bates remarked that many Africans in Tanganyika followed Kenya events more closely than their own because of the circulation of the Kenya paper

79

Table 8

Interterritorial Circulation of Kenya Newspapers, 1963

	Tanganyika		Uganda	
	Daily	Weekly	Daily	Weekly
English language:				
E. A. Standard	670	1,780	400	1,900
Daily Nation	1,560	5,100	330	3,700
Reporter Magazine		1,400	—	1,100
Total		8,280	730	6,700
Swahili language:				
Baraza		7,220		5,100
Taifa		1,200	720	1,370
Total		8,420	720	6,470
Total English and Swahili	2,230	16,700	1,450	13,170

Sources: Letter from E. A. newspapers, August 23, 1963; interview, Circulation Manager, *East African Standard,* July 29, 1963; letter from *Reporter,* July 30, 1963.

Baraza.[53] By 1963 this was no longer true. According to the paper's circulation manager, the reason for the decline was the growth of interest in local events.[54] This is an example of the disintegrative impact which separate political development had on transnational society in East Africa.

EDUCATION

Education was an important social factor in East African integration for two reasons. First, its general low level helps explain the importance of the elite in the unification process. Second, shared educational experience was a source of unity among the East African elite.

East Africa had a much smaller educated class than existed in British West Africa. Ghana, with about the same size and population as Uganda, had twice the number of secondary school students in 1950 that Uganda had in 1960. Nigeria, with about four times Tanganyika's population in

1959, had twenty-two times as many secondary school students. While Nigeria had several hundred university degree holders in 1948, Tanganyika had approximately 70 Africans with university degrees in 1959.[55]

In 1958, 656 Kenyans, 622 Ugandans, and 174 Tanganyikans were in their twelfth year of education. For boys (the figure for girls was much lower) this represented .61, 68, and .14 per cent of their age groups in Kenya, Uganda, and Tanganyika respectively.[56] As will be seen in Table 9, the educational pyramid remained extremely narrow at the top.

Table 9
African Education, 1961–62

Schools	Kenya	Uganda	Tanganyika	East Africa
Primary and intermediate	828,000	413,000	506,000	1,747,000
Secondary	6,400	6,700	5,800	18,900
University of East Africa (1962)	275	306	146	727
Universities outside of East Africa (1962)	1,075	889	221	2,185

Source: EACSO, *Report of the Africanization Commission* (Nairobi, 1963), pp. 38, 98–99.

Although Ugandan secondary schools attracted a certain number of Kenyans, interterritorial education was mainly at the higher level. Uganda's Makerere College, founded as a trade school in 1921, upgraded and made into an interterritorial institution after 1937, and granted university-college status in 1949, played an important role in helping form an interterritorial elite. Its greatest impact was in the 1940's and 1950's. Before that, only 129 of its 793 graduates had come from outside Uganda. Indeed, up to 1953, nearly half the total alumni were not merely Ugandans, but Baganda.[57] By 1960 its students were drawn in roughly equal thirds from the three territories.

With the great increase in students receiving higher education elsewhere, however, the impact of Makerere is bound to diminish in the 1960's. In 1956 a technical college was founded in Nairobi and upgraded to a university college two years later. In 1962 another university-college was started in Dar es Salaam. This increased diversification of higher education can be seen in Table 10.

Table 10

African Higher Education

Territory	Makerere	Royal College	Dar es Salaam	Abroad	Total
Tanganyika 1958	209	27	—	80	316
1962	113	16	17	221	367
Kenya 1959	285	72	—	350	707
1962	185	116	13	1075	1389
Uganda 1959	259	55	—	400 (?)	700 (?)
1962	244	90	11	889	1234

Sources: *Report of the Africanization Commission*, p. 98; International Bank for Reconstruction and Development, *The Economic Development of Tanganyika* (Dar es Salaam, 1960), p. 168; Makerere University College, *Reports for 1958–59, 1962–63*; interview, Registrar's Assistant, Royal College, December 5, 1963.

This table probably underestimates the number of students abroad, particularly for Tanganyika. The important point is the growing diversification of higher education in East Africa and the proportionately greater number of students going to overseas universities. This is another example of social changes outside the arena of conscious political decisions which seemed to be disintegrative in their long-term effect. Nonetheless, in 1963 the important point was the past integrative effect of Makerere. In 1960, 11 of 30 Uganda Legislative Council members were Makerere alumni, as were 8 of 17 members in Tanganyika and 7 of 14 elected members in Kenya. In 1963, 20 of the 49 cabinet ministers in the three countries were Makerere graduates.

One can draw only limited conclusions from a description of this social background to East African efforts to federate: (1) The limits on the ability to communicate and respond were much greater during the abortive attempts to unify East Africa in the 1920's. (2) In most matters considered (except labor migration), East Africa was more integrated than Greater East Africa—in other words, there were geographical limits to the transnational society. (3) Various historical and economic developments helped explain the different positions taken by the three territories in 1963. (4) The social changes lumped as "social mobilization" were creating problems such as unemployment, requiring attention and action by the leaders in the national states. Certain social changes in newspaper readership and higher education seemed to indicate a trend away from greater integration in East Africa.[58]

But it is also important to notice what one can *not* conclude. These social factors, whether taken alone, or even collectively, were insufficient to explain the decisions which were made in 1963 affecting integration. Any one of them could have been overcome by conscious willed action. They merely constituted the situation within which the elites manipulated their ideology and interests. In other words, these social forces, the growth and disintegration of transnational society, provide no explanation or "key" to understanding unification. There was no "automatic" social process—automatic in the sense that it was divorced from conscious political decisions. Social integration is a precondition, not a substitute, for political integration.

IV

Political Integration

For 40 years the Imperialists and local settler minorities tried to impose political federation upon us. Our people rightly resisted these attempts. Federation at that time would have led to one thing—a vast White-dominated dominion . . . We are convinced that the time has now come to create such central political authority.

Kenyatta, Obote, Nyerere
June 5, 1963

Political integration is the process leading to political community—a condition in which a group of people recognizes mutual obligations and some notion of a common interest.[1] Political integration is related to power structure—armies, police forces, budgets, and communications networks—in two ways. First, community is asserted to legitimize a power structure, to make certain uses of force acceptable. Second, the way in which a power structure develops influences how a political community grows.

We can see this clearly in East Africa. Africans asserted that the colonial power structure was illegitimate, that it was unrelated to the feelings of community among the people it ruled. But asserting this idea was not enough to bring about change. Successful nationalism involves organization as well as ideas. When nationalist institutions were established in East Africa, they were built at the territorial (not the East African) level because British colonialism had constructed the effective power structure (which the African elite wished to capture) at the territorial level. Once they had captured it, the African leaders had to use the territorial power structure to "build a nation," to create the community that they had claimed. This put strains on the weak East African structure of cooperation.

If Britain had been able to build a stronger East African power structure (and she failed largely because of the absence of community among the "races"); or if Julius Nyerere had been able to persuade his Ugandan and Kenyan colleagues to form an East African nationalist organization, as he tried to do in 1958, the major steps toward political integration would have been taken before independence. In the event, Britain created only a weak cooperative structure in East Africa, and this was reflected in the regional nationalist organization, Pafmeca, which was a weak framework for cooperation among nationalists.

At the time of the federal negotiations, partial political integration already existed. East Africans debated together in the Central Legislative Assembly of the Common Services Organization, and the cooperative framework led them to recognize certain obligations and common interests. Similarly, Pafmeca had, in the words of the Nairobi declaration on federation, led to "common objectives and ideas and . . . the essential spirit of unity" among nationalists.[2] But political disintegration was a strong possibility so long as separate power structures were consolidating the national interests and communities which had been asserted in the struggles for independence.

The problem of political integration after independence was less the reconciliation of differences in such modern and poorly rooted institutions as legislatures, nonpolitical civil services, and regional administrations (which are em-

85

phasized in classical federal theory),[3] than it was a matter of relations between political organizations which were building separate nations. Institutional differences would have faded in 1963 had the leaders of the three countries been able to create the single East African party which so many of them confidently stated that they would.[4] To understand these problems, we must go back and start at the beginning.

COLONIAL POLITICAL INTEGRATION

However defined, no single tribe or group had been sufficiently powerful to impose either a power structure or sense of community on East Africa in the precolonial era. The nomadic Masai and the Bunyoro and Buganda kingdoms all covered considerable areas at one time or another, but they left no unifying memory of ancient empire such as exists in parts of West Africa. Nor was the precolonial influence of Zanzibari traders sufficient to create the necessary power structure, community, or myth.

Britain became interested in East Africa after involvement in Egypt in the early 1880's, and German initiative in East Africa in the mid-1880's aroused British concern over control of the sources of the Nile.[5] The original British vision of East Africa was North-South, centered upon the Nile, with what is now Kenya of only incidental interest. Nonetheless, the Anglo-German agreements of 1886 and 1890 split the area on an East-West line, a situation not reversed until the defeat of Germany in World War I.

Because of the colonial division, the first attempt to unify East Africa was concerned with what is now Kenya and Uganda. In 1901 Sir Harry Johnston, who had been sent to East Africa as Special Commissioner, recommended that what are now Kenya and Uganda be merged. Sir Clement

86

Hill, head of the African Department of the Foreign Office, disagreed on the grounds that the new unit would be too large, and substituted a plan to transfer Uganda's Eastern Province to Kenya (then called the East African Protectorate) in order to bring the newly completed rail line under one administration.

Had Johnston's proposal been accepted, the great energies devoted to unification during the next sixty years might have been spent on other problems. It is ironical that personal animosity rather than compelling reasons probably caused Hill's action.[6] The extent of the irony was deepened by the transfer of Uganda's high-lying Uashin Gishu and Trans-Nzoia areas to Kenya in 1902, since this set the basis for the later reliance on African agriculture in Uganda and on European agriculture in Kenya. This difference in the racial basis of economic and social policies was to be the major pitfall in later colonial efforts at unification.

The two territories diverged rapidly after the transfer. In 1902 there were fewer than a dozen Europeans farming in the East Africa Protectorate. The next year, Sir Charles Eliot, Commissioner of the East Africa Protectorate (who had agreed to the territorial transfer on the condition that it should not rule out further amalgamation), sent an official to South Africa to recruit white settlers to farm in Kenya in order to create revenue for the new rail line. In 1906 the Colonial Secretary pledged that, as an administrative matter, the highlands of Kenya would be reserved for white settlement, and by 1911 there were 3175 Europeans in Kenya. Moreover, they were very politically conscious Europeans. From its foundation in 1911 until the depression of the 1930's, their Convention of Associations, sometimes called the "Settler's Parliament," generally overshadowed the official Legislative Council which had first met in 1907.[7]

In contrast, in Uganda the 1900 Buganda Agreement negotiated by Sir Harry Johnston established African individual land tenure, a land-owning class, and a special position for Uganda's central kingdom which remained a dominant feature of Uganda's politics even after independence. When Sir Hesketh Bell became Governor in 1905, he made it clear that large-scale European settlement would not be welcome, and that "any suggestion of federation between two such incompatible areas would be most undesirable." Bell also laid the foundation of the peasant economy by introducing cotton and investing heavily in a rural road system. In this situation, European political activity was more relaxed than in Kenya. A Legislative Council only met for the first time in 1921, fourteen years after Kenya. In general, Uganda's Europeans were cool to the idea of tying "Uganda's potential economic prosperity to the less promising future of East Africa."[8] Thus, within a decade, differences had sprung up which prevented positive action on the report of Sir Percy Girouard, who had been instructed to investigate amalgamation of East Africa in 1910.

After this initial failure the major colonial effort to build a common political framework in East Africa was the "closer union movement" which lasted from 1924 to 1931. What is sometimes called "the settlers' federation movement" was rather an imperial federation movement with which the settlers fully agreed only in 1927 when it appeared to be a means to (white) internal self-government.[9]

Leopold Amery, Colonial Secretary and leading proponent of federation, was guided less by Johnston's motives of economic and administrative efficiency than by a vision of larger empire units bolstering post-war Britain's status as a world power.[10] (Curiously, both Amery and Pan-Africanists forty years later shared a belief in the efficacy of bigness in states.)

Political Integration

The shape of the new unit was uncertain. The East Africa Commission appointed under W. G. A. Ormsby-Gore in 1924 was directed to include Northern Rhodesia and Nyasaland. Although the proposed federation was later limited to East Africa, the vision of links to the south persisted.[11] Even in 1953 a Colonial Office survey of a rail line to Central Africa, although dubious about the economic benefits, speculated that "it may be . . . that this great stretch of British Africa, an area of over a million square miles extending from Abyssinia to the Union, will emerge as a Dominion."[12]

This focus on the aesthetics of cartography was part of the weakness of the movement for closer union. The Ormsby-Gore Commission concluded that lack of communications and the expense of federal government would prevent significant benefit to East Africa. The Commission found little sense of community, knowledge regarding one another, or support for federation amongst East Africans.[13] Yet this did not prevent the closer union movement from muddling on for another six years.

Amery appointed Sir Edward Grigg to be Governor of Kenya in 1925 with instructions to pursue the question of closer union.[14] Grigg, reporting in 1927, favored further efforts but pointed out that the price of success would be progress toward (white) self-government in Kenya, "because the establishment of Closer Union must involve some considerable surrender of powers already enjoyed by the Kenya Government and the Legislature . . ."[15]

Under the leadership of Lord Delamere, who had initially been opposed to closer union, Kenya settlers had come to support the idea on the condition of a settler majority in Kenya. This they expressed in their election manifesto of December 1926. Delamere had paved the way for this acceptance at conferences of nonofficials at Tukuyu, Tanganyika, in 1925 (the difficult logistics of which we mentioned in the last chapter) and at Livingstone, Northern Rhodesia, in 1926, also the year in which the first Conference of Governors, recommended by the Ormsby-Gore Commission, had met.[16]

Meanwhile, at a conference of East African governors in London early in 1927, Sir Donald Cameron of Tanganyika, who feared the spread of Kenya's pro-European racial policy to his territory, clashed with his colleagues over closer union. In July a white paper entitled *Future Policy in Regard to Eastern Africa* was published, and another commission was appointed under Sir Edward Hilton Young to look once again into how and whether closer union should be brought about. The Commission separated the problems of closer union and a settler majority in Kenya (as Grigg had said they could not do) and recommended the appointment of a High Commissioner with considerable power over "native policy," and certain common services.[17] All this was anathema to the Kenya settlers.

Amery then sent his Permanent Under-Secretary, Sir Samuel Wilson, to East Africa to try to salvage the plan. By dropping the proposals on native policy and concentrating on services, Wilson was able to achieve some agreement on an arrangement resembling that finally established in 1947.[18] Lord Passfield, the new Labour Party Colonial Secretary, intended to implement Wilson's report, but lobbying by J. H. Oldham, Secretary of the Missionary Study Council of the United Free Church of Scotland, and Lord Lugard (and earlier lobbying by Cameron who had been in London in 1928) made this impossible.[19]

Instead, the Government issued yet another white paper (which left Kenya unchanged and proposed a high commissioner with powers over native policy and services) which was the basis for a final investigation of closer union by a Joint Select Committee of both Houses of Parliament. By this time all races in Uganda, the Tanganyika Administration, and the Kenya settlers were opposed to federation. Thus the Report of the Joint Select Committee in 1931 merely urged an expanded role for the Governors' Conferences and increased coordination of economic services. As Grigg remarked, the report was "a sedative—almost a sleeping draught."[20]

The imperial closer union movement was over—despite some echoes which rumbled on into the 1930's. It left a useful residue in the form of Governors' Conferences, common postal service and telecommunications, cooperative programs in meteorology, locust control, air services, and higher education, but it failed to establish a strong enough East African structure to ensure that a community or (later) nationalist organizations would form at that level. It failed because of the differences in economic and social policies between the territories and because of the absence of a common set of ideas which would have made these differences seem less important. The extent of the differences can be judged from Table 11 on the following page.

As the Hilton Young Commission commented, a bit belatedly: "It is not safe to allow policy in Kenya to be framed regardless of what is being done in Tanganyika and Uganda."[21] How did the British reconcile three such different territorial policies with a single colonial policy? Time and social Darwinism helped them avoid the problem. During the first decade of the century (when the crucial decisions were made), British officials regarded tribes in Uganda which had rulers as "feudal," and thus more advanced in evolution than the tribes without rulers in Kenya. Even pro-African officials felt that "the evolution of races

Pan-Africanism and East African Integration

Table 11
East African Social Policies, 1927

	Kenya	Uganda	Tanganyika
POPULATION:			
African (estimate)	2,500,000	3,100,000	4,300,000
European	12,500	1,750	5,270
Asian	31,000	12,000	20,000
LAND USAGE:			
Area alienated (sq. mi.)	10,500	250	3,400
Area in Native Reserves (sq. mi.)	48,000	no reserves	no reserves
EXPORTS:	*£ million*	*£ million*	*£ million*
Value produced mainly by Africans	.4	2.2	1.2
Value produced mainly by non-Africans	2.4	.08	1.4
FINANCIAL (AFRICAN):			
Revenue raised from tax on Africans	£542,000	£502,000	£700,000
Amount paid back to native administrations	17,000	153,000	126,000
Total expenditure of native administrations	38,000	292,000	156,000
FINANCIAL (TOTAL):	*£ million*	*£ million*	*£ million*
Revenue	2.9	1.3	1.9
Public debt, June 1928	20.6	1.7	5.2
CIVIL SERVICE:			
Number of Europeans	1772	370	727
POLITICAL INSTITUTIONS:			
Legislative Council	1907 elections 1919	1921 no elections	1926 no elections
Unofficial members			
Europeans	11	2	5
Asians	5	1	2
Africans	none	none	none

Sources: *Report of the Commission on Closer Union of the Dependencies in Eastern and Central Africa* (Cmnd. 3234), pp. 315 ff; Kenneth Ingham, *A History of East Africa* (London, 1962), Chaps. 6 and 8.

must necessarily take centuries . . ."[22] But no matter how such policy differences were reconciled by the colonial rulers, the differences were too great to permit colonial political integration.

What central structure was achieved in East Africa must be credited in large part to World War II. As Sir Philip Mitchell, the prime architect of post-war cooperation put it: "The great closer union controversy was being determined for us all at last . . ." But even the establishment of a Production and Supply Council and War Supplies Board was not accepted without suspicion in Uganda.[23] The exigencies of common defense made cooperation possible; they did not remove the obstacles to political union.

Thus, when the post-war Labour Government, in 1945, proposed its plan, *Interterritorial Organisation in East Africa* (Colonial No. 191), it explicitly proposed cooperation, not federation. Sir Philip Mitchell, who had been assigned the task of devising appropriate machinery for running common services, felt after his experience with the Governors' Conferences and joint war machinery that a central administration and legislature were necessary, though "the rub was of course the legislature, for there was no way of avoiding raising the issue of representation, which would certainly be controversial . . ."[24] Paper 191 was acceptable to all groups save certain Baganda who feared a threat to the 1900 Agreement, and the Kenya settlers who objected to its provision for equal racial representation in the proposed legislature.[25] For Kenya settlers who had just admitted the first African to their Legislative Council the previous year, the implied political advance of this formula was a severe threat, and the discussion of Paper 191 focused on this point.

In February 1947 the British Government gave in to pressure by the settlers on the representation issue and submitted revised proposals in Colonial Paper 210.[26] Africans and Asians reacted bitterly to the capitulation, and the settlers accepted only warily connections with Uganda and Tanganyika which they feared might jeopardize European leadership in Kenya. In the racial conflict the complaint of the Nairobi Chamber of Commerce that Paper 210 no longer contained provision for common commercial legislation was scarcely heard. Various other powers in the areas of industrial licensing, motor transport rates, and agricultural marketing had also been dropped.[27]

Thus the East African High Commission began work on the first day of 1948 under less than ideal conditions. Eventually, it gained sufficient acceptance (or was sufficiently innocuous) that the territorial Legislative Councils extended the life of its Central Legislative Assembly in 1951, 1955, and 1959; but there was no extension of its scope, because "the people of East Africa are not yet willing to give the necessary consent."[28] By the end of the 1950's the High Commission was becoming unacceptable to many Africans. We will discuss the crisis in cooperative arrangements further in the next chapter. Suffice it to say here that the central political integration which was achieved under colonial rule was too weak to serve as a focal point for the growth of community or of nationalist organization.

ATTEMPTS TO FORM AN
EAST AFRICAN NATIONALIST MOVEMENT

In 1963 many East African politicians hoped to merge the three main territorial parties into one. As an important Uganda minister, George Magezi, said, "I think we can dissolve the UPC, the Tanganyika African National Union [Tanu], and the Kenya African National Union [Kanu], and make one party. After all, we support each other."[29] The three parties did indeed support each other. In 1961 Tanu gave money to the UPC and to Kanu for their election campaigns. In 1963 Tanu's and the UPC's help to Kanu provoked an official of the Kenya African Democratic Union (Kadu) to remark that "there is interference in Kenya affairs from Peking, Moscow, New York, Accra and Dar es Salaam. Of all the interference, the one from the last source is the worst."[30]

In June 1963 three of the six members of the first Working Party on federation were the secretaries-general of the three parties. When asked if minor parties might be represented, Tom Mboya of Kenya replied that it had not even been considered. Earlier he had claimed that "only Kanu had created relations with other East African leaders to facilitate federation."[31] Yet, despite this claim, it soon became apparent that a merger would be difficult to achieve. Each of the parties had developed a different structure around which various political interests clustered. These different structures were born of their development in separate territorial contexts.

There were several reasons why African leaders did not build an East African organization before independence. One problem was the impact of the colonial sense of time. Independence seemed ages away. In 1930 Jomo Kenyatta had written that his Kikuyu Central Association wished to "march together as loyal subjects of his Britannic Majesty along the road of Empire prosperity."[32] As late as 1958 in Kenya, the *East African Standard* was calling for a pro-white leader like Central Africa's Roy Welensky, and some 14,000 Africans were still in detention.[33] Not until 1960 was the Uganda People's Congress founded. Even its predecessor, the Uganda National Congress (UNC) dated back only to 1952. In Tanganyika, when Julius Nyerere founded Tanu in

1954, he foresaw a fifty-year struggle for independence. Even by 1957 he still predicted twelve years to "uhuru."[34] In other words, leaders were concerned with problems other than post-independence organizational unity—at least until just before independence was achieved.

Another problem was Buganda's reliance on her 1900 Agreement and her desire to avoid entanglement with East Africa. When E. M. K. Mulira founded his Progressive Party in 1955, he argued that "it is necessary for all Africans in East Africa to unite if they are to survive the White settlers' craving for domination," but most Ugandans (particularly Baganda) agreed with the words of a 1953 Uganda National Congress resolution calling for withdrawal from the High Commission because of "Uganda's status as an African country which must develop in its way, quite apart from the other E. A. territories."[35]

Uganda nationalism was not entirely separatist. For instance, in 1953 the Uganda National Congress sent protest telegrams to Nkrumah, Nehru, and Fenner Brockway, among others, and proposed a plan for an All Africa government. On several occasions the Ugandans stressed that they opposed links with East Africa because of the absence of African control. But their greatest fear was "that the British did not really intend to allow them to become a self-governing state."[36] This pattern of increased affinity for non-East Africans when Uganda's independence was threatened was to reappear in the summer of 1963, although many of the people involved in the two situations were not the same.

The possibilities of organizing an East African movement was first seriously investigated in 1945 after the publication of Paper 191.[37] James Gichuru and Francis Khamisi, Chairman and Secretary of the Kenya African Study Union (which later changed its name to Kenya African Union) traveled to Uganda and Tanganyika to explore the possibilities of a common African approach. They received a cool reception. Khamisi had known the Katikiro (Prime Minister) of Buganda when the latter was in Nairobi during World War II, but this gained the visitors nothing more than a five-minute interview during which they were told of Buganda's desire to avoid entanglement in East African politics.[38]

In Dar es Salaam, the Kenyans visited the Tanganyika African Association (TAA), an organization founded in 1929 with Governor Cameron's blessing. The TAA was a loosely federated and poorly organized group of clubs, mainly for lower civil servants. It did not hold its first mass meeting in the capital until two years later (to protest Paper 210), and it had only 2,000 members in 1948.[39] The visiting Kenyans found that they had to lecture to an apathetic meeting of twenty or thirty Tanganyikans on what Paper 191 was. The response to this Kenyan initiative was so poor in both Uganda and Tanganyika that the Kenyans made no efforts toward coordination after publication of the more objectionable Paper 210.[40]

East African nationalists made a second attempt at organizing in October 1950. Two Tanganyikans and three Ugandans met with several Kenyans in Kiambu, near Nairobi. Central Africans had been invited but were unable to attend, and fear of the impending Central African federation was a major factor in bringing the East Africans together. One source claims that the group discussed formation of a Republic of East Africa and an African National Congress organization under Kenyatta. Others remember more limited discussions which were hampered by the disparity between political organization in Kenya and its two neighbors.[41] By the time parties were started in Uganda (1952) and

Tanganyika (1954), the Kenya Emergency had destroyed nationalist organization in Kenya.

The third major effort to form an East African organization was made at the beginning of the "big push" in East African nationalism in 1958. After abortive attempts in 1957, East Africa's leaders met in Mwanza in September 1958. This conference not only founded Pafmeca, but also sent Nyerere and Mboya to bring unity among the parties in Uganda. Nyerere and Mboya were unable to reconcile the Uganda parties during their November visit, much less get acceptance of Nyerere's plan to form an East African organization with paid full-time officials.[42] As a result, Pafmeca remained an analogue, on the nationalist level, to the weak political integration of the colonial power structure. Pafmeca was important, as we will see at the end of the chapter, but in a very limited way. Real power and real nationalist organization were in the three territories, and the difference in the territorial settings resulted in the creation of organizations which were not easily merged into one.

THE NATIONALIST MOVEMENT IN TANGANYIKA

Tanganyika, last of the three territories to gain a Legislative Council (1926), a ministerial system (1957), and a nationalist party (1954), was nonetheless the first East African territory to achieve independence (1961).

Part of the explanation lies in social factors unique to Tanganyika. We noted in the preceding chapter the importance of the Swahili language. While too much should not be made of the difference between German direct and British indirect rule, the Germans did diminish the legitimacy of a number of tribal leaders.[43] Perhaps most important, the only one of Tanganyika's 120 tribes which numbered over a million persons—the Sukuma—was a loose federation a great distance from the capital. Tribes like the Chagga and Haya which experienced the greatest economic development had neither the numbers nor the central location of the Kikuyu in Kenya or the Baganda in Uganda.

Moreover, the Tanganyika Africans never had the example of turbulent immigrant politics that Kenya has had. The Asians in Tanganyika did not have a strong association which could challenge the Europeans as they did in Kenya. The Europeans, divided ethnically and geographically, only began organized political activity after the Second World War, and only in the Northern Province did they bear much political resemblance to Kenya settlers.[44] Thus, Tanganyika gained a reputation as a territory without politics and enjoying racial harmony. Both were myths engendered by the comparison with Kenya. As late as 1958 Julius Nyerere was refused service in leading hotels in Dar es Salaam.[45] And the Northern settlers, in particular, were vehement in opposition to the racial parity formula recommended by Governor Twining's Committee on Constitutional Development in 1951.

Twining's policy was multiracialism—meaning communal equality rather than the individual equality of one man, one vote. He implemented it by expanding the Legislative Council to 61 in 1955, including 10 non-officials from each race; and by covertly aiding in the formation of a multiracial party, the United Tanganyika Party, in 1956. This was bitterly opposed by Tanu, which stood for "undiluted democracy." The banning of Tanu branches and the persistence of the multiracial policy on the local level caused continual friction between Tanu and the colonial government until after Tanu-supported candidates won a majority of the seats in the first elections in 1958–59.[46] Only when the

99

British government accepted the principle of an African majority in 1959 did tension and bitterness diminish.

But if the history and constitutional development of Tanganyika explain part of its rapid progress in the late 1950's, a large part also must be credited to the structure of Tanu. While the press image of Tanu as one of the most effective mass parties in Africa was overly generous, there was no doubt that other parties in East Africa in 1963 bore no likeness to it.

Tanu did not start so promisingly. Until 1957 it was a caucus-type party with narrow recruitment, outstanding local leaders, and little bureaucracy. When Julius Nyerere transformed the TAA (of which he had become president the previous year) into Tanu in 1954, he inherited some 15,000 members (primarily in the capital, Mwanza, and the Northern Province), but the organization was loosely structured and relied heavily on tribal associations.[47]

Given Nyerere's initial vision of a fifty-year struggle, there appeared no immediate need for a mass party, but events intervened. The 1954 Visiting Mission of the United Nations Trusteeship Council treated Tanu as the voice of African opinion, much to the government's chagrin. This gave Tanu publicity and stature beyond anything that had been enjoyed by the minor civil servants of the TAA. Nyerere's trip to the United Nations in New York the following February was another focus for publicity and fund-raising.

At this time Tanu was partly self-organizing in the villages, where local malcontents were emphasizing the racial aspects of colonialism. Although the party claimed to have 100,000 members by the end of 1956, the men who succeeded Nyerere's chief deputy, Oscar Kambona, as Secretary-General when Kambona went to Britain to study, were not notable organizers.[48] Early in 1957 Nyerere complained that the government was "picking on our minor officials to close whole branches"—a reflection both on Twining's policy and on the poor internal discipline of Tanu at that time.[49] By the end of the year ten branches had been closed.

Tanu changed in 1958.[50] One cause was the approach of the first elections designed to return ten members of each race to the Legislative Council. In January Nyerere persuaded a skeptical Annual Conference at Tabora that Tanu should participate in these "multiracial" elections.[51] The other important change was in party administration. Edward Kisenge, former government clerk, Tanu provincial chairman, and an able administrator, became Secretary-General.

Up to that time the party had been built on other units—tribal, cooperatives, or old TAA branches, plus autonomous village groups formed without the help of headquarters.[52] While opposed to tribalism, Tanu had been careful not to attack chiefs if it were possible to bring them into the party.[53] Kisenge made two important changes in Tanu—centralization and bureaucratization. For the first time, secretaries from the district level on up were paid regular salaries, and chairmen were given allowances. A secretary became a career man who could be shifted from one area to another, and Kisenge (helped by the existence of Swahili as a lingua franca) made it a policy to shift people.[54] Thus secretaries had to rely on central party, not local, support.

By the end of 1958 Tanu had a fleet of ten landrovers and 800 officials receiving some form of monetary compensation.[55] The big gain in Tanu membership came after its strength had been demonstrated in the elections of September 1958, showing that, in nationalist organization particularly, nothing succeeds (before independence) like success. Tanu's election victory killed any hopes for success of the Council of Chiefs which the government had started in 1957, and many chiefs joined Tanu with their followers.[56] From 300,000 in July 1958, the party grew to claim a million members in June 1960. The *Tanganyika Standard* reported that Tanu had 1.3 million members at the time of independence. In 1963 party officials claimed to have something between one-and-a-half and two million members in some 1200 sub-branches.[57]

Despite some loss of personnel caused by the rewarding of party officials with government jobs or scholarships after independence, Tanu maintained its network of paid officials who reported regularly to its efficient headquarters. Some observers argued that post-independence changes— such as merger of the party secretary at provincial and district level with the colonial governmental post of commissioner, and the proclamation of Tanu as the single legal party—were symptoms of the increased importance of the government rather than of the party.[58] However that may be, political integration in Kenya or Uganda could not compare with what Tanu had achieved in Tanganyika at the time of the federal negotiations in 1963.

THE NATIONAL MOVEMENT IN UGANDA

One reason why Uganda was different from her East African neighbors was the number of cleavages in her society. Among the most significant were those between the African, Asian, and European races; between Protestant, Catholic, and Muslim religions; between Nilotic-speaking Northerners and Bantu-speaking Southerners; between tribes with strong rulers and tribes without them; between educated participants in the modern economy and uneducated participants in the traditional economy; between those who wished to defend, and those who wished to destroy, traditional political organizations.

Tanganyika had some of the same cleavages—in particular, the religious, racial, educational, and traditionalist ones. The important difference was that Tanganyikan political organization became structured in such a way (after the major increase in the party bureaucracy in 1958) that these cleavages were not articulated, and an idea screen was created which deliberately played them down.

The failure to create the same type of nationalist organization in Uganda cannot be explained without some description of the status of Buganda as the central province in the country. In 1963 the Baganda accounted for nearly a fifth of Uganda's population, or about twice as many people as the next largest tribe (the Teso). In area, Buganda is a centrally located and fertile fifth of the total land in Uganda. Kampala, the national capital and largest city, is in Buganda; and through immigration Buganda's population became more than a quarter of the country's total. Moreover, per capita African income in Buganda was £19.3 in 1961, compared to the next highest average of £12.8 in Bunyoro and £4.8 and £4.3 respectively in the northern areas, Acholi and West Nile.[59]

In contrast to the Kikuyu in Kenya, the Baganda experienced little urbanization or destruction of their traditional system, and Ganda political activity was preoccupied with Buganda's internal disputes. Until the 1950's political groups formed in Buganda were concerned with issues resulting from the 1900 Agreement, rather than with Uganda-wide issues such as self-government.[60]

The focus on internal issues did not mean that Buganda failed to change. On the contrary, the province had more wealth, education, and baptisms than other parts of the country. But its modernization was on a tribal rather than an individual level.[61] New layers were added to the old. This was possible because the destruction of hereditary chief-ships by powerful Kabakas (kings) in the nineteenth century had created a hierarchy based on instrumental rather than inherent value except at the very peak, in the Kabaka-ship. The result was what Apter calls a "modernizing autocracy"—able to tolerate considerable change so long as that change did not threaten the Kabakaship.[62] Given the low levels of urbanization, of labor organization, of overseas education, and reasonably good opportunities for a career in the Buganda government, the traditional system proved remarkably able to absorb the changes brought by the colonial power.

Even after 1950, when Africans achieved parity of un-official representation in the Uganda Legislative Council (the first parity in East Africa), Buganda remained inward-looking. To simplify a complicated matter, in 1953 a liberal governor, Sir Andrew Cohen, attempted to gain the Kabaka's support for "progressive" but unpopular reforms aimed at building a central governmental structure for Uganda. The Kabaka refused to cooperate and instead seized upon the pretext of the Colonial Secretary's informal remark about eventual federation of East Africa to put forward demands for *Buganda's* independence.

Cohen's response, deposing of the Kabaka, stunned Bu-ganda and restored the monarch's popularity (which had begun to wane). In the words of one observer: "People were walking around dazed, unable to believe the news that their king had been flown away . . . even those who did not understand the issues involved or who were opposed to the feudal nature of the office were solidly behind him."[63] Two years later, when the British realized the futility of their act and restored the Kabaka, there were two differences in Buganda politics. First, the Kabaka was stronger than he had been before; second, federation became associated in the minds of the ordinary Baganda with a threat to the Kabaka.[64]

In March 1952, the year before the deposing of the Kabaka, Ignatius Musazi, a Muganda, onetime teacher, and more recently founder of a cooperative which became the Federation of Uganda African Farmers (FUAF), formed Uganda's first political party, the Uganda National Congress. With a constitution (written in 1954) patterned on the Convention People's Party of Ghana and with aims which included eradication of tribal barriers and unity under an African government, the UNC was a radical departure from past Uganda politics.[65]

The UNC was more parochial in its support and organization. Half the FUAF district directors became UNC organizers, and the two organizations shared the same office in Kampala.[66] In expanding, UNC leaders relied on such local issues as clan politics in Busoga and Acholi, opposition to formation of a game park in Toro, and FUAF problems in Lango and Teso. In Tanganyika, Tanu had also capitalized on local issues. The difference was that the UNC never built a strong bureaucracy and so remained dependent on this type of support.[67]

The core of the party was the twenty or so members of the Central Committee in Kampala. Meetings were loosely organized, and various leaders often packed them with their own supporters. Leaders maintained contact with branches by tours and visits, and branches often refused to accept centrally nominated officers or pay dues to the center. An early observer estimated UNC membership at something between 15,000 and 50,000. Its support was much wider.[68]

This poorly organized party, which had originally supported Cohen's reforms, became the Kabaka's defender after the deportation, to its short-run gain but long-run destruction.[69] The deportation destroyed a unified nationalist movement in three ways. First, by enhancing the position of the Kabaka, it made it difficult for the nationalist organization to establish itself as the source of legitimacy. Second, it turned the attention of the Baganda leaders of the party away from touring the country (their main form of contact with the active branches of the North), inward to Buganda intrigue. Third, it delivered the UNC into the hands of its enemies, the neotraditionalist "king's friends" who had gained control of the Buganda government in 1955. The neotraditionalists broke the party as a political force by shattering the prestige of its leaders with (presumably) false accusations, and by stirring up Ganda nationalism.[70]

Buganda boycotted the first elections to the Legislative Council in 1958 through fear of being absorbed into a unitary Uganda government. This further weakened the UNC. Although four of the eleven members elected in 1958 had run as UNC candidates (making it the largest party in the Council), they were elected as individuals. Within two months, one had quit to join several independents from the West and East to form a new party, the Uganda People's Union (UPU). The seven members of the new party then became the largest party in the Council, though not in the country. The fact that most of what remained of the UNC was in the North, was confirmed by two party splits in January and August 1959, in which the Baganda leaders Musazi and Joseph Kiwanuka were expelled, leaving control of most of the party in the hands of a northern leader, Milton Obote.

Political Integration

Because of these failures of the UNC, the party with the most widespread support in 1959 was the Catholic-based Democratic Party (DP). Religion had always been more important in Uganda politics than in Tanganyika, from the religious wars and factions at the end of the nineteenth century to the separatist movements of Joswa Kate Mugema and Reuben Spartas.[71] The Democratic Party, which started in Buganda in 1954 and in the rest of the country in 1956, was originally more a Catholic pressure group than a party. In part, its origins were philosophical and related to Catholic Action, but it also represented a social group which felt underprivileged and at that time might have been absorbed by a more dynamic and better organized nationalist movement.[72]

In 1958, as the elections approached, the militant nationalist lawyer and ex-soldier, Benedicto Kiwanuka, was elected president, and the DP became a proper political party. It expanded rapidly, though continuing to rely on mission schools for its branches and on teachers for its candidates.[73] In 1958 it returned one member to the Legislative Council and gained a quarter of the vote; in 1961 it won a majority of seats in the Council but not a majority of the votes; and in defeat in 1962, it captured 46 per cent of the vote outside Buganda (which did not hold direct elections).

The Democratic Party won a majority of seats in the expanded Council in 1961 because a Buganda boycott of the elections permitted the 35,000 (of an eligible 983,000) Buganda voters brave enough to register and vote despite considerable intimidation, to elect unrepresentative candidates to the twenty-one seats from Buganda.[74]

This result was so intolerable to the Buganda government that it formed an alliance with the Uganda People's Congress (UPC) which Obote had formed from his UNC and

107

the UPU collection of notables in 1960. The alliance was a strange one of left and right against the middle, and there was little love among the partners.[75]

A central feature of the alliance became known at the London constitutional conference in September 1961. Buganda would be allowed to elect its national members indirectly through its Lukiko (parliament) rather than submit to direct elections. The result was a 65-to-3 seat victory for the newly formed Kabaka Yekka (Kabaka Alone) movement over the DP in the Lukiko elections early in 1962. Subsequently, the Lukiko selected twenty-one Kabaka Yekka members to join the thirty-five newly elected UPC members in the National Assembly, where the two groups formed the independence government. After independence the instability of this coalition became one of the major concerns in Uganda politics.

Within Buganda itself, modern political organization developed slowly. In 1959 neotraditionalists who feared that the recently appointed Constitutional Commission might destroy Buganda's special position, and progressives who had seen their organizational bases destroyed, joined and hoped to influence the Uganda National Movement, a popular boycott movement aimed primarily at Asian traders. When this movement was broken by the colonial government, Ganda political activity focused on secession threatened for the end of the year. Though the motions were carried out, the threat collapsed when Buganda emissaries failed to gain international support and the important neotraditionalists withdrew from the movement.[76]

In June 1961 S. K. Masembe-Kabali led a group of loyalist Baganda who were worried about the position of the Kabaka in forming the Kabaka Yekka movement. They were later joined by progressives like J. S. L. Zake and

William Kalema who had opposed secession but were unable to build parties of their own. Finally, the movement received the approval of the Kabaka and of important neotraditionalists like Michael Kintu and Amos Sempa.[77]

Kabaka Yekka's organization was slight and it relied heavily on Buganda chiefs. A year after foundation, it had funds of £50 and no constitution.[78] When a constitution was promulgated and officers elected in September 1962, the Kabaka intervened to ensure neotraditionalist control of the movement. Despite persistent rumors and various committees appointed to determine the future of the movement, during its first two years Kabaka Yekka proved remarkable in its ability to include strands as diverse as the Bawejjere (Common Man), who combined radicalism and traditionalism, and the ultratraditionalists who wished to "purify" the movement.[79] All these elements could be disciplined with the threat of accusations of disloyalty to the Kabaka— a method which was used to control the leader of the Bawejjere. Not until after the federation announcement in June 1963 did eight of its 21 members of Parliament, including most of the progressive strand, join the UPC. That they were able to do so was an indication that the power of the system built on the Kabaka was beginning to wane now that alternative employment and a government willing to use force existed in Uganda.[80]

At the time of the federal negotiations the UPC was gradually extending its power. It won the last district council (Ankole) away from the Democratic Party in 1963, and enough Members of Parliament crossed the aisle to give the UPC a small majority in its own right. But important social groups—the Baganda and many Catholics—maintained organizations of their own outside the major nationalist party —organizations which could not be ignored, as the DP proved when it won a victory in the municipal elections in the spring of 1964.[81]

Not only was the country less integrated, but the UPC itself was a far less cohesive and organized party than Tanu. In appearance alone the contrast was great. The visitor to Tanu entered a modern three-story building built by the party for its own use. Up the road was an even bigger and better building lent by the party to the University. In contrast, the UPC inhabited a dozen or so rooms on the third floor of an office building. Both headquarters partook of the aura of chaos created by the inevitable hangers-on, but there was more of a sense of administration about the Tanu headquarters. This impression was borne out in the finance, discipline, branch activity, and communications of the two parties. A number of important people within the UPC wished to change this and make the party more like Tanu. Other influential figures opposed such changes, which would have shifted the balance of power within the UPC. Merger into a single East African organization would have raised these same internal problems. Diversity within the major nationalist party as well as within the country made Uganda's political integration into East Africa difficult.

THE NATIONALIST MOVEMENT IN KENYA

If UPC headquarters were unimpressive compared to Tanu's, those of Kanu were even worse. The same could be said of Kanu's organization. Yet more so than in Uganda, Kanu leaders felt that their party was like Tanu. This paradox is explained by Kenya's forty-year history of nationalist organization which made Kanu a party with the following —but not the organization—of a mass party.

This history of political activity, however, was limited to part of the country, primarily to the centrally located

Kikuyu tribe which suffered the greatest disruption from the white man's rule. Although Kanu had wide support among other tribes, its two solid pillars were the Kikuyu near Nairobi and the Luo from Nyanza Province, near Lake Victoria, which together accounted for 35 per cent of the population of Kenya.

Because the pastoral tribes and coastal people changed more slowly, they came to fear the dominance of the two main tribes, and were harder for Kanu to penetrate. They formed the main strength of the Kenya African Democratic Union (Kadu). Unlike Uganda, where the nationalist movement failed to integrate the most important group, in Kenya it failed to integrate the less important groups.

The Luo and Kikuyu were not united in a nationalist organization until after 1950, but as early as 1921 they were both responding to similar post-World War I conditions, such as an increase in poll and hut tax, the requirement of a special pass for Africans outside their reserves, and a reduction in African wages. That the Kikuyu reacted more strongly is partly attributable to their social structure, but partly to their closer contact with settlers and thus greater insecurity over land.[82] Even after the Carter Commission of the early 1930's concluded that 104 square miles of Kikuyu land had been alienated, and compensated the tribe by adding 265 square miles from another area to its reserve, the political myth of land theft remained vital to Kenya nationalism. So did the hard facts that African population was expanding and that the white .07 per cent of the population in Kenya controlled between 20 and 40 per cent of the best land.[83]

In 1920 Kikuyu chiefs and other conservatives formed a Kikuyu Association to present their grievances, but more important was the Young Kikuyu Association which a government telephone operator, Harry Thuku, founded the following year.[84] As Kenyatta later described the organization, "Each member of the committee went out and told the most important man in a village, and he would pass it on to all his people, and also send a messenger to the next village . . ."[85]

Thuku tried to extend this system by founding an East African Association and traveling to Nyanza Province.[86] Although his idea of a larger organization never materialized, his example had helped lead to formation of a Young Kavirondo Association, primarily among mission-educated Luo, in 1921.[87] In 1923 Archdeacon Owen of the Church Missionary Society in Nyanza Province converted the organization into the welfare-oriented Kavirondo Taxpayers' Welfare Association with himself as first president. This mainly Luo organization declined in the 1930's, and there was not a strong nationalist organization in Nyanza Province until the 1950's.

In 1922 the Kenya Government arrested Thuku, Kikuyu rioted in Nairobi, and Thuku was then deported for eight years. Kikuyu organization re-emerged in 1923 in the form of the Kikuyu Central Association (KCA) which was concerned over the right to grow coffee (denied to Africans), the release of Thuku, printing of laws in the Kikuyu language, and a paramount chief for the Kikuyu. After the fillip given to it by a controversy with the Church of Scotland over female circumcision in 1929, the KCA claimed 10,000 members, of whom 8,000 had paid their six shilling dues. When the KCA was banned in 1940 it had 7,000 members.[88] In addition, several other Kikuyu organizations had developed in the 1930's (including one led by a now chastened and more conservative Thuku), among them separatist churches and independent schools. Moreover, rudimentary organizations were developing among the Kamba, Taita, and Luhya.

Political Integration

When Eliud Mathu formed the Kenya African Study Union after his appointment in 1944 as the first African in the Legislative Council, he inherited no files, funds, or officers from these earlier associations, but he inherited something equally important—a people familiar with political organization.[89]

In 1946 Jomo Kenyatta, who had gone to London as a petitioner for the KCA in 1931 and had lived in exile since, returned to Kenya. The next year, when James Gichuru stepped down as president of the Kenya African Union ("Study" had been dropped from the name) in favor of Kenyatta, the organization, headed by three officers who served without salary, had 70,000 members mainly in Kikuyu but also in Kamba, Luhya and coastal areas. Mathu and Gichuru had been less successful in their attempts to interest the Luo in the party.

By the beginning of the Kenya Emergency in 1952 (a year before the remnants of KAU were banned), the party had 100,000 members in nearly 100 sub-branches.[90] There were still only three people in the Nairobi office and no paid officials, but Kenyatta had managed to interest important Luo, particularly Oginga Odinga, a former veterinary officer who built the Luo Thrift and Trading Corporation and was later to become the first head of the Luo Union.[91]

On the other hand, Kenyatta failed to solve two problems. One was a resentment of Kikuyu domination which led several officers to quit KAU.[92] The other was the growth of a fully alienated element which became increasingly important after "moderates" like Tom Mbotela was defeated for re-election in 1951.

The name "Mau Mau" was first heard in March 1948; the first "Mau Mau" murders were early in 1952. In October of that year a State of Emergency was proclaimed, and for the next three years the Central Province was in a state of war and civil war which caused the deaths of 13,500 Africans, 95 Europeans, 29 Asians, and the detention of 80,000 Africans. Britain sent special forces to Kenya, but the colony had to bear nearly half the Emergency cost of £55 million.[93]

Considerable controversy exists over the origin and control of "Mau Mau." A British government report attempted to show that Kenyatta planned and controlled it, and that his public denials were made with tongue in cheek. Others dispute this.[94] For instance, Josiah Kariuki claims that there was no organization as such, but that the name "Mau Mau" came to be applied to those who took a widespread and spontaneous "oath of unity." Some committees existed among the "passive wing"—the majority of whom continued to live in the reserve or town—to help channel supplies to the minority fighting in gangs in the Aberdare and Mount Kenya forests. But even the official Corfield Report admits that the organization was "somewhat loose" and that "apparently neither the Council of Freedom nor its subordinate bodies controlled the forest gangs."[95]

"Mau Mau" had little organization and was confined primarily to the Kikuyu, Embu, and Meru tribes of the Central Province, but there was no question of its popularity there. Some administrators estimate that nearly 90 per cent of the Kikuyu took the first oath, which was "relatively mild" and designed, "by using the age-old Kikuyu magic symbols, to inspire nationalistic aspiration in the people . . ."[96] This widespread participation explains how Kanu was later able to become a mass party without impressive organization. It also explains the fear of Kikuyu domination which was to plague Kanu.

Although it was closely tied to Kikuyu protest and involved a strong element of agrarian concern, the Kenya nationalist movement was less parochial than its Uganda counterpart. Leaders of KAU opposed East African federation only on racial grounds. Otherwise, they spoke of "uniting all the African people in East Africa . . ."[97]

During the height of the Emergency the trade union organization, of which Tom Mboya had become secretary in 1953, served as a substitute for political organization.[98] In June 1955 Africans were allowed to form political organizations at the district level. With the removal of Kikuyu leadership from Nairobi because of the Emergency, a younger generation of Luo leaders emerged and formed new organizations. Most important of these were Clement Argwings-Kodhek's Nairobi District African Congress and Mboya's Nairobi People's Convention Party.

These district parties were the only organizations in 1957 when the first eight Africans were elected to the Legislative Council (under a multiracial constitution which gave Europeans representation equal to the other two races combined).[99] No sooner were the eight Africans elected than they refused to work with the constitution. The Colonial Secretary announced a new constitution ("to last ten years") which increased African representation by six, to equal that of the Europeans. Nonetheless, the African leaders still rejected "multiracialism" in favor of "undiluted democracy," and in 1958 the tempo of African politics increased markedly.

In 1959 the African members boycotted the Legislative Council until the Colonial Secretary agreed to a new constitutional conference in 1960. At that conference, held at Lancaster House in London, Britain conceded an African majority and Kenya became certain that it would follow the pattern of the other East African countries.

Both Kanu and Kadu were founded in 1960 after the ban on territorial parties was lifted. Earlier attempts to form a multiracial Kenya National Party had met with only partial success, and at two meetings at Kiambu in March and May of that year, various leaders representing largely district followings formed Kanu. They used the old KAU colors and symbols and elected Gichuru as the first president.

Although Ronald Ngala and Daniel arap Moi had been elected officers of Kanu, they helped five minority groups which had refused to join Kanu, form Kadu—Kenya African Democratic Union—a month later.[100] Ngala cited the shouting down of Kalenjin leader Taita Towett at a Kanu meeting as proof that "Mboya was out to form a coalition of the Kikuyu and Luo tribes and dominate all the other tribes in Kenya."[101]

Given the nature of African "nationalism," situations such as that in Kenya, where one or two tribes are dominant politically, are likely to breed a reaction and make political integration difficult. The new nationalist idea tends to look like the old enemy in a new set of clothes. As Ngala remarked of Kanu's opposition to Kadu's policy of regional autonomy, "The end result of a 'non-tribal and unitary system' would be to place the Kikuyu in complete power, thus giving Kenya almost undiluted tribal domination."[102]

With its natural majority, Kanu easily won the 1961 elections, gaining two-thirds of the vote. But its insistence on the release of Kenyatta led the Governor to rule for a time with the minority Kadu party. After this proved unsatisfactory, Kenyatta was released, another conference was held in London, and a Kanu-Kadu coalition government was formed. In May 1963 Kanu again handily won the elections, fought this time largely over the policy of "majimbo," or regional autonomy, which Kadu had succeeded in incorporating in the 1962 constitution. In June Kanu formed the independence government and in September they were able to get Britain to modify the regional aspects of the consti-

tution. Nonetheless, the failure of the nationalist movement
to integrate the elements which formed Kadu left its mark
on Kenya's constitution, just as a similar failure was written
into Uganda's.

The same factors which led to the creation of Kadu—
uneven tribal development, the district as the level of organization after the Emergency, and the importance of Legislative Council notables—also prevented Kanu from becoming a highly integrated party. The multiple strands which
went into Kanu—Kenyatta's charisma, the Africans released
from British detention camps, Odinga's strength in Central
Nyanza, Mboya's trade union and Nairobi support, Paul
Ngei's following among the Kamba—remained separate to
a considerable extent because Kanu's natural dominance
meant that there was no need for them to come together.
Moreover, individual leaders had no trouble raising funds
from foreign "Cold War" sources, and these funds remained
in their personal control.

By 1962 many observers expected Kanu to fall apart. In
the 1961 election its candidates had run against each other.
Public sparring between Odinga and Mboya was as old as
the party, as were complaints about under-representation
of the Kamba, confusion in branch elections, and problems
of controlling spontaneous youth wings.[103] In September
1961 several "Old Guard" ex-detainees joined the party and
threatened to "reorganize" it. At the end of 1961 Kanu's
Treasurer, William Malu, told the Annual Conference that
the party had been dead broke since April, had a debt of
£3,500, and existed thanks to loans from Odinga and Mboya.
The head office did not even have a telephone. A party report said Kanu had 500,000 members in thirty branches,
but that the branches sent neither reports nor funds to the
central offices, whose workers had not been paid in six

months. The party relied on its Parliamentary Group for its existence, and members often failed to attend the Governing Council.[104]

A new constitution at the end of 1961 did nothing to solve the problem, nor was Kenyatta's charisma sufficient to overcome the differences. In the summer of 1962, party officials, youth wingers, and previously sympathetic trade unionists challenged what they felt was Kikuyu domination of the party and openly defied Kenyatta.[105] When Paul Ngei quit Kanu in the autumn of 1962, he took the majority of the Kamba, Kenya's fourth largest tribe, with him into his African People's Party. But this proved a blessing in disguise, for the possibility that Kanu could now lose the coming election helped party organization immeasurably.[106] Discipline in the 1963 election was greatly improved over 1961. However impressive, the changes in Kanu were less organizational than personal. Headquarters remained a shabby place manned by six workers. Yet in Kikuyu areas Kanu retained its support without organization. Unknown politicians with the Kanu label were able to defeat well-known ex-detainees of the 1963 election. In the chaos of the 1961 election, candidates were deterred from quitting the party by their constituents' loyalty to it.[107] Kanu was better able to raise funds by special appeal than by regular dues, according to one observer in the Central Region, because every Kikuyu identified himself as a Kanu man and did not need to pay dues to prove it, but was ready to help the party when it needed him.

The history behind Kanu explains why Kenyans, whose political integration in the form of constitution, party system, and major party, was more like Uganda's than like Tanganyika's at the time of the federal negotiations, nonetheless considered themselves closer to and more like Tanganyikans—a fact which was reflected at the bargaining table.

Had the federal negotiators reached the point of discussing a merger of the political parties, the going would have been more difficult than the East African leaders expected. As Table 12 shows (see pp. 120–121), power was distributed differently on both the decision-making and administrative sides of the three parties.

Various politicians had developed vested interests in these differences of power structure. Fitting the parties into a single mold would have shifted the internal balance of power in each party. This was particularly true of the UPC which despite its weak structure was more than a mere collection of notables to be dissolved on the whim of the leaders. Kanu, with a weaker structure and many party officials promoted to government jobs in mid-1963, could more easily have changed. Once again, Uganda was odd man out in political integration. In such circumstances the best that could be hoped for was a coalition of the three parties. The basis for such a coalition—but little more—had been prepared by the Pan-African Freedom Movement of East and Central Africa, more commonly called Pafmeca.

THE PAN-AFRICAN FREEDOM MOVEMENT OF EAST AND
CENTRAL AFRICA (PAFMECA)

"East African relations," said Godfrey Binaisa of Uganda, "began at Mwanza in 1958." Tanganyika's Oscar Kambona saw Pafmeca as "the political side of our movement toward federation just as EACSO is the economic side." And Tom Mboya wrote soon after the Mwanza meeting that history

Table 12

The Operative Structure of the Three Major Parties at Mid-1963

	Tanu		UPC		Kanu	
	Size	Meets	Size	Meets	Size	Meets
I. DECISION-MAKING						
(1) Central or Executive Committee	19	weekly	20	fortnightly	12–14	irregularly
(2) National or Governing Executive, or Council	58	every 3 months	60	every 2 months	60	every 3 months
(3) Annual Conference	120	yearly	1,000	two years	250	yearly
Most important level for policy formation	(2)		(1 and 2)		(1)	
Importance of this level relative to Parliamentary Group	more important		slightly less important		less important	

Table 12 (continued)

[121]

	Tanu	UPC	Kanu
II. ADMINISTRATION			
1. Number of regular headquarters staff	30	10	6
2. Regional (Provincial) Branches	10	—	—
3. District Branches	60	14	38
4. Constituency Branches	—	60	—
5. Sub-Chiefdom, Gombolola, or Location Branches	1,200	500	175 (?)
Levels with salaried officer paid by the central party	Headquarters, Region, District	HQ officials received an allowance	HQ officials irregularly received salary. ¼ of Districts had salaried official, usually paid by a notable
Most important level	Headquarters, Region, District	District	District

Sources: Uganda People's Congress, *Constitution* (Kampala, 1962); *T.A.N.U. Sheria na Madhumuni ya Chama* (Dar es Salaam); "Constitution of the Kenya African National Union (Kanu)" (Nairobi, Mimeographed, 1962?); interviews with party officials.

would record "that this was the place where the Pan-African ideal took real shape in terms of an organization pledged to set objectives and a course of activities and action to achieve them."[108] These statements overestimate the importance of Pafmeca. Important it was, but more as a symbol than as an organization or movement.

Except for two people, Kanyama Chiume of Nyasaland and E. M. K. Mulira of the unimportant Progressive Party in Uganda, most of the twenty-one leaders who met at Mwanza from September 16 to 18, 1958, were from three countries—Tanganyika (seven), Kenya (five) and Zanzibar (seven). The inclusion of Central Africa and virtual nonparticipation of Uganda meant there was no hope of founding a movement that would become a powerful East African organization rather than just a meeting-place for leaders. Uganda, as we have seen, was wrapped up in internal problems. Neotraditionalists were destroying the parties in Buganda, and the UNC was in chaos. Upon returning to Kampala, Mulira felt compelled to issue a statement denying that he had discussed East African federation at Mwanza.[109]

The leaders at Mwanza accomplished two things: they agreed to form Pafmeca and they jointly worked out certain fundamental ideas. In retrospect, the ideas seem diverse and obvious, but it must be remembered that this was before the first All African Peoples' Conference (AAPC), at a time when multiracialism and white dominance still prevailed in East Africa. Several leaders have said since that working out their positions on African unity, traditionalism, racialism, alien minorities, democracy, trade unions, and similar general ideas which became incorporated in the Pafmeca Freedom Charter, in the presence of other nationalists, was a great moral and psychological help. East African federation was discussed briefly and termed irrelevant.[110]

The organizational aspects were more limited. The common symbols agreed upon never became effective. Nor were the missions to unify the parties in Uganda and Zanzibar (agreed upon at Mwanza and attempted later) of much importance. Tanu looked after the Pafmeca office and secretarial work, and for the first two years the Pafmeca organization was little more than a department in the Tanu headquarters. In the beginning it did not even have a separate room. I. M. Bhoke Munanka, a Tanu official, became its first secretary. When Munanka was imprisoned early in 1959, Jeremiah Bakempenja, Nyerere's secretary, took on Pafmeca as an extra duty. After April 1959, when Nyerere succeeded Francis Khamisi as Chairman, Bakempenja tended to treat Tanu and Pafmeca as one for administrative functions. In 1961, when another Tanu official, T. A. K. Msonge, became Pafmeca's Secretary and was given a separate room in Tanu headquarters, Tanu still handled Pafmeca's typing and auditing of accounts. Postage was paid from Pafmeca funds.[111]

Even in 1960, when the Chairman, Tom Mboya, was in Nairobi, this arrangement caused few problems, largely because there was little to Pafmeca except conferences. Almost the only activity was planning conferences, appealing for contributions to bolster its perpetually short funds, and writing letters to newspapers. At the end of its first year of existence, during which it had revenue of £750, Pafmeca had £230 in assets. Only Tanu and two Zanzibari parties had paid most of their £25 entrance fee and £250 annual subscription.

Pafmeca activity is reflected in the expenditures. The Mwanza, Zanzibar, and Moshi Conferences accounted for 80 per cent of expenditure; the futile mission to unify the parties in Uganda cost 14 per cent (£70); and postage, telegrams, and taxi fares came to only £12.[112]

Pafmeca's original constitution said it was to be open to all nationalist, labor, and cooperative organizations which conformed to a policy of Pan-Africanism and liberation of Africa. Actually, none but political parties joined. Pafmeca was to have an annual general meeting in August of each year, with not more than five delegates per organization. An executive body, the Coordinating Freedom Committee (CFC) elected by the Annual Conference, was to meet every four months with one representative per organization. Each territory was to have its own Territorial Freedom Committee. There were to be four officers, two elected by the Annual Conference and two appointed by the CFC.[113]

In practice, Pafmeca's role as a leaders' forum, rather than as an organization for gaining control of a government, meant that its constitution mattered little. Only two of the four officers were appointed and it became the practice to hold CFC meetings at the same time as general meetings or at the convenience of leaders. Distinctions between types of meetings became blurred. Territorial committees never materialized, and limits on delegates at meetings were flexible.

Pafmeca's second meeting was in Zanzibar in April 1959, and it was concerned largely with Zanzibar problems. Of sixteen people attending, nine were Zanzibaris, five Tanganyikans, and two Kenyans. No Ugandans or Central Africans attended. The third meeting, at Moshi, Tanganyika, in September 1959, had originally been planned for Uganda but was banned by the colonial government which was having trouble with the Uganda National Movement boycott at that time. Thirty-four delegates from thirteen parties in six territories (including Ruanda-Urundi and the Congo) came to Moshi. Most important, a strong Uganda delegation, including both Benedicto Kiwunuka and Milton Obote, attended a Pafmeca conference for the first time. In addition to resolutions, which were more Pan-Africanist in tenor than they had been previously, the conference recommended coordination of tactics, establishment of a Pafmeca newspaper, an AAPC office in East Africa, and further delegations to bring about unity in Uganda.[114] None of these ideas materialized once the leaders had left the conference.

The fourth Pafmeca meeting, a CFC meeting in June 1960, struck a new note by stressing the eventual intention of Pafmeca countries to federate. Four months later in Mbale, Uganda, a full annual meeting endorsed the idea of a Pafmeca federation and decided that a paper should be prepared on East and Central African Federation. This, like another resolution to improve the organization of Pafmeca, was never carried out.

The first signs of the expansion that was later to dilute Pafmeca in the one area where it was effective—common ideas—appeared at the Mbale Conference. Nearly 70 delegates from 14 parties in 11 countries (including South Africa and Mozambique for the first time) came to Mbale. So also did Abdoulaye Diallo, Secretary-General of the AAPC, as an observer. Central Africans attended for the first time, and the disappearance of the old East African nature of the organization was symbolized when Sikota Wina of Northern Rhodesia challenged Tom Mboya for the chairmanship.[115]

Pafmeca met once in 1961. In January the heads of member organizations (including the Central Africans) met in the Kanu offices in Nairobi much to the chagrin of, and with many protests from, Kadu. The leaders discussed Nyerere's 1960 speech on East African federation and decided that the issue must wait until each territory had an African government. They also decided to ask Mbiyu Koinange, then head of the Bureau of African Affairs in Ghana, to become Secretary-General of Pafmeca. Subsequently, there were elections in Kenya and Uganda; and Tanganyika began to prepare for independence at the end of the year. Leaders had no time for conferences.

During the Tanganyika independence celebrations in December 1961, assembled leaders decided to expand Pafmeca into Pafmecsa (Pan-African Freedom Movement of East, Central and Southern Africa) and to hold the next meeting outside East Africa for the first time.[116] That meeting, at Addis Ababa in February 1962, elected the first non-East African Chairman, Kenneth Kaunda of Northern Rhodesia. Of the sixty delegates at Addis Ababa, only twenty per cent were East Africans, and of the fourteen countries represented, only half were East and Central African. In a foreword to the published conference speeches, Koinange noted that Pafmeca [*sic*] now spoke for 100 million Africans in five-and-a-half million square miles of land—that is, half of Africa.[117] The conference attracted four Ghanaians among the sixteen observers, and John Tettegah, head of the Ghanaian group, expressed his country's first public concern about Pafmeca dividing Africa.[118]

Among its many resolutions, the Conference urged admission of Ethiopia and Somalia to the East African Common Services Organization, and eventual East African federation including Ethiopia and Somalia (and South and Central Africa after their independence).[119] In November 1962 Ethiopia, Somalia, and Zanzibar were invited to send observers to the East African Central Legislative Assembly at Kampala. Their observers all made fraternal speeches expressing interest in federation, but the East Africans, who for a year had been unable to solve the economic problems posed by Zanzibar's application for admission to EACSO, did little

126

about the other two countries with whom their communications and trade were slight.

This dilution of the regional focus of Pafmeca was not compensated by proportional improvements in its organization. A constitutional change provided for membership by the government, rather than the parties, of an independent state. Governments were to pay £1,000 yearly subscription. In October 1961 Koinange complained that Pafmeca had £10 in the bank, existed on the generosity of Tanganyika, and would need £10,000 a year "to penetrate actively in fostering the Pafmeca spirit . . ."[120] He never received anything like that amount. The greatest new source of revenue was the Ethiopian Government which paid for the lavish Addis Conference. It also paid its £1,000 dues, as did Uganda and Tanganyika. But few parties paid their reduced subscriptions of £50, and Pafmecsa headquarters was never certain whether parties were members or not. Early in 1963 Pafmecsa consisted of a staff of four (secretaries promised by Ethiopia never arrived) working in a government-owned house in Dar es Salaam. Work consisted mainly of writing letters, issuing press releases, and coordinating refugee political groups from Southern Africa.[121]

Pafmeca—even before it was diluted into Pafmesca— could in no way be compared to the three territorial parties in East Africa as a factor in political integration. As Milton Obote said in explaining his absence from the first two Pafmeca meetings, he had more important work to do at home than talk to groups like Pafmeca.[122] Even in its efforts to coordinate the activities of territorial parties and to establish central symbols, slogans, and news media, Pafmeca never got beyond the symbol of its own existence.

Pafmeca was important, however, in one area of political integration—the integration of political ideas. As Bakempenja said: "Pafmeca could only mean moral support because we had no funds; but it meant that leaders had to express their ideas before other nationalists who might suggest ways of meeting problems." Or, in the words of Uganda Minister of State, Grace Ibingira, "It made it impossible for leaders to follow a completely territorial policy." It also made East Africans familiar with each other's personalities. As Michael Kamaliza of Tanganyika observed: "Suspicion or fear by a leader could set back federation by ten years. We are lucky that we got them to know each other beforehand." Of course familiar personalities can clash as badly as unfamiliar ones, but at least the element of the unknown was removed.[123]

East African political integration—the creation of a political community in East Africa—was not carried sufficiently forward before independence to be free from severe threats of disruption from the growth of the territorial communities which were being built by the new territorial states. Such an East African political community failed to develop because the power structure—armies, police, budgets, radio, and so forth, which the nationalists wished to capture—had been built primarily at the territorial level.

The colonial government had developed the power structure at the territorial level because the difference between the territories, which sprang up early in the century, made their lack of community too great to permit establishment of a strong central East African structure. African nationalists built organizations to capture the government at the level which was important—the territorial level. Once developed, it proved difficult to integrate these territorial nationalist organizations into more than a loose framework for debating common ideas (Pafmeca).

Political Integration

Moreover, nationalist organizations developed differently in the three territories. Their success and failure in integrating all important internal social groups were subsequently written in the constitutions which Britain gave to each of the new countries—constitutions which would have to be reconciled in federation. Thus Tanganyika whose well-developed organization, Tanu, integrated nearly all important social groups in the country, had a constitution providing strong central powers and considerable flexibility. In Uganda, the early nationalist organization (UNC) foundered on the rock of Buganda traditionalism, and its successor (UPC) was unable to integrate two important groups, the Baganda and many Catholics. As a result, Uganda received a decentralized quasi-federal constitution. In Kenya the long history of Kikuyu nationalism gave Kanu great strength in the absence of organization but it also explained Kanu's failure to integrate various other tribes—though in this case, unlike Uganda, not the most important ones. Consequently Kenya received a constitution with regional autonomy, midway between those of Tanganyika and Uganda in centralization and flexibility. These differences were reflected at the bargaining table in the summer of 1963.

But the poorly rooted constitutions, commanding little loyalty of their own as institutions, were less important than the political facts they represented. Institutional differences would have faded had it been possible to form a single East African nationalist organization. That it proved impossible to do so, as we have seen, meant that the political integration of East Africa was both partial and fragile when the leaders decided the time had come to form a federation.

V

Economic Integration[1]

What is good for the whole of East Africa is not necessarily good for each of the parts.

> A Uganda Cabinet Minister
> November, 1962

In 1961 a Nigerian newspaper commented, with reference
to the economic integration of East Africa, "These three
States have stolen a march on the older African States. They
have achieved one of the main objectives of pan-African
nationalism, without tears."[2] The extent of economic integration inherited by the three countries was impressive. Yet
their difficulties in maintaining or expanding it casts doubt
on the sufficiency of economic integration without political
integration.[3]

THE EXTENT OF INTEGRATION

In 1963 Kenya, Tanganyika, and Uganda were indeed
remarkable for the extent of their functional cooperation
through their common market and the East African Common Services Organisation (EACSO), in which they participated as sovereign states.

East Africa was sometimes compared to the European
Economic Community (EEC). Such a comparison can be
misleading, for in some ways East Africa was much less
integrated than Europe, in others perhaps more so. Also it

is important to remember that the historical and social contexts were very different. Nonetheless, a crude comparison is useful.

East African economic integration included an impressive range of common services which had no counterpart in the EEC. Furthermore, the East African countries shared a common currency—although the price they paid for it was a rigid monetary policy since their efforts at setting up a Central Bank were plagued with difficulties.

The trade of the East African common market countries among themselves represented a smaller proportion of their total exports than in Europe: one fifth as opposed to two fifths. In part, this reflected the underdeveloped, agricultural economy of East Africa, with the long-standing bias of their trade toward the industrial countries, especially Britain. The East Africans were more fully integrated than the Europeans in the common tariff aspects of their market, but this was partly a reflection of the relative ages of the two customs unions. The East African union dated back to 1927, the EEC to 1957. The East Africans also had a greater degree of mobility of labor and capital in their common market; but there was no provision, as there is in the Treaty of Rome, for the gradual improvement of mobility, and in practice it was diminishing in East Africa.

Turning to institutions, the Authority of EACSO was composed of the three heads of government, while six foreign ministers generally formed the Council of the EEC. The EACSO Authority was limited to unanimous decisions, but the qualified majorities of the EEC Council seem to make little difference in practice. The small Central Legislative Assembly of EACSO, which met three times a year, possessed some legislative power (subject to approval by the Authority), while the European Parliament, meeting six times a year, has only advisory status. Unlike the CLA, the European Parliament has the power to make the Commission of the EEC resign.

In three important ways the East Africans were considerably less integrated than the Europeans. East Africans had a treaty referring to their common services but not to their common market, and they had nothing comparable to the Treaty of Rome, which lays down a schedule of stages in the progress toward fuller economic integration.[4] Second, there was no East African judicial body, such as the Court of Justice of the EEC, which is explicitly charged with trying infringements of a treaty or of the unwritten practical arrangements which make up the common market. Finally, and most important, the bureaucracy of the EEC is incomparably stronger *vis-à-vis* the representatives of the sovereign states than was that of EACSO. Only a unanimous vote of the Council of the EEC can override a decision of the Commission. The Commission can investigate infringements of cooperative arrangements and initiate proceedings in the Court even against the member governments themselves (which it has done). The vast responsibility of working out the implications of the Treaty of Rome means that the Commission of the EEC has considerable executive powers.

Nothing like this existed in EACSO in 1963. There was a single Secretary-General and his staff, with virtually no executive powers of their own, as against nine EEC Commission members, each dealing with a department, like a Minister. Any single state could veto EACSO decisions. While it is true that the Secretary General and his staff were, like the Commission, a lobby for closer integration, they were an incomparably weaker lobby. But in such totally different circumstances all comparisons with European institutions must be regarded with caution.

Economic Integration

Nearly all the two dozen or so services shared by the East African territories, which involved 21,000 established jobs and accounted for approximately eight per cent of the gross domestic product (GDP) of East Africa, were administered by the Common Services Organisation, which took over in December 1961 from the colonial East African High Commission.[5] The change was significant, despite the complaint of a Tanganyikan M.P. that "it is merely a change of wording."[6] The administration of the services was little altered. At the beginning of 1963, 97 per cent of the 274 most senior posts in the organization were still held by expatriates.[7] The important changes were in the policy-making machinery and its relationship to the politics of the new African elite.

British policy had tried to minimize the political implications of the High Commission; Lord Hailey claimed in 1956 (just as interterritorial frictions were beginning to increase) that "the fact that it is so largely functional in its operations seems so far to have saved it from the tension in the political field which was forecast."[8] In 1955 and 1959 the High Commission came in for severe criticism in both the Tanganyika and the Uganda Legislative Councils. Milton Obote argued that it cut into the sovereignty of the people of Uganda;[9] and the Tanganyika Federation of Labour voted for its dissolution. Despite this situation, Julius Nyerere and Oscar Kambona were not in favor of scrapping colonial interterritorial cooperation, as in British West Africa, and pressed for the London Conference of June 1961 which established EACSO.[10]

It was agreed that each of the three chief elected Ministers should sit in rotation as chairman of the organization, instead of the Kenya Governor, who had been the sole chairman until then (although, in practice, since 1958 the Governor of the host territory had taken the chair at each meeting). The other major changes were the provision of triumvirates of territorial ministers to oversee the services; the expansion and popularization of the Central Legislative Assembly; and the adoption of the "Raisman pool" (described below) to give the organization a separate source of funds.

Perhaps the major difference was one of atmosphere. Territorial civil servants have said that committees became more effective because they felt somewhat more assured of political support. Jomo Kenyatta told the new CLA that they were "a completely new body" and that EACSO could be a framework for political association.[11] A Tanganyikan M.P. commented that EACSO was "a far cry from out-and-out Pan-Africanization" but that it was "a beginning toward that unity."[12]

The four ministerial committees (Communications, Finance, Commercial and Industrial Coordination, Social Services and Research) were composed of one minister appointed by each territory. Each committee was responsible for the supervision of services in its field, although occasionally committees held joint meetings. Committee meetings, for which the EACSO secretariat prepared papers and agenda, were generally held every three months. Each minister had a veto which, if exercised, meant referral to the Authority for decision. If the Authority disagreed, the matter was dropped.

In practice, informal communication rather than constitutional rights made committees run smoothly. During the first year of their operation, no one exercised his right of veto, although in at least one case this involved some sacrifice by a Tanganyikan minister.

Nonetheless, the absence of a veto was not always significant. Papers were often withdrawn or ministers refused to admit items on the agenda. In other words, part of the reason that there were no vetoes was because issues were evaded. This was particularly true of the Commercial and Industrial Coordination Committee. Unlike the Communications Committee, which had to exercise its executive functions within a given period of time (and dealt with an area more free of frictions), the Commercial and Industrial Coordination Committee achieved very little. It came to what one member called "evasive agreements, because in the absence of executive power it did no harm to agree." A year after its inception, its agenda was still a perpetuation of the agenda of the first meeting, and efforts to introduce such controversial subjects as trade agreements were thwarted.

The Central Legislative Assembly of forty-one members and a speaker was larger than its predecessor but still limited to expenditure, not revenue, powers. Nonetheless, the new body was more representative and more active. Whereas the old CLA met twice in 1960, passing seven bills, the new CLA met three times in 1962 and passed twenty-two bills. (Eight of these were appropriation bills and several others merely defined procedure.)

Of the forty-one members of the CLA, two were *ex-officio:* the Secretary-General and Legal Secretary. Of the remaining thirty-nine, twelve ministers represented the four ministerial committees, and each territorial legislature chose nine of the twenty-seven others. The practice was for the ruling party (or, in the case of Uganda, coalition) in the territory to appoint CLA representatives from its own members, though not always from among members of Parliament. Despite the presumed ideological similarity of the ordinary members, they tended to regard themselves as territorial representatives rather than as an opposition to the ministers. There was no clear government-opposition pattern of seating. There was a cross-territorial grouping of younger members, but nothing like that of the European Parliament. The CLA tended to avoid votes, but the level of debate was sometimes high, and criticism of the administration of EACSO was quite pointed during question periods.

Bills and motions had to relate to the specific functions allocated to EACSO, and simple majorities were sufficient for passage. The Authority retained the right of veto, and unless a bill was signed into law in all three territories within three months, it lapsed. The chairmen of the ministerial committees would lay the budgets for the various services before the house, and, without CLA passage of appropriations bills, EACSO could not spend. Here again, though, the real power lay with the Authority, which had to consent to any CLA appropriations bill before it became law.

EACSO was responsible for 21 organizations or institutes plus various services provided by its secretariat. The services fell into two main financial categories: the self-contained, or self-financing, services of Railways and Harbours (EAR & H), Posts and Telecommunications (EAP & T), and East African Airways (EAA); and the services directly administered by EACSO and financed from its General Fund. The latter were more numerous, but smaller in financial terms. EAR & H, EAP & T, and EAA had gross expenditure in 1962 of nearly £40 million. Expenditure for all the General Fund services in 1961–62 was slightly over £6 million.[13] A secretariat staff of six principal officers and some 100 senior officials worked in the organization's Nairobi headquarters building. The first Secretary-General, A. L. Adu, an able Ghanaian administrator, was succeeded by Dunstan Omari, a senior Tanganyikan civil servant, at the beginning of 1964.

Economic Integration

Functionally, the services were classified under five heads, as will be seen in Table 13: communications, financial, social, research, and economic and administrative services.

Table 13
EACSO General Fund Services, 1963

Services	Number of senior staff	Per cent of Gen. Fund budget
1. Communications: Meteorology and civil aviation	200	15
2. Financial: Income tax and customs and excise tax collection	1000	25
3. Social: E. A. Literature Bureau	8	1
4. Research: 11 research institutes (5 medical, 5 natural resources, 1 industrial)	185	13
5. Economic: EACSO Treasury (Statistical Department, Economic Division), London Office	30	5

The former High Commission had included defense, but the East African Navy was abolished in 1962.[14]

Communications, which included the three self-financing services, were by far the most important single aspect of EACSO. All three were run as large, autonomous public corporations. EAR & H was a giant by any standards. According to its Manager, only 23 firms in Britain had a comparable capital investment. Its 1962 revenue of £26 million was greater than the 1962–63 recurrent revenue of either the Uganda or the Tanganyika Government, invested capital was over £100 million, and with nearly 50,000 employees it was the largest employer in East Africa. EAP & T, with £7 million revenue and 7,000 employees, and EAA with £6.4 million, were not on the same scale, but the budget of each was as large as the General Fund—of which the most important services were tax collection, meteorology, and civil aviation, and the 11 research institutes.

The budget for the General Fund grew steadily, from £500,000 in 1948 to £7.4 million for 1963–64. This latter figure included £400,000 for a new item, the University of East Africa, and £350,000 for Africanization and compensation of prematurely retired officers.[15] The pattern of expenditure altered somewhat over the years, with revenue collection and civil aviation generally increasing, and locust control no longer accounting for nearly a third of expenditure as it did in the mid-1950's.[16]

The importance of EACSO was not necessarily increasing at the rate indicated by the growth in the General Fund, which included the unique expenditure on premature retirements and was somewhat inflated by price increases. Moreover, without the self-financing services, the economic impact of EACSO was modest. The General Fund services represented only about 1.5 per cent of East African GDP and this did not increase significantly. A more significant index of increased importance would have been greater powers over economic coordination. EACSO affected too many vital matters to be clear of politics, yet, unlike the Commission of the EEC, was not a sufficiently autonomous or powerful bureaucracy to help create its own political environment.

THE COMMON MARKET

The East African common market dated back to the Kenya-Uganda customs union of 1917, which was fully joined by Tanganyika in 1927. This was earlier than any of the common services, except the railways. Although some criticism arose as early as the 1920's and 1930's, the period of greatest growth in the East African market, in the late 1940's and 1950's, was the period of greatest problems. Severe frictions were not a product of independence in the sense that they were the result of African control, but of the approach of independence with its increased territorial consciousness and responsibility. Some civil servants dated the beginning of more serious frictions from the appointment of territorial ministers (1954 in Kenya, 1955 in Uganda, 1957 in Tanganyika), who asked their civil servants to justify actions from a territorial point of view. In 1960 the Chairman of the Uganda Development Corporation said that there had been a decline in cooperation for the past five years. He attributed part of the cause to the removal of commercial people from interterritorial committees and their replacement by officials responsible to governments.[17] The very growth of internal trade, since so much of it contributed to the boom in Kenya, gave an edge to the allegations of overbearing attitudes on the part of some Kenya ministers and officials.

In November 1959 the Governor of Uganda declared that economic cooperation between the East African territories had reached the lowest ebb of his experience, and placed part of the blame on the inflexibility of ministers. The Administrator of the High Commission added that the High Commission, although supraterritorial in theory, was in practice an agency of three governments which were drawing apart and seeing things from territorial points of view, and he did not know how long it could last.[18] In addition, changes in the world economy over the preceding seven or eight years intensified the potential clashes of interest which usually exist within a common market.

In 1958 the Uganda Government, worried about declining revenue, proposed a system of fiscal compensation for loss of duty on imports now supplied by Kenya to the other two countries. After protracted local negotiations broke down, the Colonial Office appointed an economic and fiscal commission, which sat during 1960–61 under the chairmanship of Sir Jeremy Raisman. Its main conclusions were that the common market had benefited East Africa as a whole and should be retained; that residual impediments should be reviewed and, where possible, eliminated; and that an income pool should be set up, each territory contributing 40 per cent of company income tax and 6 per cent of customs and excise revenue. Each would receive an equal share (one fifth) of the pool, thus compensating Uganda and Tanganyika out of Kenya's bigger contribution; and three fifths would be paid to EACSO for central finance of the common services.[19] This cost Kenya approximately two thirds of a million pounds while it benefited Uganda a quarter and Tanganyika a third of a million. The settlement provided half of EACSO's revenue for General Fund services.[20]

The Raisman report failed to end all criticism. The three colonial governors accepted it primarily in order to keep open the possibility of federation.[21] Several members of the Uganda People's Congress, later to become cabinet ministers, claimed that Uganda did not benefit sufficiently. In contrast, there was virtually no criticism of the report in the Kenya Legislative Council.[22]

After the independence of Tanganyika and Uganda, African leaders tended to be ambivalent about the common market—praising it in principle but complaining about its implications in detail. The common market became elevated to the position of a slogan, particularly when East Africans decided to reject associate membership in the European Common Market. For some the East African common market was the first step to a larger unity, while for others it represented a compromise between cooperation and separation. Yet despite its political acceptance, frictions continued to develop within the common market, and its unwritten rules became more uncertain.

As we have noted already, the East African common market rested not on an elaborate treaty, but solely on administrative practice. The two essentials of a customs union are the complete elimination of internal tariffs and a uniform scale of tariffs on imports from the outside world.

To increase these benefits derived from the free movement of goods, a common market requires also freedom of movement of capital and labor, and roughly similar commercial, fiscal, and social policies. A common currency is not essential, but may simplify matters. Thus a common market may be defined, as in the Raisman Report, as "the absence of fiscal or other administrative barriers to the movement of goods or factors of production between the territories which make up the common market area."[23]

Until 1963, East Africa was free from currency problems. An East African Currency Board, the majority of whose members were Treasury officials from the four East African countries and Aden, was created in 1919 when world silver prices made the rupee (and East African exports) too expensive. Originally the Board followed a very rigid policy, only issuing local currency against foreign exchange held. In 1955 and 1957 it was given authority to invest up to £20 million (about one third of its assets) in local securities, and in 1960 its headquarters were transferred from London to Nairobi. Nonetheless, it remained too rigid an instrument of monetary control to suit Tanganyika. In 1963 the East African governments considered the report of a German expert commissioned by Tanganyika which recommended a two-tiered local and central bank to replace the Currency Board. The East Africans reached no agreement, and it seemed possible that the monetary union which had saved the market from a large area of difficult bargaining might soon be broken.[24]

Within a market area, welfare is maximized by the classical free-trade system of specialization according to comparative advantages. But whether the market area as a whole is better off than before depends on whether the value of the trade created by the absence of internal barriers is greater than the value of trade diverted from lower-cost (outside) suppliers to high-cost (internal) suppliers. According to Jacob Viner, "The primary purpose of a customs union, and its major consequence for good or bad, is to shift sources of supply, and the shift can be either to lower or higher cost sources, depending on circumstances." He then went on to use the East African common market as an example of the wrong kind of customs union: "The customs union operated to create a protected market in Tanganyika for the produce of the small colony of British planters in Kenya, for whose welfare the British Government has shown a constant and marked solicitude."[25]

The Raisman Commission, however, concluded that the common market had benefited the whole of East Africa and that although the benefits had not been equal, none of the territories would have been better off on its own. The Commission supported its conclusion by citing trade figures to prove the unity of the market and economic growth figures to show the benefits.

In 1949 East African trade was of relatively minor importance to all three territories. Although it never became a large proportion of their world trade—in 1959, the interterritorial trade of approximately £20 million was only a sixth of East Africa's external exports of £120 million (4 and 24 per cent respectively of Gross Domestic Product)—it grew more steadily than external trade, and by 1962 its relative importance in the economy had trebled in Kenya and nearly doubled in Uganda and Tanganyika, as Table 14 shows.

Table 14
Kenya, Uganda, and Tanganyika: Interterritorial Trade
as a Percentage of Their Total External Trade

	1949	1962
Kenya	7	22
Uganda	12	22
Tanganyika	9	16

Sources: East African Customs, *Annual Trade Report, 1949*, pp. 23 ff; EACSO, *Economic and Statistical Review*, June 1963, Table D 19.

There was also considerable absolute growth of East African interterritorial trade in the 1950's. It rose in every post-war year except 1955–56. Trade in food, tobacco, and beverages, and in manufactures, grew especially rapidly, the latter doubling between 1954 and 1957 (the increases being most notable in blankets, clothing, shoes, bags, cycle tires, steel doors, and hollow-ware). The total real output of East Africa was also growing during this period.[26]

But the correlation of growth in internal trade and real output with the existence of the common market does not imply a causal connection:

In order to deduce statistically the beneficial effects of the common market it is necessary to show that, in its absence, the levels of inter-territorial output, etc. would have been lower than, in fact, they have been. This, of course, is an impossible task when a common market has been in existence as long as that of East Africa. Once therefore, the inherent unity of the market has been demonstrated the case for its retention must rest solely on the advantages deduced by economic theory.[27]

Nor was the unity of the market asserted by the Raisman Commission entirely convincing. The trade figures seem to show two markets, or perhaps one with two halves; Uganda/ Kenya and Tanganyika, or Uganda/Kenya and Tanganyika/ Kenya. Between 1959 and 1962, Uganda's exports to Tanganyika increased only slightly while Tanganyika's already small exports to Uganda declined considerably. And while Kenya's exports to Tanganyika were increasing, Tanganyika's to Kenya remained at virtually the same level. Meanwhile, trade between Kenya and Uganda was increasing in both directions, as shown in Table 15.

Table 15
Interterritorial Trade

	1962 exports £ million	Percentage change 1959–62
Kenya to Tanganyika	10.0	+54
Kenya to Uganda	7.2	+41
Uganda to Kenya	5.4	+47
Tanganyika to Kenya	2.0	+ 5
Uganda to Tanganyika	1.7	+ 5
Tanganyika to Uganda	0.4	−40

Source: *Economic and Statistical Review,* June 1963, Table D 17.

One reason for these trends was that half the population and more than half the purchasing power of East Africa was located in the Lake Victoria basin and the Kenya Highlands.[28] The other reason was the rail system, which directly linked Uganda and Kenya but before 1963 only indirectly brought in Tanganyika. It costs less to transport cloth from Bombay to Dar es Salaam than to ship from Uganda's textile plant at Jinja to Dar.[29] The early pattern used by commercial firms to subdivide East Africa stressed the regional aspects of the market; for instance, the Bukoba area of Tanganyika was handled from Kampala. With increasing national consciousness and freight rates, however, these patterns tended to be broken up.

The East African market became proportionately less important for Tanganyika after the customs union was formed. In 1922 Kenya and Uganda imported goods worth £60,000 from Tanganyika—about 5 per cent of their total imports—and Tanganyika's exports to Kenya and Uganda were 25 per cent of her very low domestic exports of £1.3 million. By 1939 this proportion had fallen to 19 per cent and by 1949 to only 5 per cent; in 1962 her exports of £2.4 million to Kenya and Uganda were still only 5 per cent of her total exports.[30]

The experience of civil servants in the departments of Commerce and Industry of the three territories confirmed this pattern. Tanganyikans reported a tendency of outside investors to wish to cover their costs by sales within the 10 million-person Tanganyikan market. Only then did investors look for profits from the rest of East Africa—almost as a bonus. Kenyans and Ugandans, on the other hand, reported that the larger market was extremely important to their prospective investors, particularly the part along the Kenya/Uganda railway which was susceptible to careful calculation of transportation costs.

One writer has suggested that the benefits of the common market were potential rather than actual, since tariff barriers would not have presented many obstacles to existing patterns of trade.[31] And it was in its potentialities that the strongest arguments for the common market lay. Professor A. J. Brown, a member of the Raisman Commission, estimated the importance of the East African market for potential local industries by a comparison with Britain. Uganda's money income was about 1/190 that of the United Kingdom, whereas the East African market, with two-fifths of the population of Britain, had 1/50 the money income. Brown estimated that either Uganda or Tanganyika on its own could hope to develop, for its internal market alone, the types of industry which accounted for 35–40 per cent of British manufacturing output. The East African market could support industries of a type which accounted for 70–80 per cent of British output. Brown may have overestimated the possibilities, because comparable British firms could rely on the external economies of outside services, which were not available in East Africa. Nonetheless, the contrast between the eventual limits of the separate markets and of the combined East African market was important, and the theoretical arguments seemed much more clearly in favor of a united East African market.[32]

Some economists have questioned the figures in the Raisman Report that purport to show that Kenya grew faster than the other territories; others have queried whether, even if true, Kenya's growth could be attributed to the common market.[33] Nevertheless, there were fairly strong theoretical and practical grounds to believe that the benefits of the market system were disproportionate. What was more significant politically was the prevalent *belief* that Kenya had benefited more. For example, the then deputy leader of the opposition in Tanganyika (a European) complained in 1960, "We do not appreciate our people being exploited for the benefit of industries in Kenya."[34]

The location of new industry certainly favored Kenya. Branches of industry and commerce tend to cluster, so that within a free-trade area the centers of urban and industrial growth are likely to behave, to quote a vivid metaphor, "like inter-connected soap bubbles—the largest absorbing the rest."[35] As a result of previous development, and a system of protective tariffs which in the early days met the needs of Kenya alone, the country was enabled to acquire a commercial leadership which was still unchallenged in 1963.

By 1958, of 474 companies registered in East Africa, 404 were in Kenya, and some 70 per cent of total manufacturing activity was centered in Kenya.[36] In 1960 Kenya's output in manufacturing and repairs was valued at £21.6 million (or 10 per cent of Gross Domestic Product) compared with £7.3 million and £5.9 million for Tanganyika and Uganda (both about 4 per cent of Gross Domestic Product). The World Bank Report showed how the East African market became of increasing importance to Kenya: during the 1950's, her imports from Tanganyika and Uganda doubled, to £7 million, while her exports to them nearly quadrupled, to £12 million.[37] This trend continued, as Table 16 shows.

Table 16
Kenya Exports (£ million)

	To East Africa	To rest of world (including re-exports)
1958	10.7	33.2
1959	12.3	38.4
1960	13.8	40.2
1961	15.9	41.7
1962	17.2	44.5

Source: *Kenya Trade and Supplies Bulletin,* March 1963, p. 97.

Thus, while Kenya's external exports were increasing by a third, her exports to East Africa were increasing by nearly two thirds. In 1962 Kenya sold nearly two and a half times as much to her East African partners as she bought from them.

The Raisman Report was also criticized for its conclusion that "although the extent to which Kenya's extra income has been spent in the other territories is small, it has been large enough (if they are taken together) to compensate them for their purchasing from Kenya at more than world prices . . ."[38] The World Bank Report on Uganda disagreed: "When Uganda's exports are examined product by product, it is difficult to establish the connection between higher incomes in Kenya and increased exports from Uganda." On the assumption that industry was likely to be located in Kenya, the Mission concluded that "the current disadvantages of adherence to the common market loom large in Uganda while the alleged advantages seem rather nebulous."[39] Nonetheless, the Mission advocated that Uganda remain in the market partly for the sake of its future potential advantages and partly for the existing benefits of the common services.

The World Bank Mission to Tanganyika similarly concluded that Tanganyika should remain in the common market, but added, "from the point of view of Tanganyika, an argument may be made for some measure of 'infant industry' protection not only against imports from overseas but against imports from other members of the customs union, and in particular from Kenya." Again, they emphasized the importance of the potential of the market, not its present performance.[40] Similarly, the report of the Economic Commission for Africa (ECA) team, requested by Tanganyika in 1962, said that the importance of the common market was probably overestimated; while Tanganyika has not benefited to any marked extent, there were no absolute disadvantages, and it would be better to remain in the market in hope of increased benefits in the future.[41]

Two factors helped compensate Uganda and Tanganyika for any short-run disadvantages: the Raisman distributable pool system, and the effect of political uncertainty in Kenya.

Economic Integration

It has even been argued that after the Lancaster House Conference of February 1960 the natural economic advantages of Nairobi as an industrial location were offset by the political disadvantages;[42] but in general the effect was quite small. Many civil servants and businessmen considered that political uncertainty caused outside capital to hold off investing in East Africa entirely rather than invest in a territory other than Kenya. Although sugar, tobacco, and shoe companies set up plants in Tanganyika, this was more to satisfy Tanganyikan aspirations for industrialization than to escape Kenyan instability and would perhaps have occurred in any case. Any neighboring gains from the Kenya recession were probably more than offset by its ill effects on the area as a whole.

The Raisman solution was only a stopgap. For instance, Uganda benefited to the extent of just one per cent of her annual budget, while the problems of trade diversion and location of industry remained unsolved. The distributable pool of revenue was intended to provide the Common Services Organization with an independent source of revenue for the General Fund services, thus reducing the territorial political pressures. But EACSO civil servants reported that this made little practical difference. The main trouble was that the causes of friction had not been removed by a report that was "much less concerned with the concepts of 'Uganda, Tanganyika and Kenya' than the governments of these territories are."[43]

THE PROBLEM OF STABILITY

An important question both for theory and for the practical politics of East African federation was whether the status quo could be maintained indefinitely. Were the bene-

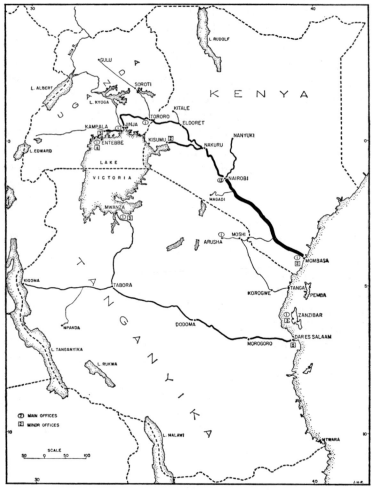

East African economic integration in early 1963, showing rail lines and distribution of EACSO offices. (The rail lines are drawn in rough proportion to their economic significance.)

fits of economic integration available for a considerable period of time without the sacrifices and problems of political integration? One theorist has suggested that a high level of economic integration either spills over into political union or regresses to a customs union or the sharing of one or two services: "Economic unions only, or economic with a minimum of political integration, are unstable not because they are likely to disintegrate but because their capacity to form consensus is out of balance with the need for it."[44]

Tanganyika's Vice President, Rashidi Kawawa, stated that "economic union can operate effectively only if it is supported by a political union"; and Joseph Nyerere predicted that the common market could not survive without federation.[45] On the other hand, early in 1963 the government of Buganda expressed both its opposition to federation and its explicit approval of EACSO. Implied was the threat that politicians reaching for the second bird of federation in the bush might lose the bird of cooperation in the hand.

It is important to distinguish institutional stability from a stable economic and socal situation. The latter did not exist in East Africa. The forces of instability were economic, administrative, and political. Economic problems could be divided into those which primarily affected the market on the one hand and the common services on the other. The former were the more important, and fell into four main categories.

Economic Foreign Policy

One of the necessary conditions for a successful common market, a common external tariff, existed long before independence. Suspended duties and a system of rebates to manufacturers on certain imported materials always accounted for some discrepancies, but the duties were suspended on only a few items (mainly meat, maize, and bottles) while there was increasing coordination of the rebate system between the territories. There were also half a dozen or so differences in tariff rates, as there was no common tariff legislation and all rates had to be passed by the three separate legislatures. The costs to consumers of the trade diversion arising from the external tariff had always troubled the common market. Protection of Uganda textiles had created problems in the past; and in 1962 difficulty arose over Tanganyika's request to protect a prospective tire manufacturer.

Nevertheless, it was generally agreed that the Tariff Advisory Committee—six permanent secretaries from the three countries, who met every three months to consider applications submitted in advance—was one of the most successful instruments of coordination, despite the considerable number of disagreements they had to try to reconcile.

A new source of friction in economic foreign policy was the signing of separate trade agreements. During the colonial period, trade with the Communist countries and with Japan was restricted by import licensing. After Tanganyika became sovereign, several Eastern countries requested trade agreements. After Kenyan and Ugandan protests at the unilateral consideration of the first of these, Tanganyika agreed to forward the drafts to Kenya and Uganda for comment. But Tanganyika gave no assurances that their comments would be respected, and the actual negotiation was not multilateral. Tanganyika turned down an attempt by the ministerial Commercial and Industrial Coordination Committee to discuss trade agreements. She also rejected the idea of a standard formula which would have prevented special concessions; and soon afterward she signed a trade agreement with Burundi without even consulting her common market partners. An agreement with Japan was sent to her partners for comment; but their objections and long delay caused a certain amount of chafing in Tanganyika.

Since these trade agreements did not include concessions in tariff rates, it might be argued that they did little harm to the common market beyond creating a sense of pique at their unilateral negotiation. But the breach of the licensing system had two important effects. First, there was the obvious point that the Czechs, for instance, could sell unlimited quantities of glass in East Africa, or Japanese competition might wipe out certain textile manufacturers in Kenya. Uganda also raised the question of dumping, which, despite legislation against it in East Africa, is difficult to prove against state trading countries. Second, there was a loss of the bargaining power which was available to Uganda and Kenya in converting the inherited restrictions into a system of mutually beneficial trade. This was not so easy after outside countries had gained unlimited access to the East African market through Tanganyika. Ugandans and Kenyans were particularly galled that the Japanese agreement was being negotiated with Tanganyika though most of Japan's current trade was done with Kenya and Uganda.

Fiscal Coordination and Development Planning

Restraints on fiscal policy were nothing new. For instance, in 1962 Uganda found herself unable to increase the tax on expensive cars as the World Bank Mission had recommended, and was also unable to avoid imposing a politically distasteful sugar duty. The finance ministers and their civil servants spent considerable time on coordination before each budget, but the coordination was entirely on the side of revenue, not on that of expenditure.

This raised few problems while all three economies were proceeding at roughly the same colonial pace, one which was maintained for the first three years of independence by development plans based on reports of the International Bank for Research and Development. But Tanganyika's first three-year plan—largely a composite of departmental capital estimates—ended in 1964. Early in 1963 Tanganyika appointed a French Director of Planning and established a Ministry of Planning with the intention of creating a much more comprehensive plan incorporating a definite development strategy. In the same year, Uganda put development planning under the Prime Minister's office and increased the expected plan expenditure. Kenya set up an advisory planning commission with a Parliamentary Secretary in the Treasury and a Cabinet Planning Committee, and announced a six-year plan to commence in 1964.

The first problems arose in Tanganyika, not only because of her earlier independence, but also because of the distribution of the important centers of population and purchasing power around the perimeter of the country. This made it extremely difficult, for instance, to spend for the benefit of the Northern Province, since the second round of expenditure on goods and services might be drained off to Nairobi and have little impact on the Tanganyika economy unless measures were taken to close the border. A prerequisite of planning is a knowledge of the effective boundaries of the unit for which one must plan.

Another problem of comprehensive planning that might take somewhat longer to develop was that of foreign exchange. Deficit financing had not been considered by the East African treasuries, but a time would come when it would be found useful. For this reason, or because service charges on foreign loans and capital equipment imports would become more important, it might be necessary to protect the balance of payments by import and exchange restrictions, if development plans themselves were not to be curtailed. But neither exchange restrictions nor inflationary pressure can be limited to one section of a common market, and without some agreement on common policy it was unlikely that the suggested central bank would be able to function effectively. Yet a common development policy could hardly be achieved without a substantially closer degree of political union.

In 1962 the three governments agreed to the appointment of an Economic Adviser to EACSO, part of whose brief was to investigate the possibilities of an East African plan. In the view of the first Economic Adviser, the difficulty of planning was only a symptom of the decline in cooperation, the cause of which was the high expectations of rapid industrial development which the politicians required the planners in each separate country to fulfill. The first necessity was some form of political agreement or compromise on the distribution of industry in East Africa; but this proved elusive. On the other hand, so long as the politics of planning remained unsettled, separate planning steadily aggravated the problems of cooperation.

Location of Industry

Perhaps the thorniest problem was the location of industry within the common market. Originally it was intended that an industrial council should license firms in certain scheduled industries, guaranteeing them a market, though not necessarily a monopoly, for a given period of time, subject to certain conditions, and direct them to suitable locations according to an East African plan. When the Council was set up in 1948, however, both the over-all plan and the direction of location had been dropped.[46] Uganda (despite her benefits in textiles), and particularly Tanganyika, felt that the licensing system was resulting in too much industry going to Kenya, and refused to pass the legislation necessary to allow new industries to be added to the schedule. Thus the schedule applied only to textiles and blankets, steel drums, glassware, enamel hollow-ware, and metal window and door frames; and no new industries were added after 1955, despite a number of attempts, particularly by Uganda with respect to cement and fertilizers. The Raisman Commission and all three World Bank reports recommended the scrapping of the licensing system; but Tanganyika changed her position. Both in August 1962 and in May 1963 the then Minister of Commerce and Industry, George Kahama, opposed motions against the system in the CLA because it could now be used "to correct the imbalance." Tanganyika's approach was to attract industry to her own country first and then try to add it to the schedule, while the Kenyans tended to favor adding an industry to the schedule and then allowing it to choose its own location.

The Industrial Council, which granted licenses and kept in touch with the licensed enterprises, was composed of the Permanent Secretaries of Commerce and Industry of each territory, the Financial and Legal Secretaries of EACSO, a non-official appointed by EACSO, and two non-officials from each territory—a total of twelve men. It met from two to four times a year, and spent about two thirds of its time on various textile problems. In 1963 twenty-three out of thirty-two extant licenses were in textiles. The initiative on location rested with the firms concerned, not with the Council, which could not therefore be accused of favoring Kenya.

For the majority of industries which were not subject to licensing, there was very little coordination, except what occurred by chance during the busy sessions of the ministerial Commercial and Industrial Coordination Committee, the Tariff Committee, or through informal contacts. Some problems were bound to arise from the lack of coordination and information, and a good example was the paper industry. In the early 1950's Uganda investigated the possibilities of a paper industry but subsequently dropped the project. Several years later a Kenya report on the prospects of pulp and paper-making recommended waiting until demand increased. Meanwhile Kenya invested £2.5 million in softwood forests.[47] In 1961 she started keeping monthly figures on the market and, after another survey in 1962, decided to go ahead. In the meantime Uganda made plans for a small paper plant, unaware of the existence of the Kenya project, which would have made Uganda's uneconomic. When the Uganda plans were reported in the press, some hasty official telephone calls made it clear that the Kenya project would still go ahead, and this caused considerable resentment in Uganda. The matter might have been solved by coordination at lower levels, but the increasing pressures on the civil service made it more difficult than ever to spare men for new committees.

More serious were the problems arising from deliberate government pressures that affected the location of industry, regardless of the general East African interest, resulting in economic waste and political bitterness. Cement was the most frequently quoted example. Uganda started the first factory; Kenya blocked the scheduling of the industry and started two factories of her own. In 1963, in spite of existing overcapacity in the industry, Tanganyika put pressure on a Kenya producer to start a cement factory near Dar es Salaam. Similarly, Tanganyika took advantage of international competition in oil to attract a refinery to Dar es

Salaam, despite existing plans for a larger one, with more than sufficient capacity for the East African market, in Mombasa.

Tanganyika's sense of her own economic backwardness and comparative disadvantages in relation to Kenya was a major cause of these actions. For instance, Joseph Nyerere told the CLA that Tanganyika should not be stopped from having textile, cement, refining, and sugar industries just because Kenya and Uganda had them, or "Tanganyika will end with nothing because everything we want you will be able to find in Kenya or Uganda." Similarly, the *Tanganyika Standard* advocated "a time for selfishness" until East Africa was ready to federate; "Investors should be encouraged to think of Tanganyika as something other than a territorial offshoot of Nairobi."[48]

Nor was Tanganyika alone in these practices. Early in 1963 Kenya told a Uganda sugar producer to invest directly in Kenya or it would find someone else to do so and he would lose his Kenya market. It was true that a market did exist for the extra production; in 1961 Kenya imported 33,000 tons of sugar from Uganda and 26,000 tons from abroad. But it mattered to Kenya that production should take place there rather than in Uganda. Furthermore, the new Kenya government was faced in the short run with worse economic problems than those of Tanganyika, particularly unemployment, as Kenya went through a once-for-all shift from settler agriculture to a more broadly based economy. Thus compromise was not so easy as might at first appear.

Free Flow of Factors

As we noted above, for a common market to achieve the benefits of internal specialization, it must permit the free flow of factors of production and follow roughly similar social and economic policies. No formal obstacles blocked the movement of capital within East Africa, nor was there any restriction on the movement of African labor, except on the entry of specified Kenya tribes into the congested Northern Province of Tanganyika. In 1961, 11 per cent of Tanganyika's 440,000 workers came from outside, including 6,000 from Kenya. In Uganda, nearly 10 per cent of the 1961 labor force of 221,000 came from Kenya and Tanganyika (18,000 were Kenyans).[49] Since the flow of labor into Kenya was slight, the net effect of labor movements was to benefit Kenya rather than compensate Uganda and Tanganyika for the location of industry in Kenya.

Yet this was where the conflict between the short-term pressures and the long-term interests of the electorate became most apparent, or to put it another way, where the lack of political unity to reinforce the East African economy was more serious. For trade unions had—as had very few other bodies—the organization, the funds, and the membership that enabled them to put serious pressure on the government.

Unions were organized on a territorial basis. Each country had its own minimum wage legislation, and was faced with its own version of unemployment and the disinclination of school-leavers to take up farming. As each government responded to pressures to alleviate the situation, there was a risk that its welfare measures, if significantly better than those of its neighbors, would be wiped out by an influx of their unemployed workers. As one Uganda trade union leader said, pleading for restriction on the entry of Kenya workers: "It is the Uganda Government's duty to ensure that its own people are given happiness first."[50] Some Uganda ministers, who were Pan-Africanists and in favor of the common market, did not hesitate to criticize Kenyan labor in Uganda, particularly Kenyan leadership of Uganda unions.

Attempts to create a common East African labor policy were not notably successful. Labor ministers of the three territories met twice in 1962, in Kampala and Dar es Salaam, and recommended the creation of a new labor triumvirate for EACSO. This was finally agreed upon, but the new body was only to have powers to deal with EACSO labor, not a common labor policy. The latter seemed politically impracticable as long as Tanganyika labor legislation was unacceptable to Kenya and Uganda union leaders.

Similarly, our discussion of industrial licensing, above, emphasizes the prevailing political reluctance to allow a free flow of capital. In one case, in 1963, when a Ugandan entrepreneur announced his intention of investing in Kenya, he encountered severe criticism from Uganda politicians.[51]

Problems of the Common Services

Another threat to stability arose from controversy over various aspects of the common services. These problems proved much less significant than the frictions arising from running a common market without common political machinery, but there were problems nevertheless.

Under the High Commission, the self-financing services experienced somewhat less criticism than the non-self-financing services, which had to undergo scrutiny by four legislatures (the CLA and three territorial ones) at budget time. Among the self-financing services, civil aviation probably came off best, since East African Airways was run on commercial lines and, with some government protection, managed to make a profit. Nevertheless, certain problems arose, such as the need to ensure "a more reasonable distribution" of trunk routes as between Nairobi, Entebbe, and Dar es Salaam.[52]

Railways and Harbours came off less lightly. As the largest employer, EAR & H faced the strongest unions, and was vulnerable to accusations of Kenyan control because of the predominance of railway activity and employment in Kenya. During 1959–60, the Tanganyika Railway African Union advocated breaking up EAR & H to make it more responsive. But the Minister of Communications, on another occasion, told the Tanganyika Parliament that a separate rail administration would cost the country 15–20 per cent more than the existing system, or about £675,000.[53]

Questions continually arose about the purposes and relevance of the research services, the distribution of their benefits, and their employment policies. For example, in 1962 a Ugandan complained in the CLA that 62 EACSO scientists were employed in Kenya and only 23 in Uganda.[54] In 1960, when Kenya and Tanganyika felt fiscal pressures, the first economy they suggested was the termination of certain common research services.[55] In the same year, territorial units of the Statistical Department were decentralized partly because of Ugandan and Tanganyikan feelings that they were not getting the details they wanted. Kenyans felt that this was a retrograde step, but there still was adequate coordination in the production of most indices, except perhaps the immigration figures.[56]

Less successful was the East African Navy. Formed in 1950 as a successor to the Kenya Royal Navy Volunteer Service, it consisted in 1961 of two minesweepers and several smaller ships, 17 officers and 200 men. It was based at Mombasa and cost some £94,000 a year to run, or less than two per cent of the General Fund budget. Without public discussion, Tanganyika announced its opposition to the service because the Mombasa base limited its usefulness to Tanganyika and because cooperating with a colony on defense raised a problem of sovereignty once Tanganyika had become independent.[57] Uganda and Kenya considered keeping the service on a modified basis—for example, as a self-supporting marine police force, maintaining buoys and lighthouses—but eventually the plan was dropped.

The Marine Fisheries Research Organization in Zanzibar almost met the same fate. The first meeting of the Social and Research Committee in February 1962 decided to close the organization on the grounds that its benefits were slight —again, it seemed, on the initiative of Tanganyika. Partly because the director was able to get outside funds, the order was rescinded, but the research program suffered a serious setback.[58]

Even the new University of East Africa, although not precisely a service, encountered interterritorial problems. Ugandans complained in the CLA that the newer colleges were duplicating existing facilities, and ministers engaged in behind-the-scenes political controversy over the distribution of funds.[59] Uganda was concerned at what she regarded as a curtailment of university development at Makerere College in Kampala when the other territories were striking out on their own.

Perhaps the most serious example of the problems that could arise from inequality of benefits came in the case of the semiofficial East African Tourist Travel Association. Without warning, the Uganda Government announced its withdrawal of support in February 1963, on the grounds that Uganda's share of the total tourist revenue of £6 million was only £800,000, or 9.5 per cent, while she paid

£6,000, or 25 per cent, of the costs of the organization. Kenya paid 52 per cent of the costs and received 67 per cent of the revenue (£5.7 million), while Tanganyika came out about even. Critics of Uganda's unilateral action were themselves accused of being "divisive" by Uganda CLA members, one of whom said that Uganda's action was necessary in conditions of "cutthroat competition," and alleged that Tanganyika ministers placed their territorial interests before those of the East African Common Market.[60] This illustrates the difficult atmosphere within which the services had to function, and the way in which they were affected by the problems of the common market as well as by political relations.

Administrative Problems

The administrative framework of cooperation was only a partial structure, and even had it been more complete, an administration is only as good as its informal communications network. While civil servants could not directly thwart the politicians' wishes, their attitudes could modify or exaggerate political attitudes, particularly in the day-to-day matters that make cooperation truly effective. When political directives were ambiguous, these influences were correspondingly more important.

One of the greatest problems affecting official attitudes might be summed up in a phrase frequently heard in East Africa—"the Nairobi mentality." Used by non-Kenyans, it seemed to connote a sense of superiority, a willingness to make common decisions without consultation, and a dislike for "provincials," although to skeptical Kenyans it merely indicated a rather far-fetched sensitivity in Tanganyikans and Ugandans. Although some Kenya civil servants denied it, others admitted that there was an aspect of snobbery about the Kenya service. Insofar as this was a reflection of European snobbery, it might be expected to vanish with the Africanization of the respective civil services. But there was also an inherent problem of the relations between any capital and the provinces. For effective functioning, every bureaucracy must make a number of small decisions at headquarters quickly and without prolonged consultation; and each such decision is a possible source of pique that those outside the center have not been consulted.[61]

Furthermore, both EACSO and the Kenya civil service had their headquarters in Nairobi, and had more opportunity for informal contact. As one official put it, "When you have to get information right away, it is an awful temptation to ring up down the road rather than wait for a scratchy connexion with Dar." Moreover, Kenyan officials, with years of experience working in the largest commercial center of East Africa, had an advantage at interterritorial meetings, and sometimes tended to become impatient with the inexperience of Ugandans and Tanganyikans. The EACSO problem was intensified by the high proportion of Kenyans among its African staff. This was not likely to be alleviated by Africanization, for with increasing opportunities in the home civil services, EACSO found it difficult to recruit more than a few Ugandans and Tanganyikans. Of some forty superscale Africans serving EACSO in mid-1963, nearly thirty were Kenyans. Thus it was not surprising that on several occasions Ugandans advocated transfer of parts of EACSO headquarters to Uganda.[62]

Still another problem, and one of the limitations of the ministerial triumvirate system, was the physical divorce between ministers in territorial capitals and the EACSO civil servants in Nairobi. Unlike a territorial civil servant, his counterpart, the EACSO official, could not personally

164

"get hold of his minister" and had to rely on paper communication. Personal briefing of ministers occurred mainly at budget time and in relation to questions in the CLA. Otherwise, memoranda and background papers were prepared by EACSO civil servants, but were discussed by ministers with their own officials who naturally tended to emphasize local interests and viewpoints. As a Tanganyikan civil servant put it, "Those East African civil servants don't understand *our* problems."

The pattern of administrative cooperation fluctuated over the years. During World War II and in the early postwar period, the existence of a large number of controls made close administrative cooperation an absolute necessity. Thus, although interterritorial rivalries existed, they were limited. Controls were relaxed, particularly in Uganda and Tanganyika, during the early 1950's; in 1955 the Production and Supply Council, staffed by officials and representatives of commerce, was replaced by the Committee for Economic Coordination, which included ministers each of whom was responsible to his own government. The pressures of territorial responsibility were stronger than had been anticipated. When Sir Ernest Vasey, long a Kenya minister, was invited to take a Ministry in Tanganyika, he dashed the hopes of some former colleagues by becoming very Tanganyikan.

As government bureaucracies grew, more demands were made on the administrators' time, and tasks increased. With the approach of independence and the premature resignation of many officials, the pool of experience decreased. As one new Tanganyikan official put it, "It took me four days just to read up the past files on one case, and I have twenty I am responsible for." It seems that lack of experience in interterritorial negotiations and fear of being accused of sacrificing national interests made many of the new African officials more intransigent than their predecessors. One official complained: "Nowadays people come here late for the Ministerial meetings, rush through the agenda, and are off immediately afterwards, leaving you little time to solve problems quietly."

Nonetheless, the low point in cooperation came in the years just before the end of the East African High Commission. With a lack of political support for the whole framework, relations became not so much a question of doing something when it did not hurt as of doing something only when it meant partisan benefits. The Industrial Council was barely working, about one in fifteen cases got through the Tariff Committee, and the Committee for Economic Coordination had virtually ceased to function. As a participant explained, every time an application was considered in the Industrial Council, the civil servants were "looking over their shoulders" and "by the time we got down to anything . . . it escaped."[63]

In contrast to this, administrative coordination was somewhat better under EACSO, although there was very little difference in administrative structure between it and the High Commission. Nor could the change be attributed to Africanization, because Africans were still a minority on most of these committees. The great change was one of climate; diminished territorial resentment was purchased at the price of greater territorial control. The situation was still far from satisfactory, and little bargaining was done in terms of an East African interest. It was notable that the role of hector in interterritorial meetings, which was mainly Kenya's when she was enjoying her economic boom in the mid-1950's, was later assumed by Tanganyika, which might be said to have been enjoying a political boom in the early

1960's. Kenyans and Ugandans often complained that Tanganyika took the initiative in most meetings by announcing her intentions and expecting the rest of the meeting to fall into line.

An important difference in the past had been the ultimate existence of a common political control. While too much should not be made of this, thanks to the Colonial Office practice of letting the men in the field make decisions, the common origin of the colonial civil servants provided both a source of informal communication and a limit on the extent to which any controversy could go. Two things partly replaced this common origin after independence: First, there was the past influence of Makerere. In 1963 some two thirds of the African civil servants at EACSO were Makerere graduates. Second, most African civil servants had a common outlook on nationalism, race, and African unity. Yet what effect this had at the bargaining table was uncertain.

Political Problems

Apart from the possibility of major clashes of ideology or interest, which would change the whole framework of cooperation, there were various political problems connected with state sovereignty. The restraints on power essential to cooperation were difficult for new rulers, who had just ousted a colonial government, to accept. More specifically, separate national flags, songs, and heroes tended to reinforce national separatism in matters of East African common interest.

On a less emotional plane, sovereignty means the responsibility of a government for the defense and welfare of a group of people within certain territorial boundaries. If the political future of East African cooperation were assured, the governments were not failing in their sovereign task by permitting a high degree of interdependence. But if that future were uncertain, the governments would have to take account of it. For instance, the Uganda Government would have to insure against total reliance on rail links to the sea through Kenya, which might mean investing in a system of communications directed more toward the Congo and Sudan. Or the Kenya Government, in the face of uncertainty, might feel that it should ignore the advice of the World Bank and develop a new hydroelectric plant on the Tana River rather than increase its dependence on power from Uganda.[64]

Another type of political problem was the friction and restraint which accompanied tripartite decision-making. Dr. Kiano, Kenya's Minister of Commerce and Industry, summed this up nicely: "Every time we wanted to take a decision, a firm decision in the field of economics, we had to get the approval directly or indirectly from our neighbors, and if they did not believe the way we did, well that just had to be put on the shelf."[65] Such irritations and restraints detracted from the atmosphere necessary for compromise and provided opportunities for backbenchers and members of the opposition to embarrass the government at home.

Political uncertainties and frictions tended to affect economic decisions that might otherwise have been straightforward. An example of the problems and embarrassments involved occurred in 1962, when the Uganda cabinet, with local elections looming, refused to accept the five cents per pound increase in the excise duty on sugar agreed to by the three Ministers of Finance. The Uganda Minister of Finance notified Kenya of this only a few hours before the Kenya budget speech. His own budget was presented without the sugar duty; and to make matters worse, he softened the impact of the other taxes by pointing out that the government had deliberately avoided raising sugar prices, which would have hurt the poorest people. Strong protests by Kenya that she would lose £500,000 through smuggling were backed up by Tanganyika, and there were threats of refusal to buy Uganda sugar—one of Uganda's major exports to the rest of East Africa.

Eventually, the Uganda Government had to swallow its pride and accept a compromise increase of three cents per pound. The Leader of the Opposition asked, "Is Nairobi or Dar es Salaam going to make decisions for Kampala and Entebbe?" and, if every decision had to be consulted over, what was the purpose of fighting for Uganda's independence? Other members objected to a decision imposed on their government.[66] Two months later, the Prime Minister told his UPC party conference, which had just adopted a resolution supporting East African cooperation, that they must be aware of the price they had to pay for it, which had been brought home to them in the National Assembly "only recently in a very brutal manner."[67]

What was surprising was that by 1963 there were so few open political problems. But even a small problem like the sugar duty raised a whole spectrum of comments in the Uganda Parliament about the alleged ill-treatment of Uganda's cement and textile industries, and suggestions of greater orientation toward Sudan and the Congo. A loose system of cooperation was forever vulnerable to any small quarrel which might set off a chain reaction. One reason why the sugar tax problem passed as easily as it did was that the government won the local elections anyway.

East African economic integration was liable to many threats of disruption in the economic, administrative, and political fields. By far the most serious were the problems of the common market. But the danger was that so many of the other frictions depended on a favorable political atmosphere for their alleviation. A breakup of the common market would destroy the atmosphere which made the General Fund common services possible and might even affect the three self-financing communications services. The Secretary-General of EACSO emphasized that the common market and services must be kept distinct, at least in theory, and that even if the difficulties should prove insurmountable in the first, there was no reason why the second should not remain as a future nucleus, or even as a set of separate corporations.[68] Although a number of services were directly related to the common market, there was no theoretical reason why the Secretary-General should not have been right. But theory must take account of political reality. There were problems, even in running the common services, and they would become more important in an intolerant atmosphere. In 1960 a Tanganyikan minister declared that the "fairly large measure of dissatisfaction" felt within Tanganyika with the customs union reflected upon the High Commission Services.[69] It was likely that this would be true of future problems as well.

An improved EACSO structure with greater executive and coordinating powers might be more viable. But it is difficult to imagine necessary improvements which would not require a very considerable political agreement. And such political agreement proved to be more elusive than the leaders of the three sovereign states imagined when they announced their intentions to federate. On the other hand, if the hope of political federation were given up, or if only two of the countries were to federate, it is not inconceivable that an agreement could be reached to maintain the three important communications services as separate corporations with interterritorial governing boards. Again, however, the assumption of political goodwill is crucial.

In 1963 the East Africans had a system of economic integration which was remarkable in Africa—but the stability of the system was doubtful. A number of political leaders, particularly in Tanganyika and Kenya, were aware of this. At the end of the year, after the failure of the summer negotiations, Tanganyika began exploring the costs of going it alone and the problems of establishing a separate currency. Subsequently, in the spring of 1964, Tanganyika made public its complaints about economic integration and after a series of hastily convened conferences, the East African leaders agreed to allow the use of import quotas to equalize the benefits of the market. Whether this breach of the common market would prove to be a successful compromise was highly uncertain. In short, economic integration was not automatically leading to political integration in East Africa. If anything, time seemed to be on the side of disintegration. It was impossible to avoid recognizing that conscious political decisions are the link between economic and political integration and that the future depended primarily on the personalities and ideologies of the East African political leaders who were responding to these pressures and problems.

Part Three

PAN-AFRICANISM
AND DECISIONS

VI

The Failure to Federate in 1963

"You are not ready," is the same argument the imperialists have always used . . . Is it not going to be the most curious piece of irony if we, the African Nationalists, who have always wanted unity, were to inherit and use this argument to perpetuate colonial divisions?

Julius Nyerere
East African Federation (1960)

In June 1960 Julius Nyerere made his famous offer to delay Tanganyika's independence if it would mean that all three East African territories could come to independence together as a federal unit. This speech brought federation to the forefront of East African politics for the first time since the Closer Union Movement of the 1920's.

Before Nyerere's speech it was definitely not politic to support federation openly. According to the *East African Standard*, "Four or five years ago, the word 'federation' was spoken in a hushed voice, if at all, so explosive was its application to the East African political scene." Indeed, Nyerere himself had inserted a clause in the original Tanu constitution pledging opposition to federation until the demand for it came from Africans. In Uganda, not only were the Baganda hostile to federation because they associated it with a threat to the Kabakaship, but important non-Baganda like B. K. Kirya promised "to fight against federation."[1]

Pan-Africanism and East African Integration

By 1958 Nyerere and Mboya favored federation, and their pioneering views were linked with Pan-Africanism. Nyerere's convictions about federation and Pan-Africanism developed simultaneously as he realized the importance of unity in bringing about success in Tanganyika. Mboya favored federation for the "greater political strength within Pan-Africa that a larger political unit would possess."[2] These two leaders were so far ahead of their colleagues at that time that neither mentioned his support of federation at the Mwanza conference in September. In December a few East Africans discussed federation informally while they attended the All African Peoples' Conference in Accra, but Ugandans did not participate, and the *Uganda Argus* said in summing up the situation at the end of the year: "It can be said quite confidently that there is no substantial body of opinion in any territory now in favor of federation."[3]

Not only was federation unpopular at this time, but the colonial institutions for interterritorial cooperation were coming under increasing criticism. In Uganda, Milton Obote and George Magezi were critical, and even the Democratic Party was advocating secession from the High Commission. Similarly in Tanganyika the High Commission was criticized in the Legislative Council, and the Tanganyika Federation of Labour (TFL) passed a resolution calling for its dissolution.[4]

Two changes in 1961 helped prolong the life of the interterritorial institutions. Pan-Africanism had little to do with the first of these changes, the implementation of the Raisman Report (discussed in the previous chapter). In the words of one Tanganyikan, it was a "technicians' adjustment worked out primarily by expatriates."[5] Ugandans and Tanganyikans accepted a less than optimal solution for the sake of maintaining East African cooperation, but this was the same basis upon which the three colonial governors agreed to the report.

The second adjustment, the agreement on the Common Services Organization, occurred after Africans had the initiative in Tanganyika and owed much more to Pan-African motivations. According to Oscar Kambona, "EACSO was Nyerere's idea. Nkrumah had destroyed the common services of West Africa, and we felt that this was a mistake that we wanted to avoid. We saw these services as mainly political."[6] As early as May 1960 Nyerere answered criticism of the High Commission by suggesting that it be reformed and made to serve the cause of unity, bolstering his argument with the good Pan-Africanist statement that "the bigger we have these units, the better . . ."[7]

Organized labor, the strongest and best organized group in Tanganyika, opposed Nyerere on this policy, and the story of their opposition is an interesting example of the way the ideology of Pan-Africanism affected an interest group. Many trade unionists felt that it was in their economic interest to dissolve the High Commission because national services would be more responsive to their pressure.[8] The Tanganyika Railway African Union (TRAU), the strongest union and leader of the opposition to the High Commission, had just suffered from a prolonged rail strike in which the failure of interterritorial labor cooperation had left it bearing the brunt of the burden.

In July 1960 TRAU and the Tanganyika African Postal Union (TAPU) were urging the breakup of the High Commission. At the same time, Nyerere had just urged federation publicly and was justifying it at Tanu rallies on the Pan-Africanist grounds that if Tanganyika tried to stand alone, "our laws may be dictated by Russia, by the United States, by Britain or by France."[9] Through private discussion, Nyerere won Rashidi Kawawa (then President of the TFL) and Michael Kamaliza (who later succeeded Kawawa as president) to his point of view by convincing them of the connection between the High Commission and eventual federation.[10]

Others remained unconvinced. In August the TRAU Annual Conference resolved that Tanganyika should secede from East African Railways and Harbours. On the other hand, Kamaliza's Transport and General Workers Union urged reform of the High Commission. Kasanga Tumbo of TRAU and Jacob Namfua of TAPU then accused Kamaliza of failing to follow the TFL policy of advocating complete dissolution of the High Commission. At the end of the month, shortly after Tom Mboya flew to Dar es Salaam for talks with the trade unionists about the High Commission, the TFL Governing Council softened its opposition and urged withdrawal unless certain reforms were made.[11]

Tumbo remained skeptical at first. He reported after talking with Nyerere in November that "the Chief Minister is seriously committed to his ideals, [but] the struggle against the High Commission will continue until regionalization of this public service is achieved." By stages, however, Tumbo's opinion began to conform with the majority's. A TRAU conference in April 1961 agreed to retention of other common services so long as Tanganyika withdrew from the railways. By May 1961, Tumbo was supporting decentralization rather than dissolution of the High Commission and finally by October, he reluctantly supported the establishment of EACSO.[12]

The Failure to Federate in 1963

What role did Pan-Africanism play in this diminution of labor opposition? According to Kamaliza, "We argued with [our opponents in the TFL] in terms of Pan-Africanism and the absurdity of breaking the High Commission when we would just have to build it again. Most of them listened, particularly Namfua, but Tumbo wanted publicity and support."[13] But in retrospect Namfua felt that the arguments which won him over were that it would be very expensive to run the services alone. In his discussions with Tumbo, Namfua said, he stressed the need for patience while politics in Uganda and Kenya improved, but he did not relate this to African unity as such.[14]

Another limitation on a too simple explanation of the role of Pan-Africanism in diminishing labor opposition was that Tumbo considered himself a Pan-Africanist and supported federation. For more than a year Tumbo was able to maintain a belief in the common ideology and a separate position in defense of his group's interest—much as Uganda politicians were later and more successfully to do. But Tumbo's opposition did gradually soften, in part at least because of the burden of arguing a unique interpretation of the ideology against a consensus. And, in general, the unitarist implications of the ideology put the labor opposition on the defensive. By May 1961 the government was able to refuse Kamaliza's request for TFL representation at the London conference which established EACSO. Kamaliza was later able to rationalize this on the good Pan-Africanist grounds that the people leading the government *were* the workers.[15]

On federation itself Nyerere was less successful. In his speech to the Second Conference of Independent African States at Addis Ababa in June 1960, Nyerere focused on the dangers of separate sovereignties and offered to postpone

Tanganyika's independence for a few months "rather than take the risk of perpetuating the balkanization of East Africa."[16]

The reaction in East Africa was disappointing. Mboya supported Nyerere, but in Uganda not only the Kabaka's government, but Obote and the Democratic Party as well, stated that Uganda was not ready for federation. Even Tanu headquarters issued a statement that Nyerere was expressing his personal views, a position the headquarters reversed only after Kambona fully supported Nyerere. Minor groups in Tanganyika quickly seized on Nyerere's offer to delay independence to attack Tanu.[17] Support from Kanyama Chiume (a founder member of Pafmeca) in Nyasaland was offset when Dr. Banda announced that East Africa could not be allowed to hold things up in Nyasaland.[18]

Although Kanu urged federation in their 1960 manifesto, Kadu in Kenya, most Ugandans, and minor groups in Tanganyika continued to say that federations would have to wait until after independence. More important, Nyerere could get no assurances about independence dates for Uganda and Kenya when he went to England in November. When the Pafmeca leaders met in Nairobi in January 1961 they agreed to support federation, but only after each country had an African prime minister.[19]

After this a number of groups openly declared their support of federation. They included Asian parties in Kenya and Uganda, the Kenya African National Traders and Farmers Union, the Kenya African Chamber of Commerce and Industry, and the Association of Chambers of Commerce of Eastern Africa. The Governor of Kenya announced that the three East African governors had met and discussed how to help the African leaders form a federation if that was what they wanted.[20] But Nyerere's plan to federate before separate sovereignties clouded the problem had already failed. The people who mattered, the African political elite, were preoccupied with elections, with the tensions attending the existence of minority governments in Kenya and Uganda, and the coming independence of Tanganyika. Various leaders made various statements favoring federation during the course of 1961, but nothing was done.

After her independence in December, Tanganyika's initiative on federation diminished for several reasons. First, and most important, Nyerere felt that if an independent Tanganyika pushed openly for federation, it might open her to charges of imperialism toward her neighbors and jeopardize future prospects of federation. "In this sense," Nyerere said, "independence made us less free." Soon after independence he told a press conference that federation would now have to wait until all three countries were sovereign.[21]

Second, independence brought problems demanding attention within Tanganyika, and Nyerere resigned to reorganize Tanu. Leaders had less time to think about federation. A non-African cabinet member in Tanganyika has said that commitment to federation actually increased, and cabinet members sometimes injected such qualifications into discussion as "this would have to be changed after federation." But the general effect of sovereignty was the introduction of a gap between commitment to the ideal of federation and the daily practice of East African cooperation, as we saw in the previous chapter.

Third, unlike Kenya where both parties in the unstable coalition were in favor of federation, Milton Obote in Uganda was anxious not to antagonize his Baganda coalition partners, who publicly opposed federation, until he had a majority of his own.[22] Statements made by UPC throughout 1962 were guarded and ambiguous. At the Pafmecsa conference in Addis Ababa in February, John Kakonge said that Uganda intended closer relations, but warned Tanganyika "not to upset the applecart."[23] In May, when Mwai Kibaki of Kenya moved in the CLA that immediate steps be taken toward federation, he was asked to withdraw the motion to save the Ugandans embarrassment.

In October Obote spoke favorably (and privately) about federation to African leaders visiting Kampala for Uganda's independence ceremonies, and during an important foreign policy speech in November he stressed that Uganda intended to move "not backward but forward" in her East African ties.[24] In December, Obote threatened to boycott Kenya goods if Britain did not speed up Kenya's independence— a safely ambiguous policy which appealed both to those who wanted closer, and those who wanted less intimate, relations with Kenya. A week later Obote and Rashidi Kawawa used the argument that cooperation with a colony was impossible as an excuse to break short an EACSO Authority meeting (without warning to Kadu's Ronald Ngala, who was attending for Kenya) and to announce their intention to take the matter up with Britain. Upon their return from Britain early in 1963, Kawawa and Obote announced their satisfaction. The local press reported that the East Africans had disclosed to Prime Minister Macmillan that they would initiate steps toward federation as soon as Kenya became independent.[25]

In the meantime, in December and again in January, Buganda government spokesmen reiterated their opposition to federation.[26] Moreover, the Buganda Lukiko unanimously adopted a resolution supporting cooperation, but calling federation inopportune. Obote countered with ambiguity. Answering a question in February, he replied that he had understood that opposition was to timing, not to the idea of federation, which was acceptable. Shortly afterward he told a political meeting that he was not greatly interested in federation at the moment. Nonetheless, in March Obote wrote to the Prime Minister of Somalia to object to Somali claims to Kenya's Northern Frontier District, and justified his interest on the dual grounds of Uganda's close ties with Kenya and African unity.[27]

In April Uganda announced that she and Tanganyika had entered a defense agreement for joint training and mutual assistance to which Kenya would be welcome to accede after independence. This brought renewed protest from Buganda, but was well received in Kenya. And at the end of April Obote discussed federation with Kenyatta and Kawawa, who were in Kampala for a Common Services Authority meeting.[28]

NEGOTIATIONS: SUMMER 1963

The decision to begin negotiations on federation was made at Arusha, Tanganyika, on June 1, 1963. Kanu had won the Kenya elections, and Kenya's independence government was inaugurated in Nairobi that morning. Shortly after the ceremony, three Kenya cabinet ministers, Tom Mboya, Joseph Murumbi, and Achieng Oneko, flew to Arusha to see Sekou Touré, President of Guinea, who was visiting Tanganyika, and to talk to Tanganyika's leaders about pressing Britain for an early date for Kenya's independence.[29] In the course of discussion, Nyerere suggested that they kill two birds with one stone—that they plan a federation and hold conferences on it before the Kenyans went to London to press for an early independence date. The next step was to notify Uganda. Obote was caught by surprise, but agreed readily without even consulting his cabinet, and a conference was planned for the next Wednesday.[30]

On June 5, after a few hours of discussion (attended also by the visiting Somali Foreign Minister and several East African cabinet ministers), Nyerere, Kenyatta, and Obote announced their intention to federate by the end of the year and to discuss a constitution to be drafted by a Working Party by the third week of August. They also announced that any British delay of Kenya's independence would be regarded as an unfriendly act.[31]

The leaders made this decision little more than a week after the end of the Addis Ababa Conference, which observers generally agreed had been a heady affair. This Pan-African climate may have influenced Obote in particular. He had recently been acclaimed as a militant Pan-Africanist at Addis Ababa, and he seems to have been swayed in a similar way during the EEC decisions the previous year.[32] Although he changed his view later, Obote signed the declaration that said "We hope that our action will help to accelerate the efforts already being made by our brothers throughout the Continent to achieve Pan-African unity."[33]

The final decision to federate was made suddenly, but not without preparation. As one leader put it, every time politicians had met for the past three years they had talked about federation. Kenyans and Tanganyikans claim that Obote had supported federation in conversations with them for a long time, and thus the decision only appeared to be sudden.

The Working Party—initially composed of Kambona and Amir Jamal for Tanganyika, Mboya and Murumbi for Kenya, and Kakonge and Binaisa for Uganda—first met in Dar es Salaam four days after the Nairobi declaration. After two days' discussion, the Working Party announced "agreement on every issue," and added that they had instructed lawyers to draft a constitution to be ready for a meeting in Kampala at the end of the month. They also announced that they were requesting United Nations specialists to assist on civil service and fiscal problems.[34] Shortly afterward, several Working Party members visited Uganda and discussed federation with the Kabaka of Buganda and the Omukama (king) of Toro, though the visitors made it clear that the central government in Uganda would make the decision on federation.[35] Before continuing on to London (where the Kenyans were successful in pressing Britain for independence by the end of the year), Mboya announced that plans were moving so quickly that the conference planned for the third week of August might be moved up to July.[36]

The era of good feeling was brief. It was over by the time the three leaders and the Working Party met in Kampala at the end of June,[37] though no one admitted the fact publicly until August. After a weekend of discussions the leaders met the hereditary monarchs—except the Kabaka, who failed to attend because of the affront of holding such a meeting in his kingdom at a place other than his palace—but they issued no final statement. Mboya denied that anything was wrong, but two days later Obote made a little-noticed statement that the Nairobi declaration did not commit Uganda to federation and that the questions of relationships and powers were still in the "exploratory stage."[38]

When the Working Party met for the third time, in mid-July in Nairobi, it had new instructions to prepare reports on areas of disagreement, but it was no more successful.[39] In the meantime, a number of UPC members had expressed discontent about federation during a debate in the Uganda National Assembly. Nonetheless, Mboya continued to deny any rifts, and Nyerere said he still hoped for federation by the end of the year.[40]

Later in July, the Working Party went to Zanzibar to bring up to date the newly elected government which had accepted an invitation to join the Working Party. At the beginning of August Mboya announced that the draft constitution would be ready for presentation to the Working Party at Dar es Salaam in another week, and he predicted that the "Big Three" leaders would now meet at the end of August or early in September.[41]

After the fourth Working Party meeting in Dar es Salaam early in August (which Zanzibar attended for the first time), Kambona and Murumbi issued statements that all had gone well, only minor disagreements remained, and that the "Big Three" would be meeting within a few days. But Adoko Nekyon, back in Uganda, denied that the "Big Three" would meet that week, and made the first public acknowledgment of disagreements. The subjects of disagreement read almost like the framework for the constitution that was supposed to have been agreed upon: the number and powers of legislative chambers; citizenship; division of power over foreign affairs; the civil service; the site of the capital; mineral rights; agriculture; and residual powers. As Nekyon said later, he wanted to see the "minimal alteration of territorial constitutions."[42]

In mid-August the Tanu National Executive passed resolutions supporting African unity and calling for federation by the end of the year, but the next day Tanganyika's Kambona announced that Uganda had informed the other countries that she was not ready for a meeting of the three leaders. In Kenya, Murumbi also attributed the delay to Uganda. Nekyon responded with the first public statement expressing doubt that there would be federation in 1963, and an expression of Ugandan nationalism "I am not prepared just to throw my nation into darkness," Nekyon declared, "As a small state Uganda needs certain guarantees for her future within a larger unit." Obote began a prolonged speaking tour throughout Uganda during which he mentioned domestic problems but never federation.[43]

By mid-September Nyerere publicly expressed doubt that East Africa would federate by the end of the year.[44] This doubt was reinforced when Obote decided not to meet Kenyatta and Nyerere in Nairobi on September 19, much to their annoyance, since in their view the talks had been scheduled for Obote's sake.[45] Nekyon issued a statement repeating that there would be no federation in 1963, but that it might be achieved by the end of 1964.[46]

Early in September some Kenyans and Tanganyikans discussed the possibility of going ahead without Uganda, but Tanganyika was opposed. Earlier Nyerere had said that he felt a two-state federation would be an admission of defeat at the start, thus making it less significant for Pan-African unity. On September 23 Kenyatta said he looked forward to federation "as soon as possible" and denied that any two states would form a federation without the third.[47]

For a month after the abortive September meeting in Nairobi the federation issue was quiet. Kenyans were preoccupied with getting Britain to revise their constitution in the direction of greater central powers, and Uganda was involved in the politics of making the Kabaka the first African head of state—an issue not directly connected with federation.[48]

In mid-October Obote expressed annoyance at Britain's failure to notify him of the appointment of a High Commissioner-designate to the East African Federation.[49] Nonetheless, he (and Nyerere) cabled support to Kanu in London for its stand on the Kenya constitution, and soon afterward he predicted that talks on federation would resume after the

Kenya delegates returned from London—a hint that was repeated by Uganda's Deputy Minister for Foreign Affairs, Sam Odaka.[50]

Whatever reconciliation might have been under way (and it should not be overemphasized), it was set back a few days later when the press reported a speech in which Murumbi suggested that Kenya and Tanganyika might have to go it alone, and that one reason for Uganda's delay was that some of her leaders feared they would become nonentities in the larger politics of federation. Obote then challenged the others to go ahead and demanded an explanation before he would attend any further talks. Kanu back-benchers criticized Murumbi, and Kenyatta sent Obote a message disassociating the Kenya Government from Murumbi's personal views.[51]

Although Uganda Minister of State Grace Ibingira told a University Conference on Federation in November that Uganda still intended to federate, he attended the conference on his own authority and in spite of objections in the Uganda cabinet. More important was the government statement that Uganda would go ahead with federal talks but would do nothing to jeopardize her obligations as a member of the provisional secretariat of the Organization of African Unity. Uganda aimed at "the unity of East Africa—not as a bloc, but as partners in the great effort to advance economic cooperation. . ."[52] The wheel had come full circle since Pan-Africanism had acted as an impetus to the Nairobi declaration in June.

ISSUES AND ARGUMENTS: THE ROLE OF PAN-AFRICANISM[53]

Why did the leaders fail to achieve a federation in 1963 and what did ideology have to do with it? One thing that is obvious from the public account is verified in private—the reluctant partner was Uganda. Between Kenya and Tanganyika there were some differences—for instance, on how strong a central bank to have—but on all important matters they were in agreement.

The nature of Uganda's reluctance was widely misunderstood and frequently traced to the Kabaka. For instance, the (Kenya) *Sunday Nation* believed it could "reduce the Federation problems to their basic essential—the Baganda . . . do not want to lose their individuality." A political columnist wrote that "it would be wrong to place the blame on the shoulders of Prime Minister Milton Obote . . . Buganda and the aspirations of her rulers constitute the chief obstacle"; and the Kenya Federation of Labour publicly appealed to the Baganda to change their position.[54] In Tanganyika, leaders who of course knew better deliberately did not disabuse the public of this notion in hopes of allowing Uganda leaders to save face.

Undoubtedly the Kabaka was reluctant about federation, but he was not the main cause of Uganda's reluctance. Among the most reluctant Ugandans were several men associated with the more radical side of the UPC—men who loved the Kabaka so little that they opposed Obote when he supported the Kabaka's candidacy for President of Uganda. The failure to federate in 1963 was not a stereotyped case of traditionalism vs. Pan-Africanism. Reconciling Pan-African ideology with personal and national interests, not overcoming the problems posed by traditional institutions, was the issue in 1963.

There is no doubt about the commitment of the leaders at the time of the Nairobi declaration. The legal draftsmen received firm directives to draft the constitution of a strong federation. The general atmosphere was good. A Ugandan who prepared a report on how to coordinate his department in a federation contrasted the cooperative atmosphere when he began the report with the backbiting in August when he submitted it. A meeting of monetary experts early in June seemed ready to agree on a strong central bank. By the time they next met in July the agreement had vanished.

In the early cooperative atmosphere the Working Party agreed on the rough draft of a strong federal constitution patterned on the Tanganyikan system, with a strong executive president, a vice-president and ministers. Originally it was to have a powerful lower house directly elected by population (after an interim period) and a weaker, indirectly elected upper house representing territories. The Working Party did not discuss such possibilities as a rotating presidency or a ceremonial head of state. The first president was to be chosen by agreement (presumably Kenyatta). Thereafter the President was to be declared elected if the successful parliamentary candidates who had previously declared their preference for him were a majority. Otherwise, he would be elected by a secret ballot in Parliament.

The Working Party did not discuss the possibility of forming a federation from smaller constituent units than the three states. They agreed that a central planning commission would have powers over economic planning after each territory worked out its plan subject to central coordination during a three-year interim period. Central government was to have power over labor legislation. Education, road-building, welfare legislation, and broadcasting were included in a list of concurrent powers. Not only was the list of federal powers much longer than the lists of state and concurrent powers, but any residual powers were to be the concern of the federal government. Civil service and fiscal arrangements were not covered in the draft constitution and were to be the subjects of reports by experts forwarded from the United Nations.

The Failure to Federate in 1963

During the first Dar es Salaam meeting at which these principles were established, Mboya led a Kenyan and Tanganyikan strategy of pushing hard for central powers in the belief that it was best to break through the separate sovereignties and settle the resulting problems later. Of the Ugandans, Attorney General Binaisa was somewhat dubious about so much centralization, particularly in foreign affairs, but Kakonge, though he had gone to the meeting with the idea of building upon EACSO, acquiesced to the Kenya-Tanganyika approach. As for Pan-Africanism, according to one participant, "During the bargaining, we did not refer to Pan-Africanism. It was always assumed." Or, as another participant put it, "When you agree on first principles, there is no need to waste time discussing philosophy."

After the Ugandan delegates returned to Kampala many of their colleagues in the cabinet began to have second thoughts about Uganda's place in the strong federation that was being drafted. Rumors about future positions in the federation also made Uganda leaders look more carefully at what their delegates had agreed to. Among the matters of concern that clouded the atmosphere when the leaders next met in Kampala at the end of June were fiscal considerations, the proposed institutions, the federal capital, and the civil service.

On fiscal matters, Uganda had nearly twice the sterling reserves of the other two countries combined.[55] Moreover, Uganda had a balanced budget while Kenya depended on aid from Britain to balance her budget (£2 million in 1962–63), and had accumulated a considerable debt (£76 million).[56] On institutions, Ugandans feared that with their smaller population and weak party structure they would never control the strong presidency, so they wanted a stronger upper house in the legislature and fewer central powers over civil service, agriculture, foreign affairs, higher education, and citizenship.[57]

Ugandans feared that if the federal capital were located in Nairobi or Arusha, as most Kenyans and Tanganyikans seemed to prefer, this would not only shift the center of power away from Uganda, but would also affect the location of industry in East Africa to the detriment of Uganda. In addition, Ugandans wished to find a use for their buildings in Entebbe so that they could complete the shift of their own capital to Kampala. They also felt that having the capital of the federation at Entebbe would provide tangible benefits to help reconcile the Baganda. Finally, although Uganda had led in education in the past, Kenya had more university students "in the pipeline" and was in a better position to fill positions in the federal civil service.[58]

A less tangible problem, but one which became worse during the summer, was a sense of exclusion and hurt pride among many Uganda politicians. Sociologists have speculated that units of three are unstable because they tend to polarize two against one—"two's company, three's a crowd."[59] Whatever its value as a generalization, this seemed to happen in East Africa. Although Uganda and Kenya were more closely integrated economically, Uganda—away from the Coast and with little Swahili, having a strong group with a history of opposition to federation, smallest in size and with the greatest need for safeguards—was odd man out in politics. This helps explain remarks like the following made informally by two Uganda cabinet ministers and a parliamentary secretary (non-Baganda) in September:

"I am still for federation if they stop treating us as third place and small."

"I would not be against a strong federation if they treated us as equals and stopped putting the blame and pressure on us."

The Failure to Federate in 1963

"Kenya needs us more than we need them. If they don't need us, let them go ahead without us and stop putting the pressure on us."

Bruised pride and threatened loss of identity were important reasons why the Kampala meeting differed so from the first meeting in Dar es Salaam, but this does not mean that the problems of federation could be reduced to one of personal status. If this were true, they could have been removed by assurances of a few jobs. Personal interest and identity were the keys which let national interests out of the ideological Pandora's box. Once out, they were not so easily got back in.

Unfortunately, Kenyans and Tanganyikans did not realize the extent of Ugandan sensitivities in time. Although they conceded a somewhat stronger upper house and a fiscal expert to advise Uganda during the Kampala session, this was not enough, and relations deteriorated during July to the point that the United Nations specialists from Nigeria and the Netherlands were hampered in carrying out their respective studies of the civil service and fiscal arrangements.

In 1963 Zanzibar's participation in the federal negotiations was limited to the Dar es Salaam meeting in August, and complicated matters only slightly. Not only was Zanzibar comparable in size and population to a district in one of the other countries, but its politics were heavily influenced by race (which also tended to coincide with social class). Roughly speaking, a sixth of Zanzibar's population identified themselves as Arabs, or were clearly descended from Arab immigrants; another sixth were mainland Africans, and the remaining two thirds were indigenous Africans who tended to identify themselves as "Shirazis."[60] Mainland Africans formed the core of the Afro-Shirazi Party (ASP) and Arabs the core of the Zanzibar Nationalist Party (ZNP), while the

Zanzibar and Pemba People's Party (ZPPP) offered an alternative to the minority of Shirazis who refused to join either of the other two.

Although the ASP won 54 per cent of the vote in the general elections of July 1963, a coalition of the ZNP and ZPPP won a majority of seats and formed the government which took Zanzibar to independence. Six months later the ZNP-ZPPP government was overthrown by a coup led by an illiterate mainland African who had been a minor official in the Afro-Shirazi party. It seems that this unorganized and basically racist coup anticipated another, more highly organized and ideologically oriented one, the would-be leaders of which gradually gained control of the new revolutionary government. In the face of some internal ideological disagreement, the new leaders merged Zanzibar with Tanganyika in April 1964.[61]

The Zanzibar revolution suddenly thrust the tiny country into an importance which it had not held in East Africa since the nineteenth century. The example it set helped touch a match to the tinder of soldiers' resentment at having British officers and low pay in the East African armies, resulting in the three army mutinies of January 1964. The greater Cold War involvement of some of Zanzibar's new leaders and the precipitate merger with Tanganyika added new pieces to the federal puzzle, but the initial most striking fact about the Zanzibar revolution and the army mutinies was that they did little to draw the three major countries together.

Whatever may have been the new elements introduced by the events in Zanzibar in January 1964, the little island state was a very small factor in the federal negotiations of 1963, and the main concern of its government at that point was to avoid involvement as diplomatically as possible. In the 1961 elections, Tanu politicians had openly interfered in the Zanzibar election campaign in favor of the Afro-Shirazi party, whose politicians made no secret of their close ties with the mainland.[62] Thus the government had good reason to be wary of its mainland neighbors.

When the Working Party visited Zanzibar in July it met the newly elected cabinet, outlined the draft constitution, and offered Zanzibar equal representation (twelve of forty-eight seats) in the upper house. The Zanzibar government said that it was prepared to negotiate, but when its delegates, Ali Muhsin and A. A. Baalawy, arrived in Dar es Salaam, they presented conditions which were clearly unacceptable to Tanganyika and Kenya, and angered them still further by meeting privately with the Ugandans. For most of the conference the Zanzibaris said little and let the Ugandans do their work for them. By the end of the meeting a Kenya delegate exclaimed that he did not care what became of Zanzibar, and Zanzibar was not invited to the next heads-of-government meeting in Nairobi.[63] Nonetheless, Zanzibar's minority government maintained its public commitment to federation, possibly from fear of allowing an opening for renewed mainland interference. In any case, in 1963 Zanzibar was merely an inconvenience; Uganda was a real problem.

How did Ugandans manage to defend their national and personal interests in the face of their previously stated commitment to an ideology which denied the legitimacy of "national interests?" They did so by turning to another interpretation of the ideology—Ghana's view that federation would hinder, not help, African unity.

Although East African federation had not been discussed at the Addis Ababa Conference that opposed the creation of blocs in Africa, Ghana notified the East Africans soon after the Nairobi declaration that she felt federation was not in accord with the Addis resolutions on African unity.

In mid-summer President Nkrumah sent a letter to Nyerere stating his opposition in detail. He sent copies to Obote, Kenyatta, Kenneth Kaunda (of then Northern Rhodesia), and Dr. Banda (of then Nyasaland), as did Nyerere with his lengthy reply. During the summer the Ghana High Commissioner in Uganda warned Makerere students against regional federations and answered Murumbi's October speech with a long paid advertisement. Rumors of Ghanaian influence were so plentiful that Adoko Nekyon had to deny them in Parliament.[64]

Ideological differences were not the cause of Uganda's holding back on federation, but they were quickly used by Ugandan leaders to justify their position. Gradually, however, it seems that some Ugandans came to believe the ideological arguments, and Pan-Africanism thus became a contributory factor in Uganda's reluctance to federate.

Nekyon first propounded the Ghanaian view opposing regional federation at the Kampala meeting in June. In July, two UPC members cited the same view in Parliament.[65] Somewhat later a major Ugandan leader began to doubt the sincerity of the Pan-African commitment of the Kenyans and to believe in the Ghana view. By the end of the summer some Ugandans were willing to call the Ghanaian view nonsense, but others (including some who had never been notably interested in Pan-Africanism at all) were using the same arguments as two UPC parliamentary secretaries:

We are committed to the idea of Pan-African unity and we are afraid that our economic interest in federation will clash with our ideological interest in African unity.

There will be no federation because it would prevent African unity. We must come together all at once. Federation is too much to expect.

196

The Failure to Federate in 1963

We cannot give up that much independence. African unity will be weaker than federation and we will not object to that.

Similarly, early in the summer Obote had said that the negotiations on federation were within the "spirit of Addis" which was opposed to blocs in Africa.[66] In August he allegedly told a diplomat that problems of reconciling East African federation with the Addis resolutions were merely an "embarrassment." But by October Obote asserted that there was discontent among Pafmeca members at being left out of federation, and warned that "we may be accused of going against the Addis spirit of cooperation."[67] By this time Obote may have been genuinely concerned about the impact of federation on African unity, but the outsider could not help but notice that the inclusion of Pafmeca countries at the beginning of federation would delay and dilute federation.

In other words, by the end of the summer enough Ugandan leaders were using the Ghanaian interpretation of Pan-Africanism to prevent the ideology from serving as the simple directive to federation that it had been in June. No longer was the burden of proof of ideological legitimacy entirely on those who opposed federation.[68] This new Ugandan view changed the role of Pan-Africanism at the bargaining table. While it had been a common assumption at the first Dar es Salaam talks, Nekyon's introduction of the Ghanaian view during the Kampala session forced other leaders to mention Pan-Africanism explicitly, but more as a weapon to advance a position than as a common assumption. By the time of the fourth meeting at Dar es Salaam, the leaders were sufficiently aware of their differences not to mention the ideology explicitly. Nonetheless, it was frequently referred or alluded to in public statements by both sides, thus serving to limit the boundaries of the dispute.

NATIONAL INTERESTS AND PAN-AFRICANISM

Once an alternative interpretation was available, Ugandans were able to use Pan-Africanism to justify interests opposed to federation. At the bargaining table Pan-Africanism became a sword which cut two ways. Yet the bargaining table may be the wrong place to look to discover its impact. If its main function was to establish a set of ideas which predisposed people to interpret their interests in one way rather than another, the impact of Pan-Africanism may better be judged by comparing what appeared to an objective observer to be the national interest with the perceived interest which the leaders took to the negotiations with them.

The sum of the geographic, economic, political, and ideological elements which have been historically associated with the preservation of a state is the "national interest." Although different groups may interpret it according to their own preferences "if a nation's territorial integrity is to be preserved, there can never be a wholly distinct policy based on political ideology or party creed even though they shape and influence the contours of this interest."[69]

The notion of national interest has never been precise even where nations have long existed, and it might be objected that it could not apply to East Africa where nations were so new. Moreover, some Pan-Africanists doubted whether "a nation's territorial integrity" *should* "be preserved." Yet despite the short history and absence of clarity on "national interest," East African leaders acted at least in part according to national interest at the same time that they maintained their commitment to Pan-Africanism. They avoided the inherent conflict by calling themselves "Pan-African Nationalists."

The Failure to Federate in 1963

Nyerere once called Tanganyika "a geographical expression created by the Germans and the British" and argued that it was not "an inviolable unit," but he also appealed to Tanganyikans to build a nation. Similarly, Obote once asked "What is Uganda?" but he also exhorted his countrymen to take more pride in being Ugandan because it would make the country more stable.[70] When Obote and Kawawa went to Britain to hasten Kenya's independence, they asserted that they had a right to be interested in Kenyan affairs, but when Kenyans put pressure on Uganda during the federal negotiation, Obote objected to the interference of outsiders in a Uganda decision.[71]

Internal economic problems helped develop the sense of national interest. In Tanganyika, Nsilo Swai, then Minister for Development Planning said that in planning to raise living standards, "we have been concerned primarily with Tanganyika's national interests. The emergence of a close political federation is going to alter this perspective."[72] Ugandans worried about a possible drain of their development funds to raise the standards of backward areas of Tanganyika. Nekyon spoke of Kenyan migrant labor lowering Uganda's living standard, "which is the highest of the three countries." Labor leaders spoke of the need to restrict the Uganda labor market to Ugandans at the same time that they praised federation and Pan-Africanism. Even strongly Pan-Africanist UPC Youth Wing officers complained about "Kenyan outsiders enjoying the fruits of independence."[73]

In 1962 Tanganyikans reconciled their uncooperative attitude in EACSO discussed earlier with their belief in federation and Pan-Africanism, by maintaining that everything would be different after federation. During the summer of 1963, when the connection between federation and Pan-

Pan-Africanism and East African Integration

Africanism began to threaten the slogan of "Pan-African Nationalism" for Ugandan leaders, they became more articulate about their national interests and rejected the connection between the ideology and federation. Kenyans, on the other hand, were fortunate in finding a close coincidence of ideology and self-interest. To judge the extent to which Pan-African ideology was effective we must sketch what appeared to an outsider to be the national interests of the countries.

Uganda

Economically, it was in Uganda's interest to join a strong —but not too centralized—federation. The Kenya market was important to Uganda, but with a long rail haul to the sea, Uganda was not a preferred industrial location. She needed a federation strong enough to preserve the market and to alter the distribution of industrial benefits, but she also needed to secure institutionalized political power which would ensure that her partners would have to conciliate her by distributing industrial benefits. This was the position advocated by the United Nations economist who was loaned to Uganda in the summer of 1963. Uganda's insistence on greater powers for the upper house and her pressure for the capital at Entebbe were in accord with this advice. Later government statements about extending a diluted federation to include the whole Pafmeca area seemed less in accord with her economic interest. Uganda's per capita income was slightly higher than Tanganyika's but lower than Kenya's. Nonetheless, considering Kenya's deficit, Uganda acted in accord with her own interests in hesitating over the financial aspects of federation.

In terms of strategic location Uganda was landlocked and dependent on the export of two bulky crops along a rail line through Kenya. Obote once remarked that Uganda would be the greatest gainer from federation because geography left her no other choice. After independence, Uganda began investigating the possibilities of the League of Nations Barcelona Convention guaranteeing the rights of inland states.[74]

Other Uganda politicians felt less restrained by geography, partly with good cause. Mali managed to survive without too much inconvenience after Senegal cut her rail line to the sea. Similarly, a geographer estimated that additional costs of road haulage in the event of disruption of Uganda's rail links would be less than annual fluctuations in crop prices.[75] Nonetheless, this assumed Kenya's permission to use roads or the unexplored possibilities of exporting through Stanleyville.[76] Some cabinet ministers argued that Kenya would not dare tamper with Uganda's access to the sea because of the spirit of Addis Ababa and Uganda's important Pan-Africanist friends—a rather insecure basis for an important national interest.

But Uganda also made various efforts to improve relations with her non-East African neighbors,[77] both to bolster her economic and bargaining position and in response to defense considerations. At independence, Uganda's armed forces consisted of one battalion of 1,000 troops, 400 paramilitary police and three light, unarmed aircraft. Two of her neighbors, the Congo and Sudan, had armies of 30,000 and 11,000 respectively.[78] This meant that it was in Uganda's interest to maintain good relations with East Africa and to this end Uganda initialed a defense pact with Tanganyika in April 1963.

Uganda's prime national interest, the securing of which Obote felt had been his major achievement a year after independence, was simply holding itself together.[79] To understand how this affected federation one must study the position of Buganda on federation.

Buganda remained important even after enough Kabaka Yekka members of Parliament had joined the UPC to give Obote a majority of his own. Not only was Buganda centrally located and the source of half the senior Uganda civil servants, but legal advisers believed that a strong East African federation would involve changes in the Uganda constitution which two thirds of the Buganda Lukiko would have to approve (according to the Uganda Constitution).

Predictions that federation might be the issue that would disenchant the younger generation of Baganda with the monarchy, proved premature, and leaders like Eriabu Lwebuga of the Bawejjere (Common Man) who favored federation, were kept in line by threats of accusation of disloyalty to the Kabaka.[80] Most Baganda leaders agreed that Buganda would do as the Kabaka said on federation.

It seems that the Kabaka saw the direction of policy and decided to try to minimize his losses. According to one Uganda cabinet minister, Obote had known since the autumn of 1962 that the Kabaka would agree to some form of federation. In November 1962 a Kabaka's government minister was willing to accept federation if Buganda were itself a constituent part.[81] Despite the fact that this was anathema to UPC leaders, Baganda leaders continued to press the point publicly, though in private they seemed to realize that it was more important to ensure that it was Uganda which gave up powers to the federal government and not Buganda. In July, after the Kabaka failed to meet the "Big Three" in Kampala, his Katikiro, or prime minister, Michael Kintu, told the press that Buganda was "not against unity" and would be consulted on the details of federation. Thus it seems that opposition to federation expressed early in the year must be understood in the light of a comment by a Member of Parliament from Buganda: "When a Muganda is going to do something, he says 'no' first so that he gets good terms when he says 'yes'." When the Lukiko met to debate federation (which it had opposed five months earlier) after the Nairobi declaration, it decided against condemnation.[82]

Given the lack of enthusiasm in Buganda's acceptance of federation, as well as her central position in the unity of the country, it was in Uganda's national interest to move slowly enough on federation to bring Ganda opinion along with it.

In summary, Uganda acted in reasonable accord with what an outside observer would consider her national interest during the summer of 1963. She departed from that interest when Ugandan nationalism and Ghanaian Pan-Africanism were allied. To the extent that these forces lulled Ugandan leaders into a false sense of security based on the Organization for African Unity or jeopardized the prospects of federation completely, they diverted Uganda from following her national interest. Pan-Africanism allied to Uganda nationalism fostered an overconfidence that helped cause the minor discrepancies between her "national interest" and her actions—but the effect of the ideology of Pan-Africanism was more detrimental than beneficial to federation.

Kenya

Kenya's case was simpler than Uganda's because ideology and interest so closely coincided that there were few discrepancies. Economically, Kenya had every interest in preserving the East African market—her most rapidly growing market and one within which she had nearly three-quarters of the manufacturing industry—even at the price of losing a few industries to Tanganyika and Uganda under a system of federal economic planning. Her higher per capita income (which mainly reflected the income of European settlers) was more than offset by her budget deficit, public debt, and lower currency reserves. As a net exporter of labor with unemployment at home, she had an interest in a federation which would preserve the already threatened mobility of labor in East Africa.

In terms of population, education, and strategic location, Kenya could expect to play a large role in any federation. In terms of internal unity, federation was frequently hailed as something which might diminish the severity of Kenya's tribalism and regionalism.[83] Despite disagreements between Kanu and Kadu concerning which units—central or regions —should go into a federation, it was too obviously in Kenya's interest for any party to oppose. Despite a number of threats which Kadu—justifiably—made from time to time, it considered federation above party politics.[84]

In terms of defense, Kenya had the strongest army—three battalions, 3,500 men—but it also had the highest defense costs and, in the form of the Somali secessionists in the Northern Frontier District, the worst military problem. In this area, also, Kenya would have benefited from a federation that might have spread the burden. In short, Kenya's national interest and ideology were so close that there was no occasion to use the concept of national interest to find discrepancies which might be due to ideology.

Tanganyika

Tanganyika's position was the most difficult to explain by national interest alone. Economically, Tanganyika might have gained from federation, but she had less to gain than Kenya or Uganda and was the most capable of "going it alone."[85] As we saw in the last chapter, the East African market was not vitally important to Tanganyika and, if anything, may have prevented industries from locating there until Tanganyika took her uncooperative line in the 1960's.

On the other hand, the Economic Commission for Africa estimated that separate rail and postal services would cost Tanganyika an extra million pounds a year. In finance Tanganyika should have been more wary of Kenya's deficit and debt. In the field of labor Tanganyika was a net importer (despite unemployment) and had little to gain from federation. In terms of development of backward areas, she had a slightly lower per capita income and might have expected some redistribution of income from Kenya and Uganda, but this was far from certain. In other words, in terms of economic gain, Tanganyika might have benefited from federation, but not dramatically so, and much of the benefit depended on the future potential of the East African market and an uncertain redistribution of income.

Tanganyika's political interests were similarly ambiguous. With the strongest political party in East Africa, no significant opposition, and the largest population, she would have had a powerful voice in a federation. But this might have been counteracted by the lower level of education in Tanganyika, which would have prevented her from contributing an equal share of the members of the federal civil service. Nor was it likely that federation would help economize on this scarce factor—educated manpower.[86] Moreover, in terms of internal politics Tanganyika stood to lose by federation. The freedom of action that Tanganyikan leaders enjoyed in a semiauthoritarian system would probably have been curtailed by the bargaining and compromise politics of federalism. In 1963 Tanganyika had already delayed implementation of a law to make Tanu the single legal party in order to avoid jeopardizing the federal negotiations.[87]

In terms of defense and location Tanganyika had a two-battalion army and to the south was confronted by Portuguese East Africa from which she harbored refugees; but she had neither the Somali threat that faced Kenya nor the disproportionately strong neighbor (Sudan) that Uganda had.[88]

In contrast to what an observer would regard as ambiguous benefits in East African federation, Tanganyika had a good deal to gain from closer relations with Northern Rhodesia, whose £120 million of annual copper exports might provide funds and traffic to make feasible a rail link to Tanganyika's undeveloped southwest. Northern Rhodesia was in no hurry to enter a federation, but she did remain an important interest to the south.

If Tanganyika's political commitment to East African federation was out of proportion to her national interest in it, can the inconsistency be attributed to Pan-Africanism? An alternative explanation might be that though Tanganyika had little to gain, she had nothing to lose. But this ignores the restraints on fiscal and monetary policy and the inconveniences which a number of Tanganyikans felt as they waited for the other two territories to gain independence and agree to federate. Another possible explanation for the inconsistency was that Tanganyikans were not aware of their national interest. While this may have been true at the lower level of leadership, various cabinet ministers were definitely aware that their benefits from the East African common market were limited, that their economic development plan might be diluted, and that federation would probably disrupt the efficiency of Tanganyika's political system. A third possible explanation—that the decisions were not Tanganyika's but were dictated by strong outside pressure—is not supported by the evidence.

The Failure to Federate in 1963

In other words, Tanganyika's position on federation was not completely in accord with her national interests, and it seems that the discrepancy cannot be explained without referring to the Pan-African commitment of her top leaders. According to Derek Bryceson, a European cabinet member in Tanganyika, "Ideology is undoubtedly the most important motive in Tanganyika's view on federation. Economics is second in importance and defense is virtually nil." Or, in the words of Roland Brown, the Attorney General, "Pan-Africanism is the dominant force behind it. It has little to do with economics. There is absolutely no doubt about this."[89]

This is not to argue that Tanganyikan leaders ignored the national interest completely. For instance, they did not compromise and agree to a weak federation which would have been the least beneficial option for Tanganyika. And by the end of 1963 they were beginning to reconsider whether it was possible to achieve both economic progress within Tanganyika and East African federation. In March 1964 Tanganyika expressed these doubts by demanding (and eventually receiving) changes in the East African common market, as we saw in the last chapter. But it is nonetheless true that it is impossible to understand Tanganyika's position without bringing in ideology.

This characterization of national interests and motivations is not meant to deny that there was a complex set of motives in each country—defensive, utilitarian, ideological—possessed in different degrees by different people. But in Tanganyika in 1963 the third of these motives seemed more compelling while in the other two countries the first two were probably more important. The following statements of motive, most in answer to the question "What do you personally feel are the most important reasons for or against an East African federation?" give an impression of the differences.[90]

Tanganyika:

You cannot have a continental government in Africa tomorrow, but you can start in East Africa. It is almost a duty for us to act now and show it is possible and not just a myth (*Julius Nyerere*[91]).

The main reason is that it is a step for the unity of Africa. Economics is important but definitely secondary (*Rashidi Kawawa*).

The main reason is that the world is finding larger units more successful. Also it would avoid competition in coordination of industry. Also Pan-Africanism is an important reason (*Oscar Kambona*).

Kenya:

An East African Federation would mean that the world would have to reckon with us (*Jomo Kenyatta*[92]).

Because I want a United States of Africa. Ethnically, Africa is one. (*Oginga Odinga*).

1. Economic, the common market—we are aware of the weakness of E.A.C.S.O.; 2. defense, though that is not so important; 3. the need to save resources; 4. the desire for unity and the need for East Africa to make an impact on the world; 5. Pan-Africanism and the Addis spirit (*Tom Mboya*).

Economic reasons are most important (*James Gichuru*).

Uganda:

I hate the division of Africa into small sections. Also Uganda cannot go it alone. It is simply a matter of geography (*Milton Obote*).

It is the first step toward African unity, and it will save money, for instance, on the foreign service (*Godfrey Binaisa*).

The world thinks in terms of strength, both economic and political. But if we are going to have to support Kenya's problems, we will just improve E.A.C.S.O. (*George Magezi*).

The Failure to Federate in 1963

I think our unity should come later so we can now protect our personality and fulfil our obligations to all our people who are still slaves (*Adoko Nekyon*[93]).

Pan-Africanism may be important, but for me defense and trade are the important reasons (*Cuthbert Obwangor*).

Pan-Africanism had several causal roles in the failure of East Africa to federate in 1963. In the background period, from 1958 on, it provided arguments and a sense of direction toward federation. In this way it influenced expectations, which are often more important than preferences—witness Buganda's position. In another role it provided the set of common assumptions which existed during the early meetings on federation in 1963. At later meetings it became a weapon used to defend separate interests. In still another role it helped provide the impetus of commitment which brought about the Nairobi declaration.

Probably the most important contribution of Pan-Africanism was its provision of a set of beliefs and values through which leaders perceived their interests. Although ideology sometimes elicited sacrifices or caused impulsive actions (such as Uganda's in June 1963), in most clearcut situations where there was a significant difference between courses dictated on the one hand by interest and on the other by ideology, people acted in accordance with what seemed to an outsider to be their interest. But in situations, such as Tanganyika's, in which interests were more nearly balanced, people sometimes acted against what seemed to an outsider to be to their advantage—for two possible reasons. First, their perception of the issue through ideological glasses meant that they sometimes did not see the conflict. Second, when they did see the conflict, they sometimes were willing to make small sacrifices of interest in order to further ideological values. In other words, Pan-Africanism predisposed

East Africans toward certain courses of action in cases of marginal interest.

This role of ideology in the perception of interests, long a factor in relations between more mature members of the international state system, increasingly became its major function in East Africa during the course of 1963. Ugandan leaders were unwilling to make a large sacrifice of their national interests, so they seized upon a new interpretation of Pan-Africanism: they did not reject the ideology.

National interests developed quickly during 1963, as Nyerere had predicted they would, "not because we shall appoint evil people . . . but simply because we shall be increasing the number of human beings who have a personal interest in disunity . . ."[94] Largely as a result of the failure to federate, leaders increasingly paid attention to the second part of "Pan-African nationalism" by the end of 1963.

VII

The Rejection of Association
with the European Economic Community

> If we see the East African Common Market as a first
> step towards the pan-African Common Market, then
> we must, in fact it is our duty, to go to that meeting
> as a team.
>
> —Mwai Kibaki to the C.L.A.,
> August 30, 1962

Before the breakdown of the federal negotiations, the
one major crisis in East African unity and ideological solidarity was coordination of policy toward association with
the European Economic Community.[1] The September 1962
decision to reject associate status with the EEC provides an
example of the interplay of ideology and economics in the
making of foreign policy decisions in East Africa. This case
helps to elucidate the role of Pan-Africanism in the federation movement and suggests one of its possible roles in an
East Africa without federation.

As we noted earlier, in looking for the effect of ideology
upon a particular decision, it is easy to look for the wrong
thing. No ideology, diffuse or specific, gives an exact program for all future decisions—witness the programmatic
flexibility of Lenin's Russia. And the more diffuse the ideology the more difficult it is to see its relationship to action
over a short period.[2] Rather than look for specific directives

one should look for foregone alternatives and narrowed possibilities of action. One can look at real costs (including opportunity costs) and compare them with perception of costs. One can look at the style of argument and decision.

Britain fully expected the East African territories to accept the associate status in the European Economic Community she had so painfully negotiated for them and which seemed to have been agreed upon between Britain and the EEC at Brussels in the summer of 1962.[3] As late as the end of August the East African press reported that "reliable sources" believed Kenya and Uganda were "impressed" with association but that Tanganyika had given no indication of her position.[4] Two years earlier the expatriate finance ministers of the three territories had told the Commonwealth Finance Ministers Conference in London that East Africa was not opposed to Britain's entering a trade association with Europe.[5] The British press in the three territories tended to favor East African association with EEC.

Late in 1961 the Chief Government Economist in Tanganyika had told the Chamber of Commerce that Tanganyika would benefit from closer association with the European trade bloc,[6] and, generally speaking, expatriate civil servants in the three territories favored acceptance of the associate status negotiated by Britain because of what they expected to be its economic benefits—retention of Commonwealth preference (since it was believed Britain would join the EEC), increased access to the European market, and a new pool of aid funds. As a Uganda study concluded, the benefits were tangible and the losses only speculative.

Rejection of Association with EEC

In Tanganyika both politicians and civil servants have said that the decision to reject association was purely political. The Tanganyika Treasury had given prima facie advice *for* joining (based primarily on the potential market for coffee and cotton, and on the immediate effects of not joining on tea and meat products). The Ministery of Commerce and Industry prepared a careful study only *after* the London Conference, and a civil servant was not assigned to the problem until after the decision. Tanganyika's partners found that her homework had been poorly done, and at his London press conference, Kawawa was unable to answer questions on what damage might be done to Tanganyika's products.[7]

The decision to reject association took most officials by surprise and appeared to them to be totally irrational, a view that was shared by the press. In Kenya, the *East African Standard* felt that leaders "would do well to ponder the cold realities of economics"; and in London the liberal *Economist* concluded that "to plead Western rational arguments against it is at present useless."[8]

If "rational" means weighing the costs and benefits of the probable consequences of an act, it is true that there were elements of irrationality in the decisions taken; it is *not* true that the final East African decision was irrational. Costs, benefits, and probable consequences were considered. But the conclusions of rational thought reflect the assumptions inherent in the views of the world which underlie all rational thought. What is interesting is the diverse views of the world which led East Africans to differ from the British in their evaluation of costs and benefits.

The difference in world views was not a preference among the British for "rational economics" and among the Africans,

213

for "emotional politics." Britain's economists were divided about her own entry into the Common Market, and politics played a very large part in her decision to apply. Indeed, Macmillan allegedly told the Commonwealth Conference that Britain wished to join because traditional balance-of-power theories were outdated in the days of superstates like Russia and America, and that Britain must find new ways to keep the balance. Similarly, political antipathies played a very large part for British opposition to the Common Market. None of these political hopes and fears were susceptible of more than the crudest demonstration.[9] In this sense the British and East African decisions were not so dissimilar.

The difference was that the British (at home and abroad), inhabited a world in which mature powers sought to shape institutions like the European Economic Community to bring balance and stability into the world. In their view, within a stabilized status quo, the interest of weak new states could be protected by allowing them to associate with the EEC. The obvious need of all former colonies was to establish economics and "to get on with the job," and this was much more important than "kicking against the pricks" of being associated with Europe. Associate status was designed to increase and stabilize the earnings from raw material exports for the associates. Admittedly it had originally been designed by the French to maintain ties with their former colonies, but this, the British argued, had not prevented a militant country like Mali from following its obvious self-interest. From this non-Pan-African point of view any political implications of association were only a shadow, while the economic benefits were very real.

Most of the African leaders, on the other hand, were living in a world in which they had experienced racial discrimination personally; in which their cultures had been disrupted; in which exploitation by Europeans and suspicion of the motives of Europeans formed a plausible explanation of recent experience. For Africans, the EEC was an economic group aiming at political federation and strengthening of Europe for the Cold War. Balance of power and status quo meant being treated as Europe's pawns. Associate status was a French invention to tie colonies to Europe after their formal independence. Not having experienced an assimilationist policy, territories once under British rule regarded as definitely sinister the less militant actions of some of the former French colonies. What appeared to the British to have slight political significance was regarded by the Africans as an instrument to forge political chains.

AFRICA AND THE EEC

Before looking at the decisions made in East Africa it may be helpful to sketch in the larger picture of Africa and the Common Market. President Nkrumah had labeled the EEC "a new system of collective colonialism which will be stronger and more dangerous than the old evils we are striving to liquidate." A Marxist economist writing for an East African magazine called it a "colonialist plot to irrevocably bind the African economy to that of West Europe and hence to determine and control the pace of Africa's economic development."[10]

These critics argued that the Common Market was a response to the decline of the imperial power of Europe and that association was an attempt to re-establish some of those imperial relationships. By linking unequal economies the Europeans would keep the Africans in a dependent status. Another way of putting it was that the division of labor in the customs union would emphasize the industrial capacity of Europe and the raw materials of Africa. The general catch phrase was that Africans would remain "hewers of wood and drawers of water."

Aside from the emotional dislike of such a division of labor, the critics complained that it was unfair because the terms of trade for primary goods decline when production increases. While this is not strictly true over a long period, there was enough truth in it in the latter part of the 1950's to give the argument considerable weight.[11] Moreover, the critics argued that the aid fund offered to associates was used for infrastructure projects which helped Europe to extract wealth from Africa, rather than to diversify and strengthen its economies. Finally they argued that the EEC was an openly political device in the Cold War and association was an attempt to align Africa with the Western bloc.

These criticisms were not wholly unfounded. The origins of the EEC *were* political. While the Treaty of Rome only mentioned prospects of closer union, the history of Europe that led up to that treaty shows the political intentions of the promoters. Similarly, the EEC was frequently defended as strengthening the West; and by 1962 the Europeans had been presented with both the Fouchet and Spaak plans for political union. Both sides in the Cold War often described the EEC in political Cold War terms. Associate status and participation in the Community's institutions did not necessarily mean alignment with the Western bloc. Nonetheless, events like the West German threat to cut off EEC aid to Mali should she recognize East Germany, even though this was subsequently retracted, caused justifiable suspicion in Africa.[12] Similarly, the close relations with and dependence on France of a number of the associated former French states looked suspicious to other Africans.

Rejection of Association with EEC

There was no doubt of the political origin of the provision for associating dependent territories of France, Belgium, Netherlands, and Italy with the EEC. As an American expert wrote for the Joint Economic Committee of Congress: "This provision was the result of French insistence on specially favorable treatment for the French dependencies. French insistence was an outgrowth of the close political and economic ties between France and these dependencies, ties which the French Government was anxious to maintain."[13]

Eurafrica, as an alternative vision to Pan-Africa of the future development of Africa, can be traced as far back as the 1920's, but it came into prominence only during the political arguments about European Union. In the early 1950's Jean Monnet is supposed to have referred to Africa as "France's dowry to Europe."[14] More recent expositions stressed the mutual benefits inherent in the idea, but, like most concepts and visions of geopolitics, it was never precise. Moreover, it involved fewer ideas than its rival, Pan-Africanism, and never achieved the latter's emotional appeal, particularly among British Africans. Thus Mwai Kibaki told the CLA that "the concept of Eurafrique as it has been called was viewed from objectives which had nothing to do with what should be the objectives of development in Africa. They originated from people who had other objectives."[15]

The Treaty of Rome says that association "shall in the first place permit the furthering of the interests and prosperity of the inhabitants of these countries and territories in such a manner as to lead them to economic, social and cultural development which they expect."[16] The Treaty provides for the right of establishment for all EEC states a common aid fund and free nondiscriminatory trade. Both members and associates are to remove gradually all tariffs and quantitative restrictions on each other's exports, but the associates are permitted to impose protective tariffs for infant industries and revenue tariffs, though they must submit them, with reasons, to the Council of Association (on which they are represented). According to the proposed new Convention of Association (which was in the hands of the East Africans), new tariffs "shall be a matter for consultations should the Community so request."[17] Thus there is a certain ambiguity about real power over tariffs. The Treaty left associates free to follow what policy they chose toward third states outside the Community, but they were requested not to favor them against EEC members.

This question of freedom of trade with third parties was an important factor in the East African rejection. While the treaty did not prevent it, the experience of the already associated states had been otherwise. According to one source, "Their access to sources of supply outside the Community is likely to be limited by quantitative restrictions unless measures of import liberalization toward third countries are taken which are a good deal broader than those which have been taken in the past." And, "the system has not worked much differently from the way it did under the old French paternalism. Resident French experts decided whether or not to restrict imports from Europe (which on the whole, and naturally enough, they did not) . . . French experts decided on trade relations with third countries (which remained at the same proportionately low level)."[18] These restrictions were not a necessary part of association. They reflected the dependent structure of the former French economies and the restrictions required to maintain their overvalued currency. The fact that restrictions existed in associated states was cited in the East African arguments as strong evidence that the freedom of associates was not so great as promised.

Rejection of Association with EEC

An aid fund of $581 million for the period 1958–62 was administered by the European Fund for the Development of Overseas Territories under the complete control of the EEC. But by mid-1961 less than a third of this had been disbursed, and that primarily on infrastructure, agriculture, and social services. The operations of the fund have been described as "slow, complicated and inevitably burdensome to the recipients," and a mere redistribution of "part of the burden of assistance to the former French dependencies from France to Germany."[19]

A new Convention of Association mentioned earlier was being negotiated during 1962 between the EEC and the associates (in Africa, all the former French states except Guinea, plus the Congo, Somalia, Rwanda, and Burundi). This provided for an increased aid fund of $730 million of which $230 million would be used for economic diversification and removal of dependence on single crops, and for institutions which would give the associates more say in the control of aid. These institutions—a council, a parliamentary conference, and an arbitration court—symbolized political ties for the East Africans, who were later surprised to discover, during their mission to Brussels in 1963, that the institutions had been requested by the associated states. The Convention, when finally signed in July 1963, conceded the right to form customs unions with non-associated states; but the language was even then obscure.[20] The fact that the Convention was under negotiation and not final when the East Africans made their decision to reject association increased the uncertainty and thus increased the inclination to rely on ideology and first principles.

In short, there were justifications for African suspicions of associate status. But these justifications fit into a particular frame of reference. Most African nationalists of the former British areas were in rivalry with the ex-ruler, seeking to prove their equality with Europe. African "unity" was to give not only the strength for equality, but intrinsic moral superiority over "divided Europe." Associate status meant help offered upon certification of former colonial status rather than independent need. Assimilationist policy blurred the psychological impact of this for many leaders of former French Africa but most leaders of ex-British territories felt —and resented—it.[21]

THE DECISION IN EAST AFRICA

It is difficult to say exactly when East Africans first became aware of the EEC problem. As early as September 1958 the Tanganyikan Minister of Finance had told a Commonwealth trade conference in Montreal of the difficulties for East Africa that a European Free Trade Area could create, and a High Commission official was assigned to investigate the effects of the Treaty of Rome on East Africa. Again in 1960 the Finance Ministers of all three territories had discussed British entry into Europe during a Commonwealth Finance Ministers Conference in London. At the end of the year the High Commission (with Nyerere present as an observer) decided to seek mitigation of the effects of the Treaty of Rome on six exports, but felt that East Africa's interest was not sufficiently great at that stage to ask the Colonial Office for separate East African representations at any negotiations.[22]

From this time on, High Commission data on the EEC began to accumulate; by 1962 EACSO had seven bulging files. On the political side, the Secretary-General of the All Africa Peoples' Congress had told a conference in Tunis in 1960, at which several East African politicians were present, that Africa needed her own common market and that EEC investments meant neocolonialism.[23] In general, however, it was a low-priority problem for East African politicans who were still in the process of gaining power from the colonial governments.

The Tanganyika cabinet first discussed the problem in June 1961.[24] It was discussed several times after this by the cabinet, but never by Tanu. In the same month the first stories and editorials about Britain and the EEC appeared in the press. In July the newspapers reported Nkrumah's opposition to association with the EEC on the grounds that it was an attempt to maintain artificial divisions in Africa. At the end of the year the arrival in Dar es Salaam of a High Commissioner from Ghana meant direct information and persuasion for Tanganyika but not for still dependent Kenya and Uganda.

At the end of July 1961 Prime Minister Harold Macmillan announced Britain's intention to seek admission to the European Economic Community. Early in 1962 Nyerere was consulted about the timing of the Commonwealth Prime Ministers' Conference at which the EEC would be discussed. A September date was agreed upon in April 1962. Also at this time new governments (both coalitions) were formed in Uganda and Kenya. This, together with the domestic problems in Tanganyika which had brought about Nyerere's resignation a few months earlier helped explain the delay that led the *Tanganyika Standard* to complain at the end of May that time was running out and the politicians had given no signs of their intentions.[25]

The European Economic Community became an increasingly important problem during the summer of 1962. Uganda civil servants had discussed the matter in April, and in June a government economist submitted a paper to the cabinet favoring association on an East African basis.

This became the first paper to be circulated among the three governments, although officials of their treasuries had held a few informal talks before this. During the summer the Uganda cabinet discussed the EEC three times, and the problem received passing mention in the report of the economic committee of the UPC Conference at the beginning of August. In Kenya civil servants had begun studies toward the end of 1961.

In July 1962 the Treasury of EACSO circulated the first of six studies on the economics of association which concluded (so far as it was possible) that there was an economic advantage in accepting associate status.

At the beginning of August it seemed that the EEC had agreed that certain Commonwealth territories would be admitted to associate status. According to an important civil servant, he first began to have doubts about the chances for association as the Nigerians added their doubts to those of Ghana. British memoranda informed the East Africans of the West African point of view, but there seems to have been no direct political consultation between East and West Africans. Obote later said that one reason he held back a statement of his position before he arrived at the Commonwealth Conference in London was his desire to find out what the West Africans were thinking.[26]

On August 4, 1962, the Tanganyikan Ministry of Commerce and Industry announced that association was receiving careful consideration. A week later officials of the three territories met in Nairobi for the first time explicitly to consider the EEC problem, and agreed to try to arrange a meeting of ministers. On August 22 Kenya's Minister of Finance, James Gichuru, stated that Kenya had no alternative but to accept association despite his hope for an eventual African common market.

Rejection of Association with EEC

The first attempts at political coordination on the question of association occurred at a meeting in Nairobi at the end of August. The CLA debated and passed a motion that preservation and building of the East African Common Market should be the "primary objective" to guide the governments during any negotiations. The Ministerial Committees for Finance and Commercial and Industrial Coordination met jointly and seem to have agreed that if nothing else were possible, association would be accepted. Finally, the EACSO Authority held a special meeting where they agreed to be guided by the need to maintain the East African Common Market, the need to keep trade links open, and to maintain freedom from political ties. Association was neither accepted nor rejected—partly because the leaders felt they lacked sufficient information on the terms of association and partly because of disagreement on what course to take.[27]

The last public statements before the three principal negotiators—Kawawa, Obote, Gichuru—left East Africa for the Commonwealth Conference in London bore some rough similarity. Kawawa, in an eve-of-departure broadcast claimed that a common East African approach had been worked out which would avoid political ties and maintain the East African Common Market as the first step in African unity. Gichuru said that because of the "obscure wording" of the Treaty of Rome, Kenyan association with the EEC would arouse "anxieties" about political involvement, restriction of freedom in making trade agreements and negotiating tariff concessions with outsiders, and possible hindrance of Kenya's industrialization.[28]

Obote, who had left earlier to visit Israel en route to London, had announced before he went to the Nairobi session that he was going to Britain for information and not to accept or reject association. "There is no question of my committing Uganda while I am there."[29]

Obote was the first to reach London. He was accompanied by Minister of Finance Amos Sempa (a Kabaka Yekka conservative), Minister of Economic Affairs J. T. Simpson (a European Kabaka Yekka member), and civil servants. Kawawa was accompanied by Tanganyika's Minister of Finance, Paul Bomani, Minister of Commerce and Industry George Kahama, and six civil servants (only one of whom, the Permanent Secretary of the Treasury, was not an African). They were joined two days later by Minister without Portfolio, Nsilo Swai, then Ambassador to the United Nations. Gichuru was accompanied by two expatriate civil servants. He was joined on Tuesday, the 11th of September (the second day of the conference and the eve of Kawawa's rejection speech), by Minister of Labor Tom Mboya (Kanu), and Minister of Agriculture Wilfred Havelock (Kadu, European).

Upon arrival the three heads of delegations, at separate press conferences, emphasized the need to preserve the East African Common Market, wariness of the political implications of association, and no outright rejection of association. Obote outlined three choices to be decided later. "We will go back to East Africa and take a decision on whether to join in on an East African basis, have a special form of relationship or have nothing to do with it." Asked specifically whether association was ruled out and whether there were political ties in association, Obote replied that the first question was still under consideration and that the second was being examined by Prime Ministers in Africa and elsewhere.[30]

During the week-end before the conference opened, the East African delegates agreed that Kawawa, representing the only fully independent state, would present the East African case. According to a minister, a draft paper was being drawn up in purely economic terms that would accept association if there were no "political" links. Just before the conference opened, Nsilo Swai arrived from New York. His view was that Tanganyika would not "suffer unduly" if she rejected association because existing international agreements were sufficient protection for exports, and Commonwealth preference was not of great importance.[31] As an important politician with more training in economics than any other member of the Tanganyikan delegation, it seems that his views may have done much to remove the last restraints on Tanganyika's preference to reject association.

The first day of the conference was occupied with procedure, during which the members turned down Kawawa's request that Obote be given the same rights of attendance as Central African Federation Prime Minister Sir Roy Welensky (who favored association and was a bete blanche for nationalists). The second day of the conference was devoted to the presentation of Britain's case. For the East Africans the afternoon was spent in Kawawa's hotel suite working out his speech for the next day. At this point, according to Kenyans and Ugandans, Kawawa still left the door open to association.

On Wednesday, September 12, Kawawa, to his East African colleagues' surprise, joined Ghana and Nigeria in rejecting association. In his speech Kawawa outlined the existing framework for cooperation in East Africa, pointed to the interest of other African states in it, and the necessity of African unity for independence, stability, and prosperity. He referred to the fact that "more or less the same powers" as now made up the European Economic Community had met in Berlin in 1884 to partition Africa. "It is obvious that if we join the Community we should commit ourselves to the Western bloc. Further, we believe that our association with the Community will be against the possibility of the promotion of African unity, which we highly value." On the economic side, he said East Africa "would like to negotiate trade arrangements with the Community."[32] The arguments conform closely to the characterization of Pan-Africanism in Chapter II.

The next day some East Africans expressed their surprise and said that Kawawa had gone further than expected with his flat rejection. When Colonial Secretary Duncan Sandys asked Gichuru and Sempa whether they endorsed the Tanganyikan rejection, they replied, "We reserve our positions."[33] And Gichuru added: "Mr. Kawawa spoke for us all in the sense of the East African Common Market, but I cannot commit the Kenya Government as such." Paul Bomani of Tanganyika complained that Britain was "getting at" Kenya and Uganda. As for explanations of Kawawa's action, one observer said that Kawawa would have been less categorical had it not been for the militant example set in an earlier speech by Nigerian Prime Minister Balewa.[34] As a participant put it: "Sierra Leone and the West Indies or the British Labour Party did not matter. The only real outside influences were Ghana and Nigeria."

On Friday there were further meetings in Kawawa's suite to try and iron out differences over association. At the end of the sessions Gichuru was still quoted as saying, "I am in no position to say yes or no on association," but it seems that Obote, the only committed Pan-Africanist among the Ugandans, exercised his authority and followed his preferences by fully supporting Tanganyika. In contrast to his earlier statements, he now said he was "fully convinced that the European Economic Community is not only an economic organization but also a political one and has a great deal of military designs in it." He was immediately supported by a telegram from the Secretary-General of the Uganda People's Congress who termed the EEC "a colonialist and imperialist device intended to undermine the unity, integrity and independence of African countries and subject them perpetually to European economic domination." Similar telegrams were sent to Gichuru from radical members of Kanu, but he did not have the same personal or governmental authority as Obote. At the same time, Mboya (in London) expressed his suspicions of association, and of Sandys' rejection of the possibility of special relations similar to those enjoyed by Libya and Tunisia.[35]

The following Monday, with Uganda behind him, and feeling that Kenya would support him more openly if Kanu were in control, Kawawa held a press conference at which he reiterated that "our position is absolutely decided" and that he spoke for all East Africa. As for damage to trade, his answer was, "We have something to offer. We are not just bare-handed. We produce goods which people want."[36]

After returning home Kawawa repeated that his decision was final and that "there is no question of any Government revising it." Obote claimed that he had always felt the EEC to be a "rich man's club" with political links. Not only did he agree with Kawawa but he also said that he might have gone further himself.[37] In Kenya, on the other hand, Wilfred Havelock said that Kawawa spoke for East Africa as far as politics were concerned, but that the final decision still had to be made, and Kadu Minister of Commerce and Industry, Masinde Muliro, told the Nakuru Chamber of Commerce that he disagreed with Kawawa. Three-fourths of Kenya's trade would be with the enlarged market and "if we remain outside these arrangements, the effects could in the long run be very damaging. Instead of staying clear of the politics of Europe and avoiding siding with the West it could even be that eventually sheer poverty would drive us into the clutches of the opposite camp."[38]

According to a Tanganyikan minister, it was during the EEC talks that the difficulty of dealing with a coalition government in Kenya first became intolerable to Kawawa and Obote and resulted in their premature adjournment of the Authority meeting in December and their trip to Britain in early 1963.

The important decisions were made at the end of August and the beginning of September 1962. Tanganyika came to the East African discussions at Nairobi with almost a year of independence, with greater outside contacts and a more political and decided point of view. Uganda came with a new coalition government split between Pan-Africanists and conservatives and with more "homework" done on the costs involved in the decision. Kenya came with a coalition government which had done its homework but with the less militantly Pan-African Kadu members reading a somewhat different set of conclusions from the more militant Kanu. What was interesting was the way the need for African—and particularly East African—unity was asserted and agreed upon first. Later, in London, with the support of the West Africans, Tanganyika took the lead, Obote brought Uganda into line, and Kenya remained split but unwilling openly to disrupt East African unity.

It seems, then, that Tanganyika's perception of the political aspects of association, colored by her Pan-Africanism, was the guideline for rejection, reinforcing Obote's own preferences and at least keeping Kenya acquiescent. But Tanganyika also had less to lose in rejecting association than Kenya; 73 per cent of Tanganyika's exports, 53 per cent of

Uganda's, and 37 per cent of Kenya's would have been duty-free under the common external tariff which the enlarged EEC would have applied against them.[39] Sisal, cotton, and diamonds entered EEC countries freely, while coffee faced a 9.6 per cent tariff. The same provisions applied to Uganda's major exports of coffee and cotton, and there was hope (subsequently justified) that the EEC tariff on tea would be reduced. Kenya's sisal entered freely and sales of her high-quality coffee might not be strongly affected by tariffs. Moreover, she had no competitors among the associated states in the production of pyrethrum. Her greatest problems would have been tea, meat, and canned fruit. One study concluded that the damage from the implementation of the Treaty of Rome would have been slight and that while the loss of Commonwealth preferences might be more severe, the disadvantage in tariffs that the East Africans would face would be something in the order of five to ten per cent—Kenya coming closer to ten per cent and the other two closer to five. Similarly, association would probably have meant a preferential advantage of one to five per cent, with Kenya again standing to gain more.

The Tanganyikan government was aware of these figures, and their own Treasury had told them that, aside from opportunities lost, it was mainly tea and meat that would be hurt. Similarly, politicians might have expected to hear rumblings from the sisal industry or cooperatives if cotton and sisal exports were likely to be hurt. As Swai's statement indicated, they were aware that the divergence between their interest and their ideology was of a low order of magnitude.

Finally, it is interesting both with respect to the decision itself and to the view of political decision-making outlined in Chapter I that pressure groups played almost no part in the East African rejection of the EEC. In Uganda and Tanganyika no groups offered advice. In Kenya, Havelock talked with some people in agriculture and Gichuru had a brief talk with the President of the Chamber of Commerce before the September decision. Far more important were the views of the political elite—their ideology and their perception of their interests.

THE ARGUMENTS

It is unlikely that we will discover the arguments used in private conferences among the members of the "Big Three" but they may have resembled those put forth in the CLA debate in Nairobi which are on public record.[40] Several members who attended and participated in the debate subsequently went to London for the conference.

Five persons spoke on the motion that the governments of the three territories "should be guided by the primary objective of maintaining and building the East African Common Market." Mwai Kibaki (Kenya, Kanu), who made the motion, and Semei Nyanzi (Uganda, UPC) had both taught economics at Makerere; Masinde Muliro (Kenya, Kadu) and George Kahama (Tanganyika, Tanu) were Ministers of Commerce and Industry, and Tom Mboya (Kenya, Kanu) was Minister of Labor. Four of the five speakers avowed their commitment to Pan-Africanism, though Muliro was more dubious than the others about its practicality. The only one who did not mention Pan-Africanism by name was nonetheless a strong Pan-Africanist and quoted Nkrumah in his speech.

Muliro spoke in support of the motion but warned the negotiators to remember that Kenya sold nearly three quarters of her coffee to the European Common Market, and Tanganyika half of hers. While he hoped to see political and economic integration in his lifetime in East Africa, he was doubtful if he would see Pan-Africa.

All four of the other speakers were so strongly in favor of the motion as worded that they went on, in effect, to debate the pros and cons of association in the EEC. By treating these four speeches as complementary, we can abstract an East African argument that clearly weighed costs and benefits. The gist of the argument was that, in economic terms, there were three main costs and three alleged benefits. It was felt that the costs of joining were quite considerable while benefits were overinflated. And there were, in addition, definite political costs.

The three main economic costs of associating with EEC were: trade diversion, risk of retaliation, and loss of flexibility. Trade diversion, the question of whether consumers are able to buy from lowest-cost suppliers or must buy from a high-cost partner, is an important aspect of any customs-union issue. In this case it was complicated by the possibility that high-quality European goods might be too expensive for the African consumer; that many Africans might prefer lower-priced, less well-made goods.

Three possible objections might be made to their argument. First, it was not a question of trade diversion alone; but whether the benefits of trade created by the new arrangements would outweigh the costs of diversion. This was dealt with by the East Africans under the category of benefits which they claimed were insufficient. Second, it could be argued that imports from low-cost and low-quality suppliers were only a small fraction of total imports (e.g., in 1961 imports from Japan, India, and Hong Kong were only about one-seventh of the total).[41] But this is a static argument and neglects the expansion of trade in which low-cost suppliers might become more important. Finally, there is the question of whether there need be any trade diversion. Article 133 of the Treaty of Rome says that duties on imports into the associated states shall be progressively abolished (with exceptions for infant industry and revenue tariffs). Associated states were also requested not to favor third parties over EEC states. Whether this would necessarily hinder trade with third parties was an open question. The East Africans cited the experience of the former French territories. With little knowledge and a great suspicion of the colonial French, this is where their argument became an assertion of an unverifiable system of belief.

The "risk of retaliation" was somewhat overstated in the East African argument. Kibaki claimed that setting up preferential trade arrangements with the EEC that resulted in discrimination against non-member countries would put three quarters of East Africa's trade in danger of retaliation for the sake of the one fourth done with the EEC. Since he had assumed that Britain would join the European Common Market, the figures should have been closer to half East Africa's trade going to the enlarged EEC and half elsewhere. How serious the risk of retaliation would have been is hard to judge but the objection was carefully reasoned as well as deeply felt.

The third objection was the loss of flexibility that association would mean for East Africa. In specific terms, this might mean the loss of a bargaining weapon when import tariffs had been reduced; the missed opportunity of Eastern bloc aid; and diminished relations with non-European areas where trade was growing most rapidly. The strength of these arguments is debatable. The Convention of Association is not clear about power to stop an African threat to reimpose revenue or infant industry tariffs from being used for bargaining. It was not clear that the Eastern bloc would diminish aid (which so far had been negligible in East Africa) to associated territories—it did not do so in the case of Mali. Finally, the question of where trade was expanding most rapidly depended on the time period studied. East African trade with the EEC had not changed dramatically in the late fifties, but had increased over the full decade. While it had ceased to rise after the Treaty of Rome, there was insufficient change in preferences during the period to account for the change in trade, which might better be explained by a secular leveling of European demand in the late fifties compared to the postwar period of replacement.

Against these economic costs the East Africans said three potential benefits were claimed by proponents of association: retention of the trade with Britain carried out under imperial preference (estimated at between five and ten per cent on coffee, tea, and sisal); assurance of markets in Europe for their exports; and an assured source of capital through the aid fund.

The East Africans felt these benefits were not as great as usually made out. On imperial preference in Britain, they argued that it was not that important (total trade with Britain was 26 per cent of East African exports; coffee and tea comprised one third of trade with Britain);[42] that alternative markets could be found if need be; and that, in any case, imperial preference would be kept in the short run to give them time to adjust. They doubted the value of the sheltered European market for their exports. In industrial goods they would not be able to compete with Europe, and they doubted the capacity of even a growing European market to absorb all the increase in primary products in Africa. Moreover, they expected the French to trade with their former territories in any case, and exports to Germany had increased thus far despite tariffs. Finally, they felt that the aid offered was small; $730 million divided among 18 countries came to only $2.7 million a year, or just enough to start one good factory. They felt that EEC aid was disbursed on the basis of political criteria and was largely controlled by the French. The benefits might be outweighed by possible loss of Eastern-bloc aid. And probably most important, they felt that they would receive Western aid in any case.

In other words, in economic terms, they were worried about the costs (with varying degrees of justification) and rather skeptical of the benefits of association. Contrary to the impression given by the East African press, political leaders did recognize costs but did not believe that they were "crippling," or, in the words of one magazine, that rejection of association would "lead the people to misery."[43]

In addition to this uncertain economic picture, the East Africans saw definite political costs. These were of two kinds: first, there was the feeling that the European Economic Community was to a large extent political and involved in the Cold War—in its origins as well as in the interpretations put on it by both sides. The East Africans felt that the EEC was aimed at the federation of Europe and constructed in Europe's interest. It was further argued that trade was bound to affect politics.

A second aspect of the argument was the increased dependence on one source of trade and aid that association with the EEC might bring about. While it might be necessary for the East African countries to receive aid for some time, there was a feeling of safety in numbers and greater ability to guide their own development if they had no formal ties to Europe. Finally, the institutions of the EEC seemed to symbolize the political aspect of association, in particular its French inclination. Though designed to increase the political voice of associates, the institutions symbolized to the East Africans reduced political independence and a loss of dignity. According to one of their number, only later at Brussels did they discover that the associated states had actually *asked* for the institutions.

Of these arguments, none was openly deduced from Pan-African principles. Nonetheless, several of them involved weightings of the importance of factors and these weightings were always against the EEC. We saw that in the economic arguments the questions of trade diversion, risks of retaliation, and the loss of flexibility were all respectable points but not as conclusive as they were stated to be (remembering of course, that the setting was a public debate). Similarly, the question of benefits was also played down somewhat more than the facts might warrant, though not so much as on the cost side. As for the political arguments, suspicion played some part, but it might well be argued that in light of the experience of the former French states it was justified suspicion. In other words, the effect of Pan-Africanism on the arguments was twofold. It was a subtle background which led to weighting of questionable points in one direction rather than another. It also provided a system of belief which filled gaps in fact which are inevitable in all arguments in the social sphere. It provided the general values that always underlie rational argument. The East African arguments were influenced by Pan-Africanism, but they could not because of this be called irrational.

Certain arguments were advanced in which Pan-African-ism played a more active part, but they were less convincing. One was the contention that association with the EEC would prevent industrialization in East Africa. The argument was that the internal market was too small for rapid industrialization and that East African products would not be able to compete in the European market, whether they were protected at home or not. Thus third markets were vitally important for industrialization but they might be closed to an associated state in retaliation. Most frequently mentioned in this connection was a future African common market but an effective one did not seem likely in the near future. Their desire for it may have obscured the East Africans' analysis.

Another overtly Pan-African argument used against association in the EEC by the East Africans was that it tended to split Africa and destroy hopes for an African Common Market. But surely with eighteen African states already associated, this could as easily have been used as an argument *for* association as against. For instance, in the West Indies, "one of the reasons why Dr. Williams wanted Trinidad to become an associate . . . was because of the closer contact it would have given Trinidad with her French and Dutch associates in the Caribbean."[44]

One reason why it was not read this way in East Africa was the hope, openly expressed, that the East African Common Market would be the first step toward an African Common Market. The sense of the beginning of a Pan-African market, perhaps even the hope that the former French territories would join it, may again have obscured analysis. And finally, as Mboya said later: "We are bound to doubt the value of unity imposed and decisions taken by Europe on behalf of Africa."[45]

In other words, one might say that when Pan-Africanism remained in the background as a system of value and belief, it fitted well with a careful and coordinated evaluation of interests, but that when it became a more immediate and openly expressed factor, it tended to obscure analysis. It was here, too, on the question of immediacy and timing, that the closest thing to a difference of opinion among the East African debaters occurred—between Muliro and the rest.

Aspects of irrationality and poor judgment certainly characterized the decision not to associate, particularly in Tanganyika. Examples were the absence of a study of costs until the last moment, despite forewarning on the problem; and the feeling described by a number of civil servants and hinted at by Kawawa in his press statement that "we are not poor," that they were being wooed. Also, at least one of the Pan-Africanist economists admitted privately that his economic arguments were shaky, but that he felt rejection of association to be essential for African unity.

Britain also made mistakes. Although she kept the East African governments informed of the negotiations as they went along, she did not take steps to soothe the pride of those for whom she was negotiating. The feeling that East Africans could make their own arrangements without Britain telling them what to do undoubtedly played a part in the decision. Finally, for similar reasons, the language of rejection was more extreme than the arguments used.

SEQUEL

After the September decision the East African territories gradually softened the ostensible impact of their rejection. It was announced at the time that East Africa would like a special trading arrangement similar to that enjoyed by Libya, Morocco, and Tunisia—a protocol attached to the Treaty of Rome in 1957 that those countries' products would continue to have free access to their former mother country. Mboya had mentioned in the CLA debate that East Africa might try to work out a form of association or trade agreement that ensured the unity of the East African market and its freedom of relations with other trading partners. Indeed this was really the East African position before London. Some form of arrangement was to be tried that would avoid political links, and if that failed, association was to be reconsidered. Kawawa reversed this by rejecting association and then mentioning possible trade agreements, much to the embarrassment of the Kenya government.[46]

Later, after the French rejection of British entry into the EEC, the East African countries sent a joint delegation to Brussels to attempt to work out some form of arrangement or association without political ties. (The mission had been planned shortly after the London Conference.) Its success was not impressive, although the delegation was cordially received, ironically for the political reason that France was something of an outcast among the Six at the time and was in a poor bargaining position, and so more susceptible to German, Dutch, and Italian pressures to liberalize arrangements with states not associated.[47]

In mid-1963 George Kahama announced that Tanganyika's policy would be to continue negotiations for trade concessions and "eventually when the convention comes up for review in 1968 . . . it should be possible . . . to sit down and work out a new, suitable agreement of economic cooperation . . ."[48] At the end of the year the three East African countries asked the EEC for a "formal economic relationship" which would protect their exports without contravening their "previously defined position."[49] The irony of the situation was that any reasons for the Europeans making any concessions to the East Africans would be primarily political—to maintain good will in Africa.

In short, East Africa subsequently tried to soften rejection into a third alternative to association or nonassociation. The alternative—modified association, or a special trade agreement—was present in the CLA debate and in the London talks, though Britain discouraged it, and its feasibility at that time was questionable. Obote had said that there were three alternatives, and people in Kenya seemed to think this was the agreed East African position. Even in his categorical rejection, Kawawa mentioned some other possibility. The main difference between the third alternative and association seems to have been the institutional form of the political ties in the case of association, with the resulting loss of flexibility and injury to pride of independence. The alternative—special trade agreements, for example—might also avoid the dangers of trade diversion and retaliation to the extent that those factors were important.

CONCLUSION

What was the effect of Pan-Africanism on the decision to reject association with the EEC? Probably great, but not so great that it obscured rational analysis or led to foolish actions, as the British press tended to suggest. What might have been the decision in the absence of Pan-Africanism? East African interest alone might have been enough to ensure an East African approach, but not to bring Obote so close to the Tanganyikan position or to keep Kenya quiet after Kawawa overstated his rejection.

Would there have been a rejection in the first place? If there had been suspicion of ex-colonial powers, this alone might have been sufficient for rejection without bringing in a sentiment for African unity. But there is no denying the impact of the West African views and the general climate of suspicion that was phrased in terms of splitting Africa. Mistrust of the former colonial powers did not lead Sierra Leone or the West Indies to rejection, nor could it supply beliefs to bolster or substitute for facts. "Divide and rule" had enough truth in it to be credible, and Pan-Africanism tied it to a view of history, of imperialism, and a belief about the size of states.

What did the East Africans involved in the decision to reject association say about the role played by Pan-Africanism? The answers tended to vary with the motives of the person involved. More skeptical of the importance of Pan-Africanism in the decision were several important Ugandans and some non-Africans.

Maybe it was Pan-Africanism, but each territory saw its own interests, and coordination was because of East African economic unity, not Pan-Africanism (*George Magezi*).

It was a political decision. We were worried about industrialization and jeopardizing our non-alignment, but it was not Pan-African (*Amos Sempa*).

They used their Pan-African arguments more in talk with the Europeans. Among themselves they talked more of sovereignty and political freedom (*A non-African participant*).

On the other hand:

They did talk of strengthening East African unity and attaching other states to it. They also talked of reshaping the world economy, and less frequently, of the need for large states in world affairs (*A non-African participant*).

We felt that it was a threat to African unity (*Solomon Eliufoo*).

Unity, not economics, was the most important reason (*Mwai Kibaki*).

Our decision was made largely on ideological grounds (*Julius Nyerere*).

Yes, Kawawa's Pan-Africanism played a large part. We brought the Kenya cabinet around on the grounds of the need to ensure our unity and African unity (*James Gichuru*).

Rejection of Association with EEC

It is impossible to argue that Pan-Africanism was a necessary condition for the rejection of associate status by the East African countries. Other viewpoints, particularly the belief in neocolonialism, might have resulted in the same decision. But these viewpoints were connected with and part of Pan-Africanism in this particular case, and simple anticolonial emotion was reinforced by a framework of ideas. East African unity was usually seen as the first step in Pan-African unity. The tendency to be suspicious of the former colonial powers was part of the vague set of ideas that an avowed Pan-Africanist would have expressed. The feeling of unity in strength and "the bigger the better" was also part of that set of ideas. And with full knowledge that the alternatives in history remain closed and that it is risky to try to speculate upon them, one might say that without Pan-African ideas, East Africa would have associated with the EEC. Or, putting it another way, one might have predicted in the summer of 1962 that because of Pan-African ideas, the alternative of association would not be a likely choice. Many civil servants did not make this prediction, but it is interesting that those who did, did so on the basis of the avowed Pan-Africanism of the decision-makers involved.

What light does this decision shed on the unification problem? Certain qualifications must be clearly stated, though they in themselves illuminate the role of ideology. First, among the East Africans there was more uncertainty about what associate status would mean than there was about federation. This uncertainty inclined leaders to rely on systematized beliefs and attitudes because facts were scarce and decisions had to be made. Second, there was considerable suspicion of motives—a state of mind which encourages the role of ideology because assertions of facts which can seldom be conclusively demonstrated in social

241

affairs are not accepted. For instance, Mboya later wrote that "to accept [association] we must have complete confidence and faith in the motives and good will of Europe towards Africa. Can we afford to do this?"[50] At least the federation issue was not subject to such suspicions, based as they were on race and history.

What the decision to reject association does emphasize is the importance of the political elite (rather than groups) in this type of decision, and the interrelationship of ideology and economic interests in their thinking. It illustrates both ideological acceptance and commitment. The former was evident in the phrasing and perception of the issue. The latter may have accounted for Kawawa's and Obote's otherwise surprising actions. The subsequent softening of the decision in favor of the third alternative may shed light on the Nairobi declaration on federation and subsequent blunting of the decision by Uganda. Finally, the East Africans' awareness that they did not have a great deal to lose supports the view that ideology is most effective for prediction when there is only slight divergence from economic interests.

VIII

Pan-Africanism and African Integration

> Not ideas, but material and ideal interests directly
> govern man's conduct. Yet very frequently the "world
> images" which have been created by "ideas" have, like
> switchmen, determined the tracks along which action
> has been pushed by the dynamic of interests.
>
> Max Weber[1]

In Europe, integration as exemplified by the EEC is a
response to two disastrous wars and the growth of a modern
industrial economy. Africa has had no such disastrous wars
and has largely primitive economies. Nonetheless, efforts at
integration in Africa are more than imitation or grandiose
dreams. African leaders are determined to industrialize their
countries, though "the national boundaries are both too tight
and not suitably drawn to provide the balanced markets and
supplies to permit of purely national planning in industrialization . . ."[2]

We saw in Chapter V the difference between the potential
for industrialization of Uganda compared to East Africa as
a whole. Yet 70 per cent of the African states independent in
1964 had smaller populations than Uganda; only three (Nigeria, Egypt, Ethiopia) compared in size with East Africa.
In other words, a strong case can be made for integration
in Africa—not, perhaps, on a basis of "the bigger the better,"
considering the problems of enlargement we discussed in
Chapter I—but at least on a regional level.

Pan-Africanism and East African Integration

In the current movement for African integration, these economic considerations play a subsidiary part. More important, particularly in English-speaking areas, has been an ideology of integration—Pan-Africanism. Even Nigerians, often accused of a lukewarm attitude toward Pan-Africanism, dare not ignore it.[3] Indeed, Nigeria used the ideology to attack regional cooperation among the former French states that had preferential advantages in access to the European market.[4] As we have noted above, almost as important as whether an ideology is believed is whether it is used.

Like all ideologies which become movements, the synthesis of ideas that constitute Pan-Africanism has been affected by events. Certain ideas have increased in prominence and others (like nonviolence and self-determination) have declined. Perhaps the central initial contradiction which events were bound to bring into prominence was that between Pan-Africanism and nationalism—long glossed over by the slogan, "Pan-African nationalism." This problem plagued the Pan-African movement from the emergence of a number of new estates in 1960 until the Addis Ababa Conference of 1963. At Addis Ababa the charter of the new Organization of African Unity made it clear that the Pan-African movement would henceforth involve relations between sovereign states. But in dissolving antagonistic ideological blocs, the Addis solution also cast doubt on the legitimacy of regional groupings.

Given the poorly developed infrastructure of the interior of Africa, the best prospects of "functionalist" cooperation as a strategy of integration are at the regional level. Yet even here one might doubt the success of a functionalist strategy in Africa since such a strategy assumes "the patience and the time to wait for gradual change" and "serves best when the political structure itself is stable."[5] And whatever its merits

244

as a prediction for Europe, it seems difficult to conceive of supranationalism as a new and permanent form of institution in the African context.

But if the problems of EACSO and the East African common market which we discussed in Chapter V cast doubt on the viability of functional arrangements over a prolonged period under African conditions, the background of the federation movement described in Chapter VI suggests that functionalism may work for a limited period if it is related to a sense of purpose. In East Africa, Pan-Africanism led important leaders like Julius Nyerere and Tom Mboya to see the importance of preserving the colonial functional institutions. At first they saw them as means toward a federation which would serve as a nucleus for African unity.[6] Later, after Ghanaian and Ugandan criticism, pro-federationists argued that a federation would demonstrate the possibility of sacrificing sovereignty and thus prove the reality of Pan-Africanism.[7]

Again, qualifications are important. According to participants, Pan-Africanism seldom appeared at the bargaining table when EACSO committees met; discussions were in terms of pounds and shillings. A Pan-African commitment did not make Tanganyika refrain from uncooperative acts. In the words of a Tanganyikan official, "We have a commitment to fight poverty here too." One is reminded of Dunduzu Chisiza's observation that "Pan-Africanism, as a strategy for emancipation, is unquestionably effective. But as a unifying agent for regional cooperation it is far too superficial and an operation 'roof-top'."[8] In other words, Pan-Africanism may provide the sense of purpose that makes functional cooperation possible—but only as a general background for a limited period, and as a strategy toward some form of union soon.

Given the absence of the interest groups and strong bureaucracy which theorists suggest are the motors of European integration, can ideology serve as the impetus for integration in Africa? Of the three categories of motivating forces which Wheare says created federations in the past—defensive, utilitarian, ideological—defense against a common enemy has probably received most attention, and ideology the least.[9] In June 1963 it seemed that ideology (combined with utilitarian factors) might be the major force in the creation of an East African federation. A federation movement had existed for a number of years, but most observers had believed it dead until Pan-African ideology became a new factor breathing life into it. The negotiations in 1963 provided a unique opportunity to observe the interaction of ideological and utilitarian factors in a unification movement. After the army mutinies, the Zanzibar revolution, and greater Cold War involvement in 1964, new variables clouded the relationship between ideology and economics. But in 1963 the relationship was quite clear.

Commitment to the ideology of Pan-Africanism was a major cause of the Nairobi declaration of intent to federate by the end of 1963. Not only did the meeting come soon after the Addis Ababa Conference, but such an interpretation is consistent with Obote's actions on other occasions, as we saw in Chapter VII. Although the separate territories had existed for more than sixty years and possessed separate identities, leaders were able to call themselves "Pan-African nationalists" without facing any adverse consequences because national interests were still ambiguous.

When Ugandan leaders realized what they were being asked to sacrifice in a federation, they became much more precise about their national interests and defended them at the bargaining table. To maintain the legitimacy of their interests, Ugandans retained the ideology of Pan-Africanism but seized upon the Ghanaian interpretation of it to break the link between the ideology and federation. By doing so, they removed the practical consequences of Pan-Africanism that threatened their national interests without having to give up the "Pan-African nationalist" synthesis.

Ideologies are seldom discarded, but they are frequently reinterpreted to avoid their unfortunate implications. Asians in Kenya, for example, asserted "one man, one vote" in their struggle with Europeans for thirty years, until the vast African majority entered the political arena. Then, rather than drop their principle, they qualified it and asserted "one man, one vote, for all civilized men."[10] In a similar way, Ugandans, by removing the regional implications, could remain Pan-African nationalists.

This is not to say that the Ugandan leaders were not sincere about their Pan-Africanism. Ugandans were just as willing as other East Africans to sacrifice for their brothers in South Africa. The boycott of South African trade hurt Uganda more than it did South Africa. It shut Uganda off from a market for her politically important surplus coffee crop, a market which was not subject to the International Coffee Agreement quota. It seems that sacrificing thousands of pounds is easier than sacrificing sovereignty.

What are the implications for Pan-Africanism of the downgrading of subregions that followed the Addis Ababa Conference and the failure of the promising East African attempt at unification under the optimal conditions of 1963?[11] From an optimistic view it may merely mean that some day an East African federation will be achieved through a reconciliation of national interests, with ideology playing a less significant part. As a Ugandan cabinet minister said at the end of 1963, "We hope that wisdom will prevail in the federal discussions so that decisions will be taken which respect the interests of all the states."[12] Tanganyikans were also becoming more articulate about their national interest by the end of 1963, and there was room for bargaining. The significance of the events of that year may be that whatever the future of federation, East African leaders will never allow the gap between their ideology and interests to become as wide as it was in June 1963. Similarly, taking an optimistic view of Pan-Africanism in general, the downgrading of regionalism and the East African failure may simply mean that the Pan-African movement will be limited to cooperation of sovereign states for limiting wars and coordinating diplomatic activity. Creation of such a security area, in which states might forego the use of force, would represent an impressive achievement of integration which could be attributed to Pan-Africanism.[13]

If, however, this level of integration failed to satisfy the aspirations of Pan-Africanists, and any higher degree of integration remained unlikely, except at the subregional level, then , from a more pessimistic view, the downgrading of regionalism and the East African failure may mean that there is no way short of force of overcoming the geographic, historical, economic, and linguistic barriers to African unity. In this case the ideology of Pan-Africanism may remain as a destabilizing vocabulary and myth, providing scapegoats but no solutions for serious economic problems. It may even degenerate into racialism or imperialism as so many "pan movements" have in the past. A relatively conservative figure like Dr. Michael Okpara of Nigeria has said of the possibility of an African Napoleon: "If this plan for union by stages failed, if every orderly means of consultation failed, then, if we saw someone strong enough, I would support him, because we must have African Unity at all costs."[14]

So far, this pessimistic view is premature. Regionalism has not yet failed in East Africa, much less all of Africa; and there may well be links between Pan-Africanism and integration other than those discussed here.

Moreover, we must ask to what extent it is possible to generalize from experience in East Africa. One might argue that the East African failure to federate in 1963 was simply a matter of a bungled job. When nations disagree it is not necessarily the one that says "no" that is wrong. Kenya and Tanganyika might have gone further to meet Uganda's demands and ease her feeling of being the third partner.[15] The East Africans had no definite strategy of integration, nor did they fully explore all the alternative possibilities between functionalism and federalism.

But even when this is said it remains an open question whether any institutional arrangement could have solved the complex problems which caused the failure to federate. In situations with a small political elite, an institutional compromise which leaves power in the constituent units (as was true, for example, of the West Indies Federation) runs the risk of failing to involve the important political figures with the new center—an unstable arrangement when the power of the state is necessary to create the national community the existence of which national leaders had already asserted. The failure to federate in 1963 must be attributed not only to mistakes, but also to underlying problems of political, social, and economic integration which we discussed in Part Two and which are not unique to East Africa.

As for our theories of integration, any generalizations from East African experience must be limited to situations where economies are underdeveloped; in which the society

249

has few powerful pressure groups (and these often staffed by people of another race); where leaders of newly independent states are still ambiguous about national interests; where the mass of the populace is illiterate, and communications are not fully developed. Because of these limits, and until we have more cases from developing areas, the East African experience is mainly useful as a qualification of existing generalizations. It suggests that strategies of integration based on gradualism, group theory, the predominance of economics or a welfare calculus, make little sense in these conditions. Scholars studying integration in Africa must remember the primacy of politics and not be misled by assumptions natural to "developed" societies. It is important to pay attention to social, historical, and economic factors, but too much time in the archives or statistical libraries will be spent at the cost of diversion from the main factors—the political elite and its ideology and interests.

Finally, the East African experience suggests that whether ideology helps or hinders integration, it must be raised from a background condition to the position of a major variable.

The role of Pan-Africanism is not simple. We have seen the extent to which it was an ambiguous symbol in East Africa. As African leaders become more sophisticated about their national interests, we may expect to find fewer of the sacrifices that Tanganyika made before 1963, or the impulsive decisions that Uganda made in June 1963. Nonetheless, the Pan-Africanist ideology is widely accepted, particularly among younger politicians. It provides the vocabulary and helps to establish the limits of most discourse on African integration. It helps to shape the "world images" which "like switchmen" will determine the tracks along which action will be "pushed by the dynamic of interests." Part of the ambiguous effect of Pan-Africanism in East Africa can be attributed to its diffuse nature; and part to the fact that, for this political generation, the "switches" are not fully closed but remain open to manipulation by political leaders who are also trying to build new nations. Yet even if all future efforts toward African integration are carried out within the context of national interests, scholars and other observers cannot afford to ignore the "Pan-African switchmen."

BIBLIOGRAPHY

NOTES

INDEX

SELECTED BIBLIOGRAPHY

(Some suggestions for further reading)

I. REGIONAL INTEGRATION

Balassa, Bela, *The Theory of Economic Integration.* Homewood, Illinois: Irwin, 1961.

Brinton, Crane, *From Many One.* Cambridge, Mass.: Harvard University Press, 1948.

Claude, Inis L., *Swords Into Ploughshares,* 3rd. ed. New York: Random House, 1964.

Dell, Sidney, *Trade Blocs and Common Markets.* London: Constable, 1963.

Deutsch, Karl, "Supranational Organizations in the 1960's," *Journal of Common Market Studies,* vol. I, no. 3 (1963).

—— *et al., Political Community and the North Atlantic Area.* Princeton: Princeton University Press, 1957.

Etzioni, Amitai, "A Paradigm for the Study of Political Unification," *World Politics,* October 1962.

—— "The Dialectics of Supranational Integration," *American Political Science Review,* December 1962.

Haas, Ernst B., *The Uniting of Europe.* Stanford: Stanford University Press, 1958.

—— *Beyond the Nation-State.* Stanford: Stanford University Press, 1964.

—— "International Integration: The European and the Universal Process," *International Organization,* Summer 1961.

—— and Philippe Schmitter, "Economics and Differential Patterns of Political Integration: Projections about Unity in Latin America," *International Organization,* Autumn 1964.

Hoffmann, Stanley, "Discord in Community: The North Atlantic Area as a Partial International System," *International Organization,* Summer 1963.

Jacob, Philip and James Toscano, eds., *The Integration of Political Communities,* Philadelphia: Lippincott, 1964.

255

Selected Bibliography

Kitzinger, Uwe, *The Politics and Economics of European Integration*. New York: Praeger, 1963.

Lindberg, Leon, *The Political Dynamics of European Economic Integration*. Stanford, Stanford University Press, 1963.

Viner, Jacob, *The Customs Union Issue*. New York: Carnegie Endowment, 1950.

II. NATIONALISM

Carr, E. H., *Nationalism and After*. London: Macmillan, 1945.

Cobban, Alfred, *National Self-Determination*. Chicago: University of Chicago Press, 1947.

Coleman, James S., "Nationalism in Tropical Africa," *American Political Science Review*, June 1954.

Deutsch, Karl, *Nationalism and Social Communication*. Cambridge, Mass.: M.I.T. Press, 1953.

———— and William Foltz, eds., *Nation-Building*. New York: Atherton, 1963.

Emerson, Rupert, *From Empire to Nation*. Cambridge, Mass.: Harvard University Press, 1960.

———— *Self-Determination Revisited in the Era of Decolonization*. Cambridge, Mass.: Harvard University Center for International Affairs, 1964.

Hayes, C. J. H., *Essays on Nationalism*. New York: Macmillan, 1926.

Hodgkin, Thomas, *Nationalism in Colonial Africa*. New York: New York University Press, 1957.

———— "A Note on the Language of African Nationalism," in K. Kirkwood (ed.), *Saint Anthony's Papers No. 10*. London: Chatto and Windus, 1961.

Kedourie, Elie, *Nationalism*. New York: Praeger, 1961.

Kilson, Martin, "The Analysis of African Nationalism," *World Politics*, April 1958.

Kohn, Hans, *The Idea of Nationalism*. New York: Macmillan, 1944.

———— and Wallace Sokolsky, *African Nationalism in the Twentieth Century*. Princeton: Van Nostrand, 1965.

Rotberg, Robert I., "The Rise of African Nationalism: The Case of East and Central Africa," *World Politics*, October 1962.

Shepperson, George, "Notes on American Negro Influences on the Emergence of African Nationalism," *Journal of African History*, 1:299–312 (1960).

Selected Bibliography

Silvert, Kalman, ed., *Expectant Peoples: Nationalism and Development*. New York: Random House, 1963.

Wallerstein, Immanuel, "Ethnicity and National Integration in West Africa," *Cahiers d'études africaines*, 3:129–139 (1960).

Whiteley, W. H., "Political Concepts and Connotations: Observations on the use of some political terms in Swahili," in ·K. Kirkwood, ed., *St. Anthony's Papers No. 10*. London: Chatto and Windus, 1961.

III. PAN-AFRICANISM AND AFRICAN UNITY

American Society of African Culture, *Pan-Africanism Reconsidered*. Berkeley: University of California Press, 1962.

Bascom, W.R., "Tribalism, Nationalism and Pan-Africanism," *The Annals of the American Academy of Political and Social Sciences*, July 1962.

Berg, Elliot, "The Economic Basis of Political Choice in French West Africa," *American Political Science Review*, June 1960.

Boutros-Ghali, Boutros, "The Addis Ababa Charter," *International Conciliation*, January 1964.

Chisiza, Dunduzu, *Africa—What Lies Ahead*. New York: African-American Institute, 1962.

Decraene, Philippe, *Le Pan-Africanisme*. Paris: Presses Universitaries de France, 1959.

Emerson, Rupert and Norman Padelford, eds., *Africa and World Order*. New York: Praeger, 1963.

Legum, Colin, *Pan-Africanism: A Short Political Guide*. New York: Praeger, 1962.

Lewis, I. M., "Pan-Africanism and Pan-Somalism," *Journal of Modern African Studies*, vol. I, no. 2 (1963).

Mazrui, Ali A., "On the Concept of 'We are All Africans'," *American Political Science Review*, March 1963.

Mboya, Tom, *Freedom and After*. London: Deutsch, 1963.

McKay, Vernon, *Africa in World Politics*. New York, Harper & Row, 1963.

McWilliams, W. C. and J. W. Polier, "Pan-Africanism and the Dilemmas of National Development," *Phylon*, Spring 1964.

Munger, Edwin S., *African Field Reports 1952–61*. Capetown: Struik, 1961.

Selected Bibliography

Nkrumah, Kwame, *Ghana: The Autobiography of Kwame Nkrumah*. Edinburgh: Nelson, 1962.

——— *Africa Must Unite*. London, Heineman, 1963.

Nyerere, Julius, "A United States of Africa," *Journal of Modern African Studies*, vol. I, no. 1 (1963).

Padelford, Norman, "The Organization of African Unity," *International Organization*, March 1964.

Padmore, George, *Pan-Africanism or Communism*. London: Dennis Dobson, 1956.

Rake, Alan, "Is Pan-Africa Possible?" *Transition*, June 1962.

Sanger, Clyde, "Toward Unity in Africa," *Foreign Affairs*, January 1964.

Shepperson, George, "Pan-Africanism and 'Pan-Africanism': Some Historical Notes," *Phylon*, vol. XXIII, no. 4 (1962).

IV. EAST AFRICA

Brown, A. J., "Customs Union Versus Economic Separatism in Developing Countries," *Yorkshire Bulletin*, November 1961.

Cox, Richard, *Pan-Africanism in Practice: PAFMECSA 1958–1964*. London, Oxford University Press, 1964.

Darby, Anthony, "East Africa: The Case for Federation," *New Commonwealth*, February 1961.

Delf, George, *Asians in East Africa*. London: Oxford University Press, 1963.

East Africa Royal Commission 1953–5 Report (Cmd. 9475) London, 1956.

East Africa: Report of the Economic and Fiscal Commission (Cmd. 1279) London, 1961.

Franck, Thomas, *East African Unity Through Law*. New Haven: Yale University Press, 1964.

Goldthorpe, J. E., *Outlines of East African Society*. Kampala: East African Institute of Social Research, 1962.

Goldthorpe, J. E., and M. Macpherson, "Makerere College and Its Old Students," *Zaire*, vol. XII, no. 4 (1958).

Hailey, Lord, *An African Survey—Revised 1956*. Oxford: Oxford University Press, 1957.

Ghai, Dharam, "Territorial Distribution of Benefits and Costs of the East African Common Market," *East African Economics Review*, June 1964.

Selected Bibliography

Hill, M. F., *Permanent Way*. Nairobi: East African Railways, 1949.

Hughes, Anthony, *East Africa: The Search for Unity*. Baltimore: Penguin, 1964.

Hollingsworth, L. W., *The Asians in East Africa*. London: Macmillan, 1960.

Ingham, Kenneth, *History of East Africa*. London: Longmans, 1962.

Kennedy, T. A., "The East African Customs Union: Some Features of Its History and Operations," *Makerere Journal*, no. 3 (1959).

Khamisi, Francis, "The East African Political Scene: The African Viewpoint," *African Affairs*, January 1946.

Khrishna, K. G. V., "Some Economic Aspects of an East African Federation," *East African Economics Review*, December 1961.

Kiano, Julius, "East African Countries," in Joseph Black and Kenneth Thompson, eds., *Foreign Policies in a World of Change*. New York: Harper and Row, 1963.

Lomas, P. K., "The Report of the East African Economic and Fiscal Commission," *East African Economic Review*, June 1961.

Massell, Benton, *East African Economic Union: An Evaluation and Some Implications for Policy*. Santa Monica: RAND, 1963.

Mitchell, Sir Philip, *African Afterthoughts*. London: Hutchinson, 1954.

Okondo, Peter, "Prospects of Federalism in East Africa," in David Currie, ed., *Federalism and the New Nations of Africa*. Chicago: Chicago University Press, 1964.

Oliver, Roland, *The Missionary Factor in East Africa*. London: Longmans, 1952.

Oliver, Roland, and Gervase Mathew, eds., *History of East Africa*, vol. I. Oxford: Clarendon Press, 1963.

Ord, M. W., "The Growth of Money Incomes in East Africa," *East African Economics Review*, June 1962.

Richards, Audrey I., ed., *East African Chiefs*. London: Faber, 1959.

Rosberg, Carl, with Aaron Segal, "An East African Federation," *International Conciliation*, May 1963.

Rotberg, Robert, "The Federation Movement in British East and Central Africa," *Journal of Commonwealth Political Studies*, May 1964.

Rothchild, Donald, *Toward Unity in Africa*. Washington: Public Affairs Press, 1960.

Southall, A. W., "Population Movements in East Africa," in K. M. Barbour and R. M. Prothero, eds., *Essays in African Population*. London: Routledge, 1961.

259

Selected Bibliography

Trimmingham, J. S., *Islam in East Africa*. London: Oxford University Press, 1964.

Welbourn, F. B., *East African Rebels: A Study of Some Independent Churches*. London: SCM Press, 1961.

Wraith, Ronald, *East African Citizen*. London: Oxford University Press, 1959.

V. KENYA

Altrincham, Lord, *Kenya's Opportunity*. London: Faber, 1955.

Bennett, George, "The Development of Political Organizations in Kenya," *Political Studies*, June 1957.

―――― and Carl Rosberg, *The Kenyatta Election*. Oxford: Oxford University Press, 1961.

Blundell, Michael, *So Rough a Wind*. London, 1964.

Castagno, A. A., "The Somali-Kenyan Controversy: Implications for the Future," *Journal of Modern African Studies*, July 1964.

Delf, George, *Jomo Kenyatta: Towards Truth About 'The Light of Kenya'*. Garden City: Doubleday, 1961.

Dilley, Marjorie, *British Policy in Kenya Colony*. New York: Nelson, 1957.

Engholm, G. F., "African Elections in Kenya, March 1957," in W. J. M. Mackenzie and Kenneth Robinson, eds., *Five Elections in Africa*. Oxford: Clarendon Press, 1960.

Huxley, Elspeth, *White Man's Country*. London: Macmillan, 1953.

―――― and Margery Perham, *Race and Politics in Kenya*. London: Faber, 1956.

International Bank for Reconstruction and Development, *The Economic Development of Kenya*. Baltimore: John Hopkins Press, 1963.

Kariuki, Josiah Mwangi, *'Mau Mau' Detainee*. London: Oxford University Press, 1963.

Kilson, Martin L., "Land and Politics in Kenya: An Analysis of African Politics in a Plural Society," *Western Political Quarterly*, September 1957.

Leys, Norman, *A Last Chance in Kenya*. London: Hogarth, 1931.

Lonsdale, J. M., "Archdeacon Owen and the Kavirondo Taxpayers Welfare Association," *Proceedings of the East African Institute of Social Research*. Kampala, 1963.

Selected Bibliography

Ogot, B. A., "British Administration in the Central Nyanza District of Kenya, 1900–60," *Journal of African History*, vol. IV, no. 2 (1963).

Origins and Growth of Mau Mau: An Historical Survey (Corfield Report). Nairobi: Government Printer, 1960.

Rake, Alan, *Tom Mboya*. Garden City: Doubleday, 1962.

Rosberg, Carl, "Independent Kenya: Problems and Prospects," *Africa Report*, December 1963.

Ross, William McGregor, *Kenya From Within*. London: Allen & Unwin, 1927.

Sanger, Clyde and John Nottingham, "The Kenya General Election," *Journal of Modern African Studies*, March 1964.

Savage, Donald, "Labour Protest in Kenya, the Early Phase: 1914–1939," *Proceedings of the East African Institute of Social Research*. Kampala, 1963.

Sorrenson, M. P. K., "The Official Mind and Kikuyu Land Tenure 1895–1939," *Proceedings of the East African Institute of Social Research*. Kampala, 1963.

Welbourn, F. B., "Comment on Corfield," *Race*, May 1961.

VI. UGANDA

Apter, David, *The Political Kingdom in Uganda*. Princeton: Princeton University Press, 1961.

Bryd, Robert, "A Portrait of Leadership in a New Nation—The Case of Uganda," *Queens Quarterly*, Winter 1963.

Burke, Fred, *Local Government and Politics in Uganda*. Syracuse: Syracuse University Press, 1964.

Economist Intelligence Unit, *Uganda—Background to Investment*. London, 1962.

Engholm, G. F., "Political Parties and Uganda's Independence," *Transition*, January 1962.

Elkan, Walter, "Criteria for Industrial Development in Uganda," *East African Economic Review*, January 1959.

Fallers, Lloyd, *The King's Men*. New York: Oxford University Press, 1964.

——— "Despotism, Status, Culture and Social Mobility in an African Kingdom," *Comparative Studies in Society and History*, October 1959.

Selected Bibliography

Gertzel, Cherry J., "Independent Uganda: Problems and Prospects," *Africa Report,* October 1962.

———— "How Kabaka Yekka Came to Be," *Africa Report,* October 1964.

Goldthorpe, J. E., "An African Elite," *British Journal of Sociology,* March 1955.

Ingham, Kenneth, *The Making of Modern Uganda.* London: Allen and Unwin, 1958.

International Bank for Reconstruction and Development, *The Economic Development of Uganda.* Baltimore: Johns Hopkins University Press, 1962.

Low, D. A., *Political Parties in Uganda 1949–62.* London: Athlone Press, 1962.

———— and R. C. Pratt, *Buganda and British Overrule 1900–1955.* New York: Oxford University Press, 1960.

Lowenkopf, Martin, "Uganda's Prime Minister Obote," *Africa Report,* May 1962.

Munger, Edwin S., *Relational Patterns of Kampala, Uganda.* Chicago: University of Chicago Geography Department, 1951.

Nye, J. S., "The Impact of Independence on Two African Nationalist Parties," a paper delivered at the Boston University Seminar on African Politics, 1963.

Nyhart, J. D., "The Uganda Development Corporation and Agriculture," *East African Economic Review,* December 1959.

Ochieng, Daudi, "An Economist Looks at Uganda's Future," *Transition,* November 1961.

Pratt, R. C., "Nationalism in Uganda," *Political Studies,* June 1961.

Rothchild, Donald, "The Extent of Federalism in Uganda," *Proceedings of the East African Institute of Social Research.* Kampala, 1963.

———— and Michael Rogin, "Uganda" in Gwendolen Carter, ed., *National Unity and Regionalism in Eight African States.* Ithaca: Cornell University Press, 1965.

Shepherd, George, *They Wait in Darkness.* New York: John Day, 1955.

Southall, A. W., "Micropolitics in Uganda: Traditional and Modern Politics," *Proceedings of the East African Institute of Social Research.* Kampala, 1963.

Stonehouse, John, *Prohibited Immigrant.* London: Bodley Head, 1961.

Selected Bibliography

Welbourn, F. B., "Religion and Politics in Uganda," *Spearhead*, September 1962.

VII. TANZANIA

Austen, Ralph, "The Prehistory of TANU," *Makerere Journal*, no. 9 (1964).

Arthur D. Little, Inc., *Tanganyika Industrial Development*. Cambridge, Mass., 1961.

Bates, Margaret, "Tanganyika," in Gwendolen Carter, ed., *African One-Party States*. Ithaca: Cornell University Press, 1962.

Bennett, George, "An Outline History of TANU," *Makerere Journal*, no. 7 (1962).

Burke, Fred, "Tanganyika: The Search for Ujamaa," in William Friedland and Carl Rosberg, eds., *African Socialism*. Stanford: Stanford University Press, 1964.

Cameron, Sir Donald, *My Tanganyika Service and Some Nigeria*. London, 1939.

Chidzero, B. T. G., *Tanganyika and International Trusteeship*. Oxford: Oxford University Press, 1961.

Erlich, Cyril, "Some Aspects of Economic Policy in Tanganyika, 1945–60," *Journal of Modern African Studies*, July 1964.

George, J. B., "How Stable is Tanganyika," *Africa Report*, March 1963.

Glickman, Harvey, *Some Observations on the Army and Political Unrest in Tanganyika*. Pittsburgh: Duquesne University Institute of African Affairs, 1964.

Hughes, Tony, "Profile on Zanzibar," *Africa South in Exile*, April 1961.

International Bank for Reconstruction and Development, *The Economic Development of Tanganyika*. Baltimore: Johns Hopkins University Press, 1961.

Kyle, Keith, "Coup in Zanzibar," and "More Pieces for the East African Puzzle," *Africa Report*, March 1964.

Leubuscher, Charlotte, *Tanganyika Territory: A Study of Economic Policy Under Mandate*. London: Oxford University Press, 1944.

Leys, Colin, "Tanganyika: The Realities of Independence," *International Journal*, XVII (1963).

Lofchie, Michael, "Party Conflict in Zanzibar," *Journal of Modern African Studies*, I (1963).

Selected Bibliography

Lowenkopf, Martin, "Outlook for Tanganyika," *Africa Report*, April 1961.

Mohamed, Abdul Rahman, "Election Postscript," *Africa South in Exile*, April 1961.

Mustafa, Sophia, *The Tanganyika Way*. Dar es Salaam: East Africa Literature Bureau, 1961.

Nyerere, Julius, "The Nationalist View," *International Affairs*, January 1960.

———— "Ujamaa: The Basis of African Socialism," reprinted in W. Friedland and Carl Rosberg, eds., *African Socialism*. Stanford: Stanford University Press, 1964.

Nye, J. S., "Tanganyika's Self-Help," *Transition*, November 1963.

Pratt, R. C., "Multi-Racialism and Local Government in Tanganyika," *Race*, II (1960).

Rake, Alan, "The Nyerere Story," *Africa Report*, December 1961.

Rotberg, Robert, "The Political Outlook in Zanzibar," *Africa Report*, October 1961.

Taylor, J. Clagett, *The Political Development of Tanganyika*. Stanford: Stanford University Press, 1963.

Young, Roland, and Henry Fosbrook, *Smoke in the Hills: Political Tensions in the Morogoro District of Tanganyika*. Evanston: Northwestern University Press, 1960.

NOTES

CHAPTER I: NATIONALISM, PAN-AFRICANISM, AND INTEGRATION

1. Speech to the United Nations by Kenya's Minister of Home Affairs and subsequently Vice President Oginga Odinga, quoted in *Reporter* (Nairobi) December 21, 1963.

2. Quoted in *Reporter* (Nairobi), June 8, 1963, pp. 8–9. More than a year later, a European journalist was expelled from Kenya for reporting that Kenyatta had referred to the federation declaration as a "hoax" designed to insure early independence for Kenya. The Kenya Government denied this and stated that Kenyatta's Swahili word "ujanja" should have been translated "ingenuity." *Reporter* (Nairobi), August 14, 1964. The latter interpretation seems more plausible, as we shall see in Chapter VI, but this does not rule out the possibility that East African leaders were tempted to rewrite history after a failure. See also Obote in *Uganda Argus,* June 27, 1964.

3. *East African Standard,* December 10, 1963.

4. "Collapse of the Mali Federation," *Africa Report,* December 1960, p. 5.

5. For an elaboration of this problem see Louis Hartz, "The Problem of Political Ideas," in *Approaches to the Study of Politics,* ed. Roland Young (Evanston, Ill., 1958).

6. Except at the "tribal" level and in the Somali case; and this is not to deny that it is growing. On the term "African nationalism," see James S. Coleman, "Nationalism in Tropical Africa," *American Political Science Review* (APSR) 48:404–426 (June 1954); and Martin Kilson, "The Analysis of African Nationalism," *World Politics,* 10:484–497 (April 1958).

7. *New York Times,* February 16, 1964.

8. See E. H. Carr, *Nationalism and After* (London, 1945), *passim;* and Joseph R. Strayer, "The Historical Experience of Nation-Building in Europe," in Karl Deutsch and William Foltz, eds., *Nation-Building* (New York, 1963), pp. 17–26.

9. Rupert Emerson, *From Empire to Nation* (Cambridge, Mass.,

1960), p. 103; see also C. J. Friedrich, "Nation-Building?" in Deutsch and Foltz, *Nation-Building*, pp. 31–32.

10. Hans J. Morgenthau, *The Decline of Democratic Politics* (Chicago, 1962), p. 184; Alfred Cobban, *National Self-Determination* (Chicago, 1947).

11. Lord Hailey, *An African Survey: Revised 1956* (London, 1957); Hodgkin, *Nationalism in Colonial Africa* (New York, 1957).

12. *An Address to the Norwegian Students Association in Oslo* (Dar es Salaam, 1963), p. 4. It is of some significance that both "nation" and "race" were translated by the same Swahili word (taifa) in East Africa. See W. H. Whitely, "Political Concepts and Connotations," in *St. Anthony's Papers No. 10* (London, 1961), p. 19.

13. James Coleman and David Apter, "Pan-Africanism or Nationalism in Africa," in *Pan-Africanism Reconsidered*, edited by The American Society of African Culture (Los Angeles, 1962), p. 81.

14. Hans Kohn, *Nationalism: Its Meaning and History* (Princeton, N. J., 1955), pp. 65–73; and "Pan-Movements," *Encyclopedia of the Social Sciences*, ed. E. R. A. Seligman (New York, 1937), II, 544–553.

15. Paul E. Sigmund, ed., *The Ideologies of the Developing Nations* (New York, 1963), p. 36. Sigmund argues that these ideas are sufficiently coherent to be called an ideology.

16. Simon Kuznets, "Economic Growth of Small Nations," in *The Economic Consequences of the Size of Nations*, ed. Austin Robinson (London, 1960), pp. 31–32.

17. Elliot Berg, "The Economic Basis of Political Choice in French West Africa," *American Political Science Review*, 54:405 (June 1960).

18. Inis L. Claude, *Swords Into Plowshares*, 2nd ed. (New York, 1959), p. 375.

19. M. Margaret Ball, *NATO and the European Union Movement* (New York, 1959), p. 23. See also Uwe Kitzinger, *The Politics and Economics of European Integration* (New York, 1963), pp. 4–6. These terms are not precise, and the dispute over means might better be expressed as a functional vs. a constitutional approach, with federalism as a common end.

20. Kwame Nkrumah, *Africa Must Unite* (London, 1963), pp. 218–220.

21. Oscar Kambona, Tanganyika Minister of External Affairs, interview, March 1, 1963.

22. Senghor is quoted in "The Addis Conference," *Africa Report*, June 1963, p. 4; Haile Selassie in *East African Standard*, November 4, 1963; President Azikiwe in Colin Legum's *Pan-Africanism: A Short Political Guide* (New York, 1962), p. 276.

23. Although experts from the Casablanca powers met in Conakry in January 1962 and recommended a complete customs union within five years, little was done to implement it. Nor did the avowed economic intentions of the Monrovia Bloc receive practical attention. Similarly, the Conseil d'Entente (Ivory Coast, Upper Volta, Niger, and Dahomey) was primarily political in its practice.

24. Padmore, *Pan-Africanism or Communism* (London, 1956), p. 22; Edwin S. Munger, "All African Peoples Conference," in *African Field Reports 1952–1961* (Capetown, 1961); also, Tom Mboya, interview, July 29, 1963.

25. Nkrumah, *Africa Must Unite*, pp. 142, 147.

26. Clyde Sanger, "Toward Unity in Africa," *Foreign Affairs*, 42:268–281 (January 1964).

27. Nkrumah, *Africa Must Unite*, p. 215.

28. Karl Deutsch, "Social Mobilization and Political Development," *APSR*, 55:502 (September 1961).

29. Tom Mboya, interview, July 29, 1963.

30. "A Ferment of Change," *Journal of Common Market Studies*, vol. 1, no. 3, p. 211.

31. Ernst B. Haas, "International Integration: The European and the Universal Process," *International Organization*, 15:375 (Summer 1961); *The Uniting of Europe* (Stanford, 1958), p. 28.

32. Ernst B. Haas, "Regional Government and the 'New Europe';" Keynote address at McGill University Conference on World Affairs, Montreal, October 30, 1963; see also George Lichtheim, *The New Europe* (New York, 1963); S. M. Lipset, "The Changing Class Structure and Contemporary European Politics," *Daedalus*, 93:271–303 (Winter 1964).

33. Michael Shanks and John Lambert, *The Common Market Today—and Tomorrow* (New York, 1962), p. 174; Hallstein quoted on p. 178.

34. See Karl Deutsch, "Supranational Organizations in the 1960's," *Journal of Common Market Studies*, vol. 1, no. 3, pp. 214–216; also, Roy Pryce, *The Political Future of the European Community* (London, 1962).

Notes to Chapter I

35. Haas, *Uniting of Europe*, p. xv.

36. Amitai Etzioni, "A Paradigm for the Study of Political Unification," *World Politics*, 15:67 (October 1962).

37. Amitai Etzioni, "European Unification: A Strategy of Change," *World Politics*, 16:50 (October 1963). For Etzioni's ranking of sectors, see "The Dialectics of Supranational Unification," *APSR*, 61:932 (December 1962).

38. *The Economist*, November 16, 1963.

39. Etzioni, in *APSR*, December 1962, p. 932.

40. Lucian Pye, *Politics, Personality and Nation-Building* (New Haven, 1962), p. 43.

41. M. M. Kihere, quoted in *East African Standard*, October 18, 1963; *Sunday Nation* (Nairobi), October 20, 1963.

42. Interview with President, Association for Promotion of Industry in East Africa, May 21, 1963; see also Minutes of Kampala Session, Association of Chambers of Commerce and Industry of Eastern Africa, February 6 and 7, 1961.

43. Julius Kiano, quoted in *Uganda Argus*, February 7, 1961.

44. Interview, Executive Officer, Dar es Salaam Chamber of Commerce, March 1963.

45. *Uganda Argus*, June 1, 1960. The 1961 conference of the Kenya African Chamber of Commerce supported federation but no politician bothered to attend though several had been invited. *Tanganyika Standard*, April 7, 1961.

46. Interviews, Vice-President, Uganda Trade Union Congress, December 18, 1963; Acting General-Secretary, Tanganyika Federation of Labour, November 21, 1963.

47. See *Tanganyika Standard*, January 12, 1963; or "A Case for East African Unity" prepared by the UPC Makerere Branch. The limited nature of group politics will be seen in the case studies in Chapters VI and VII below.

48. Stanley Hoffmann, "Discord in Community: The North Atlantic Area As a Partial International System," *International Organization*, 17:529 (Summer 1963).

49. Marco Surveys Ltd., Public Opinion Polls No. 1 and No. 10 (Nairobi; 1960, 1962); J. S. Nye, "Attitudes of Makerere Students towards East African Federation," *Proceedings of the East African Institute, 1963* (Kampala, 1963); Edwin S. Munger, *Relational Patterns of Kampala, Uganda* (Chicago, 1951), p. 123.

50. Letter from Dr. G. K. Park, Fellow of the East African Institute, August 10, 1963.

51. Solomon Eliufoo, interview, March 6, 1963.

52. See Tom Mboya, *Freedom and After* (London, 1963), p. 62.

CHAPTER II: PAN-AFRICANISM IN EAST AFRICA

1. See Karl Mannheim, *Ideology and Utopia* (New York, 1949), pp. 55–108; Talcott Parsons, *The Social System* (Glencoe, Ill., 1951), p. 349; Harold Lasswell and Abraham Kaplan, *Power and Society* (New Haven, 1950), p. 123; Ben Halperin, "Myth and Ideology in Modern Usage," *History and Theory*, vol. I, no. 2, p. 137.

2. See Daniel Bell, *The End of Ideology* (Glencoe, Ill., 1960), pp. 370–372; Zbigniew Brzezinski, *Ideology and Power in Soviet Politics* (New York, 1962), p. 4; Paul Sigmund, *The Ideologies of the Developing Nations* (New York, 1963), p. 3.

3. For the early period of Pan-Africanism see Colin Legum, *Pan-Africanism: A Short Political Guide* (New York, 1962), pp. 13–37; George Padmore, *Pan-Africanism or Communism* (London, 1956), pp. 105–185; American Society of African Culture (AMSAC), *Pan-Africanism Reconsidered* (Berkeley, 1962), pp. 33–78; Kwame Nkrumah, *Ghana, The Autobiography of Kwame Nkrumah* (New York, 1957), pp. 40–52; Vernon McKay, *Africa in World Politics* (New York, 1963), pp. 93–125; George Shepperson, "Pan-Africanism and 'Pan-Africanism': Some Historical Notes," *Phylon*, 23:346–358 (1962); Philippe Decraene, *Le Pan-Africanisme* (Paris, 1959).

4. *East African Standard*, October 24, 1945.

5. Interviews: Gichuru, July 15, 1963; Mboya, July 29, 1963; Mwanjisi, February 20, 1963; Nyerere, February 13, 1963.

6. See J. S. Nye, "Attitudes of Makerere Students towards East African Federation," *Proceedings of the East African Institute of Social Research, 1963* (Kampala, 1963). Similar results were obtained from interviews with thirty civil servants taking a "refresher" course at Makerere in 1962.

7. Quotations in this section not otherwise cited are from interviews by the author.

8. "The Task Ahead of Our African Trade Unions," *Labour* (Accra), June 1961, p. 28.

9. *East African Standard*, October 18, 1963.

10. *The Second Scramble* (Dar es Salaam, 1962).

11. *Uganda Argus,* August 15, 1959.

12. *Ibid.,* April 29, 1963.

13. Julius Nyerere, in *Labour,* June 1961.

14. *Democracy and the Party System* (Dar es Salaam, 1963), p. 7.

15. Nkrumah, *Ghana,* p. vii.

16. Nyerere, *Democracy and the Party System,* p. 24.

17. *Tanganyika Standard,* April 23, 1961.

18. *East African Standard,* January 9, 1945; *Uganda Argus,* November 26, 1960.

19. *Uganda Argus,* February 3, 1960.

20. See K. M. Barbour and R. M. Prothero, *Essays on African Population* (London, 1961), p. 322.

21. "Pan-African Unity and the N.F.D. Question in Kenya," a memorandum by the Kenya delegation to the African Summit Conference, Addis Ababa, 1963.

22. See Lucian Pye, *Politics, Personality and Nation-Building* (New Haven, 1962), p. 38; W. R. Bascom, "Tribalism, Nationalism and Pan-Africanism," *Annals of the American Academy of Political and Social Science,* 342:26 (July 1962); I. Wallerstein, "Ethnicity and National Integration in West Africa," *Cahiers d'études africaines,* no. 3 (1960), pp. 129–139.

23. (Obote) *Proceedings of the Central Legislative Assembly,* November 28, 1962; (Nyerere) *The Second Scramble.*

24. (Obote) *Proceedings . . .*

25. Informal poll by the author, November 1963.

26. "Kenya and Pan-Africanism," *Spearhead* (Dar es Salaam), April/May 1963, p. 14.

27. Tanganyika Information Service Press Release, March 16, 1962.

28. *Reporter* (Nairobi), June 8, 1963.

29. (Senghor) "What is Negritude?" *West Africa,* November 4, 1961; Legum, *Pan-Africanism,* p. 33.

30. Juan Comas, *Racial Myths* (Paris, UNESCO, 1958), p. 49. See also J. S. Nye, "Civil Rights for Whites," *New Republic,* October 24, 1964, pp. 5–6.

31. Ali Mazrui, "On the Concept of 'We are all Africans,'" *American Political Science Review,* 57–91 (March 1963).

32. Memorandum on "Pan-African Unity and the N.F.D. Question in Kenya" (see above, n. 21).

33. *The Second Scramble*, and *Ujamaa: The Basis of African Socialism* (Dar es Salaam, 1962).

34. *Pan-Africa* (Nairobi), September 20, 1963; "Federation," a paper for the University of East Africa Public Policy Conference, November 1963.

35. *East African Standard*, August 11 and 21, 1962.

36. "Address to the African Summit Conference," Addis Ababa, May 1963.

37. *Tanganyika Standard*, February 4, 1963.

38. *Freedom and After* (London, 1963), p. 235.

39. See Padmore, *Pan-Africanism or Communism*, pp. 18–22; Legum, *Pan-Africanism*, pp. 38–39; McKay, *Africa in World Politics*, pp. 93ff.

40. D. A. Low, *Political Parties in Uganda: 1949–62* (London, 1962), pp. 50–51.

41. Interview, June 10, 1963.

42. Interview, April 26, 1963.

43. Interview, July 25, 1963.

44. R. Bauer, A. Inkeles, and C. Kluckhohn, *How the Soviet System Works* (New York, 1960), pp. 35–38.

45. Hans Gerth and C. W. Mills, eds., *From Max Weber* (New York, 1946), p. 63. It is difficult to point to a single individual as the originator of Pan-Africanism—one reason, perhaps, for its diffuseness.

CHAPTER III: SOCIAL INTEGRATION

1. Elspeth Huxley, *White Man's Country* (London, 1953), II, 201. The "closer union" movement of the 1920's is discussed in Chapter IV.

2. Karl Deutsch, "Social Mobilization and Political Development," *American Political Science Review*, 55:493 (September 1961).

3. Carl G. Rosberg with Aaron Segal, "An East African Federation," *International Conciliation*, No. 543 (May 1963), p. 7; see also Anthony Darby, "East Africa: The Case for Federation," *New Commonwealth*, March 1961, p. 144.

4. Of course, the three countries are all in Eastern Africa and are part of the series of plateaux known as "High Africa" but this they share with others. Incidentally, Lake Victoria was an underutilized common feature. Trade on the lake in 1961 was only half the tonnage handled by the Kampala railway station alone. See Anthony M.

Notes to Chapter III

O'Connor, "Rail Transport in the Economic Geography of Uganda," unpub. diss., Cambridge University, 1963, pp. 94, 112.

5. E. S. Munger, *Relational Patterns of Kampala, Uganda* (Chicago, 1951), p. 98.

6. S. J. K. Baker, "The East African Environment" in Roland Oliver and Gervase Mathew, eds., *History of East Africa* (Oxford, 1963), I, 20–21.

7. J. E. Goldthorpe, *Outlines of East African Society* (Kampala, 1962), pp. 11–18, 285; Dennis Lury, "Brief Statistical Background to East African Federation," Paper for the University of East Africa Conference on Public Policy, November 1963, p. 2.

8. International Bank for Reconstruction and Development (henceforth IBRD), *The Economic Development of Kenya* (Nairobi, 1962), p. 163.

9. Government of Kenya, *Economic Survey 1963* (Nairobi, 1963). p. 4. *East Africa and Rhodesia*, January 28, 1965, p. 363.

10. A. W. Southall, "East African Population Movements," in K. M. Barbour and R. M. Prothero, eds., *Essays on African Population* (London, 1961), p. 182.

11. These are the figures given in East Africa Office, *East Africa Information Digest* (London, 1962), p. 13; for details see also J. E. Goldthorpe and F. B. Wilson, *Tribal Maps of East Africa and Zanzibar* (Kampala, 1960), pp. 1–10.

12. I am indebted to D. J. Parkin for information on the urban population of Kampala and to Roger Scott for information on trade unionists. See also Cyril and Rhona Sofer, *Jinja Transformed* (Kampala, 1955), p. 20.

13. Quoted in *Africa Diary*, April 28, 1962, p. 525.

14. For the resolution on Swahili, I am indebted to Dr. C. J. Gertzel for notes on the Uganda People's Congress Annual Conference, August 1962.

15. Uganda, *Proceedings of the Legislative Council*, June 7 and 8, 1960.

16. Milton Obote, interview, April 30, 1963; John Babiiha, interview, May 3, 1963; Godfrey Binaisa, interview, April 26, 1963.

17. Achieng Oneko, interview, July 25, 1963.

18. See *East African Standard*, October 15, 1958. Also, W. H. Whiteley, "Language and Politics in East Africa," *Tanganyika Notes and Records*, June and September 1957, pp. 159–173.

19. Uganda, *Enumeration of Employees, June 1961* (Entebbe, 1962); Tanganyika, *Annual Report of the Labour Division 1961* (Dar es Salaam, 1962); Kenya, *Labour Department Annual Report 1960* (Nairobi, 1961).

20. Uganda, *Enumeration of Employees;* Uganda Protectorate, *Report on African Employees, 1951.*

21. Tanganyika, *Annual Report of the Labour Division, 1961.*

22. P. H. Gulliver, *Labour Migration in a Rural Economy* (Kampala, 1955), p. i.

23. Joint Select Committee on Closer Union in East Africa, *vol. I —Report* (London, 1931), p. 14.

24. EACSO, *Economic and Statistical Review,* June 1963, Table D 16.

25. *Ibid.,* Table K 3.

26. David Walker, "The Economic Development of East Africa," Paper delivered at the International Economic Association Conference, Addis Ababa, July 1961; Uganda Government, *Background to the Budget 1963–64* (Entebbe, 1963), Table 30.

27. IBRD, *Economic Development of Kenya,* p. 106.

28. Walker, "Economic Development of East Africa (see above, n. 26).

29. Tanganyika Government, *Statistical Abstract—1962* (Dar es Salaam, 1962), Table E 3.

30. IBRD (See above, n. 27), p. 106.

31. *Report of the Commission on Closer Union of the Dependencies in Eastern and Central Africa,* Cmnd. 3234 (London, 1929), p. 315.

32. Kenya, *Economic Survey,* Tables 10 and 12.

33. IBRD (see above, n. 27), p. 106.

34. For the growth of interterritorial trade, see Chapter V.

35. Kenya, *Economic Survey,* p. 6.

36. By Greater East Africa I mean countries bordering the three East African states of Kenya, Uganda, and Tanganyika. See Benton F. Massell, *East African Economic Union: An Evaluation and Some Implications for Policy* (RAND Memorandum RM-3880-RC, Santa Monica, 1963), p. 70.

37. See, for instance, Aiden Southall, *Social Change in Modern Africa* (London, 1961), p. 1.

38. The figures in the table may underestimate the number of per-

sons in Kampala, Uganda; but it is still the least urbanized of the three countries.

39. A. G. Dalgleish, *Survey of Unemployment* (Nairobi, 1960), pp. 3–5.

40. *Ibid.*, p. 21.

41. Kenya, *Economic Survey*, pp. 31–32. In February 1964 the Kenya government announced a plan to create 40,000 jobs. The government would increase its staff 15 per cent and private employers would increase theirs by 10 per cent. By the middle of March 15,000 persons gained employment through the plan but another 120,000 still sought jobs. *East African Standard*, March 17, 1964.

42. Sir Richard Turnbull quoted in *Uganda Argus,* December 15, 1962.

43. Walker, "Economic Development of East Africa" (see above, n. 26); see also M. F. Hill, *Permanent Way* (Nairobi, 1949); and "Development of Uganda's Communications," *Spear* (Nairobi), 5:244–250 (October 1962).

44. Kenya, *Statistical Abstract 1962* (Nairobi, 1962), Table 54.

45. *Ibid.*, p. 58; Uganda, *1962 Statistical Abstract*, p. 38; Tanganyika, *Statistical Abstract—1962*, p. 61.

46. *Development Plan for Tanganyika 1961/62–1963/64* (Dar es Salaam, 1962), p. 14.

47. Lury, "Brief Statistical Background to East African Federation," p. 1.

48. Kenya and Uganda, *Postal and Telecommunications Report 1926.*

49. Kenya, Uganda and Tanganyika, *Annual Report of Postal and Telecommunications Departments, 1933.*

50. Uganda, *Information and Broadcasting Department Report, 1960.*

51. Tanganyika Broadcasting Corporation, *Annual Report 1961;* Tanganyika Information Service, "Tanganyika Fact Sheets," No. 5.

52. Interview, Public Relations Director, Kenya Broadcasting Corporation, December 5, 1963.

53. M. L. Bates, "Tanganyika under British Administration, 1920–55," unpub diss., Oxford University 1956, p. 521.

54. Interview, Circulation Manager, *East African Standard,* July 29, 1963.

55. Helen Kitchen (ed.), *The Educated African* (London, 1962),

pp. 145ff, 326ff, 364ff; IBRD, *The Economic Development of Uganda* (Entebbe, 1961), pp. 272ff.

56. J. E. Goldthorpe, "Makerere Students: Studies in the Social Origins and Formation of an Educated African Elite," unpub. diss., London University 1961, p. 88.

57. J. E. Goldthorpe and Margaret Macpherson, "Makerere College and its Old Students," *Zaire*, 12:356 (1958).

58. This does not include disintegrative trends which were deliberate political decisions, such as repatriation of Kenyans in the Uganda police force in 1963, or dismissal of mainland Africans from the Zanzibar police force, or banning of certain Kenya papers from entering Tanganyika for several months in 1964.

CHAPTER IV: POLITICAL INTEGRATION

1. On community, see C. J. Friedrich, "The Concept of Community in the History of Political and Legal Philosophy," and John Ladd, "The Concept of Community: A Logical Analysis" in C. J. Friedrich, ed., *Community* (New York, 1959), pp. 3–24 and 269–293.

2. Quoted in *Reporter* (Nairobi), June 8, 1963.

3. See K. C. Wheare, *Federal Government*, 3rd ed. (London, 1953), pp. 46–49.

4. See the next section.

5. Ronald Robinson, John Gallagher, with Alice Denny, *Africa and the Victorians* (New York, 1961), pp. 283–289.

6. Roland Oliver, *Sir Harry Johnston and the Scramble for Africa* (New York, 1958), pp. 335–337; Kenneth Ingham, *A History of East Africa* (London, 1962), pp. 207–208.

7. Ingham, *A History of East Africa*, pp. 208, 212; J. E. Goldthorpe, *Outlines of East African Society* (Kampala, 1962), p. 129; Marjorie Ruth Dilley, *British Policy in Kenya Colony* (New York, 1937), pp. 36ff.

8. Kenneth Ingham, *The Making of Modern Uganda* (London, 1957), pp. 102, 105.

9. For detailed treatments, see Donald Rothchild, *Toward Unity in Africa* (Washington, 1960), chaps. 2–5; Bernard Chidzero, *Tanganyika and International Trusteeship* (London, 1961), chaps. 2 and 3; M. R. Dilley, *British Policy in Kenya Colony*, pts. 2 and 3; Margery Perham, *Lugard: The Years of Authority* (London, 1960), pp. 674–

693; Robert Rotberg, "An Account of the Attempt to Achieve Closer Union in British East Africa," *Proceedings of the East African Institute* (Kampala, 1963).

10. Leopold Amery, *My Political Life*, 2 vols. (London, 1954), II, 360.

11. *Report of the East African Commission*, Cmnd. 2387 (London, 1925), p. 3; see also Margery Perham and Elspeth Huxley, *Race and Politics in Kenya* (London, 1956), pp. 156, 159; a report of a Governor's Conference in *East African Standard*, February 14, 1947; and *Proceedings of the Central Legislative Assembly*, January 19, 1950.

12. Colonial Office, *Central African Rail Link* (London, 1953), I, 43.

13. Cmnd. 2387 (see above, n. 11), pp. 7, 8.

14. Lord Altrincham, *Kenya's Opportunity* (London, 1955), pp. 71, 191.

15. *Papers Relating to the Question of the Closer Union of Kenya, Uganda and the Tanganyika Territory*, Colonial No. 57 (London, 1931), p. 2.

16. Dilley, *British Rule in Kenya Colony*, p. 58; Elspeth Huxley, *White Man's Country* (London, 1954), II, 84, 198.

17. *Report of the Commission on Closer Union of the Dependencies in Eastern and Central Africa*, Cmnd. 3234 (London, 1929).

18. *Report of Sir Samuel Wilson on His Visit to East Africa*, Cmnd. 3378 (London, 1929).

19. George Bennett, "Paramountcy to Partnership: J. H. Oldham and Africa," *Africa*, 30:359 (October, 1960).

20. Joint Select Committee on Closer Union in East Africa, *Report* (London, 1931); *East African Standard*, November 26, 1931.

21. Cmnd. 3234 (see above, n. 17), p. 9.

22. John Ainsworth quoted in Keith Sorrenson, "The Official Mind and Kikuyu Land Tenure, 1895–1939," *Proceedings of the East African Institute* (Kampala, 1963).

23. Sir Philip Mitchell, *African Afterthoughts* (London, 1954), p. 186; Ingham, *Making of Modern Uganda*, p. 220.

24. Mitchell, p. 214.

25. Ingham, p. 234; E. M. K. Mulira, interview, June 10, 1963; Francis Khamisi, interview, July 18, 1963.

26. The capitulation was thinly disguised. Three of the four members to be chosen by each Legislative Council were to be of the three

races while the fourth would be chosen to represent the whole Council. Since Europeans prevailed in the Councils, the practice would be racial inequality.

27. Electors Union of Kenya, "An Outline of Policy" (1946), p. 37; *East African Standard,* March 7, 14, and 21, 1947. Among Africans "210" became a bad word and the subject of protest telegrams sent by KAU. Even in 1951, Mathu referred to "paper 210 which many Kikuyu go about saying is bad." *East African Standard,* April 25, 1947, February 9, 1951.

28. J. C. Mundy, Finance Member, quoted in *East Africa and Rhodesia,* April 5, 1956, p. 1080.

29. Quoted in *Uganda Argus,* June 24, 1963.

30. *East African Standard,* December 21 and 23, 1961; Martin Shikuku quoted in *Sunday Nation* (Nairobi), April 14, 1963.

31. *Reporter* (Nairobi), June 15, 1963; *East African Standard,* October 2, 1958.

32. Letter to *Manchester Guardian,* March 18, 1930.

33. *East African Standard,* October 2, 1958.

34. See H. M. Basner, "The Beginning," *Spearhead* (Dar es Salaam), December 1961, p. 9; *East African Standard,* January 29, 1957.

35. *East African Standard,* February 10, 1955; Uganda National Congress, "Minutes of Meeting at Budonian Club," Kampala, March 7 and 8, 1953.

36. UNC telegrams in *East African Standard* files; *East African Standard,* September 29, 1953; Neal Ascherson, "The Uganda National Congress," unpublished paper in files of East African Institute of Social Research; George Shepherd, *They Wait in Darkness* (New York, 1955), p. 257.

37. There were also earlier contacts between Kenyatta and Ignatius Musazi and Semakula Mulumba of Uganda, and several Kenyans recall visits to the KAU offices by Ugandans and Tanganyikans. Later, at least two Uganda politicians, Milton Obote and Cuthbert Obwangor, participated in Kenya nationalist politics.

38. James Gichuru, interview, July 15, 1963; Francis Khamisi, interview, July 18, 1963; Francis Khamisi, "The East African Political Scene: the African Viewpoint," *African Affairs,* 45:139–141 (January 1946).

39. Margaret Bates, "Tanganyika under British Administration,

1920–55," unpub. diss., Oxford University, 1956, p. 334; George Bennett, "An Outline History of Tanu," *Makerere Journal,* no. 7 (1962), p. 16.

40. Khamisi, interview, July 18, 1963.

41. *The Origins and Growth of Mau Mau: An Historical Survey* (Corfield Report), Sessional Paper No. 5 of 1959/60 (Nairobi, 1960), p. 58; Bildad Kaggia, interview, July 17, 1963; Achieng Oneko, interview, July 25, 1963; Mbiyu Koinange, interview, July 28, 1963.

42. *Uganda Argus,* April 10, 1962.

43. See Ralph Austen, "Indirect Rule in a Tanganyika Province," *Proceedings of the East African Institute* (Kampala, 1963).

44. Bates, "Tanganyika under British Administration," p. 325.

45. *Uganda Argus,* April 10, 1962.

46. Cranford Pratt, "Multi-racialism and Local Government in Tanganyika," *Race,* 2:46 (November 1960).

47. See Martin Lowenkopf, "Political Parties in Uganda and Tanganyika," unpub. diss., London University, 1961, pp. 149ff; Margaret Bates, "Tanganyika" in Gwendolen Carter, ed., *African One-Party States* (Ithaca, N. Y., 1962), p. 415.

48. Bennett, "Outline History of Tanu," p. 19; Lowenkopf, "Political Parties in Uganda and Tanganyika."

49. *Sauti Ya Tanu,* No. 9 (Dar es Salaam, April 1957).

50. At this same time Nyerere first began to temper his original opposition to East African federation and to think favorably of it as an African policy—a reflection of Tanu's growing strength. Julius Nyerere, interview, February 13, 1963.

51. *East African Standard,* January 27, 1958.

52. Lowenkopf, "Political Parties in Uganda and Tanganyika," p. 198. Although Tanu could build on cooperatives and tribal associations, it differed from the nationalist movements in Kenya and Uganda in not having had the ground prepared for it by separatist religious movement or ex-servicemen's leagues. I am indebted to Margaret Bates for this point.

53. See R. E. S. Tanner, "Local Government Elections in Ngara, Tanganyika," *Proceedings of the East African Institute* (Kampala, 1962).

54. E. A. Kisenge, interview, March 5, 1963.

55. *Uganda Argus,* April 10, 1962.

56. Pratt, "Multi-racialism and Local Government in Tanganyika," p. 46.

57. *Tanganyika Standard,* December 9, 1961; E. A. Kisenge, interview, March 5, 1963; T. A. K. Msonge (Acting Deputy Secretary-General), interview, March 2, 1963. Membership figures include all people who have at one time or another bought Tanu cards, not who paid their dues regularly. Lowenkopf estimated the latter at between 15 and 35 per cent of the membership in 1960. I found some evidence that this became lower after independence. J. B. George reported that the party had 450,000 dues-paying members in late 1962. "How Stable is Tanganyika?" *Africa Report,* 8:15 (March 1963).

58. Nyerere announced Tanu's intention to make itself the single legal party in January 1963, but action was withheld so as not to jeopardize the federal negotiations. When it was clear that the negotiations had failed, the government took up the single-party plan again. *East African Standard,* December 4, 1963; for party decline and details of Tanu party structure, see J. S. Nye, "The Impact of Independence on Two Nationalist Parties," in J. Butler, ed., *Papers in African Politics* (Boston University Press, to be published).

59. Economist Intelligence Unit, *Uganda: Background to Investment* (1962), p. 55.

60. D. A. Low and R. C. Pratt, *Bugunda and British Over-rule* (London, 1960), p. 274; F. B. Welbourn, *East African Rebels* (London, 1961), pp. 21–22.

61. Low and Pratt, *Bugunda and British Over-Rule,* p. 259.

62. David Apter, *The Political Kingdom in Uganda* (Princeton, 1961), p. 4.

63. John Stonehouse, *Prohibited Immigrant* (London, 1960), p. 107.

64. The Colonial government had to include a promise that "federation is outside the realm of practical politics at the present time or while public opinion remains as it is . . ." in the 1955 agreement concerning the Kabaka's return. *The Buganda Agreement,* 1955 (Entebbe, 1955, p. 3.

65. Ascherson, "The Uganda National Congress"; Lowenkopf, "Political Parties in Uganda and Tanganyika," p. 49.

66. Ascherson, *ibid.*

67. D. A. Low, *Political Parties in Uganda, 1949–62* (London, 1962), p. 19.

68. Ascherson, "The Uganda National Congress."

69. See UNC, "Memorandum on Constitutional Reforms in Buganda," March 20, 1953, in files of *East African Standard.*

70. Low, *Political Parties in Uganda*, p. 25; Geoffrey Engholm, "Political Parties and Uganda's Independence," *Transition*, January 1962.

71. Welbourn, *East African Rebels*, and "Religion and Politics in Uganda," *Spearhead* (Dar es Salaam), September 1962.

72. Lowenkopf, "Political Parties in Uganda and Tanganyika"; Abu Mayanja, interview, April 25, 1963. I am also indebted to Dr. Cherry Gertzel for help on this point.

73. Lowenkopf, "Political Parties in Uganda and Tanganyika"; see also A. W. Southall, "Micropolitics in Uganda," *Proceedings of the East African Institute* (Kampala, 1963).

74. Low, *Political Parties in Uganda*, p. 46.

75. In 1960 the UPC stated "U.P.C. is strongly opposed to the political views of the Kabaka's Government . . . ," *U.P.C. Voice* (n.d.).

76. Interviews, E. M. K. Mulira, June 10, 1963; Amos Sempa, April 26, 1963; J. S. L. Zake, May 10, 1963.

77. I am indebted to Dr. Gertzel for help on this point. See also C. J. Gertzel, "How Kabaka Yekka Came to Be," *Africa Report*, October 1964, pp. 9–13.

78. *Uganda Argus*, May 21, 1962.

79. Eriabu Lwebuga, interview, January 3, 1963.

80. Dr. S. J. L. Zake and others, *Fresh Political Approach in Buganda* (Kampala, 1963).

81. Not only were Baganda not integrated into the nationalist movement, but the popular association of their success with their monarchy led other areas to demand constitutional heads or monarchs of their own (even after independence); and led the Western kingdoms and Busoga to press for semifederal status in the independence constitution. Southall calls this the "pond-ripple effect" of Buganda. See Southall, "Micropolitics in Uganda." By the beginning of 1965, Kabaka Yekka had left the government and enough DP supporters had "crossed the floor" that Kabaka Yekka Baganda formed the core of the opposition.

82. See Bethwell A. Ogot, "British Administration in the Central Nyanza District of Kenya, 1900–60," *Journal of African History*, 4:266 (1963). I am also indebted to Carl Rosberg for help on this point.

83. Margery Perham uses the first figure in *Race and Politics. . . ,* p. 54; Robert Rotberg gives the second figure in "The Rise of African Nationalism: the Case of East and Central Africa," *World Politics,*

15:80 (October 1962). See also Martin Kilson, "Land and Politics in Kenya: An Analysis of African Politics in a Plural Society," *Western Political Quarterly*, September 1957, pp. 559–581.

84. George Bennett, "The Development of Political Organizations in Kenya," *Political Studies*, 5:113–130 (June 1957).

85. Quoted in *The Daily Worker* (London), January 20, 1930.

86. W. M. Ross, *Kenya From Within* (London, 1927), p. 228.

87. Ogot, "British Administration . . ." (see above, n. 82), p. 261; J. M. Lonsdale, "Archdeacon Owen and the Kavirondo Taxpayers Welfare Association," *Proceedings of the East African Institute* (Kampala, 1963).

88. Bennett, "The Development of Political Organizations . . ." p. 121; Corfield Report, p. 47.

89. Francis Khamisi, interview, July 18, 1963.

90. *Ibid.*, and interviews, J. D. Otiende and Bildad Kaggia, July 17, 1963; Achieng Oneko, July 25, 1963.

91. Oginga Odinga, interview, July 18, 1963; KAU Kisumu Branch, "Minutes of Meeting, June 7, 1951" in files of *E. A. Standard*.

92. Of nine KAU officers in 1951, two were Kikuyu, two Kamba, two Luhya, one Luo, one Masai, and one from the Coast; but the Executive Committee was overwhelmingly Kikuyu. *East African Standard*, November 9, 1951; Corfield Report, p. 61.

93. Corfield Report, p. 316.

94. For instance, F. B. Welbourn, "Comment on Corfield," *Race*, May 1961; Montague Slater, *The Trial of Jomo Kenyatta* (London, 1955); George Delf, *Jomo Kenyatta* (London, 1961).

95. Josiah Mwangi Kariuki, '*Mau Mau*' *Detainee* (London, 1963), pp. 22–24, 34–36; Corfield Report, p. 260.

96. *Ibid.*, p. 168.

97. See "Open Letter to the Labour, Conservative and Liberal Parties," October 7, 1951; and texts of speeches by Tom Mbotela and Bildad Kaggia in the files of the *E. A. Standard*.

98. Tom Mboya, *Freedom and After* (London, 1963), p. 35.

99. G. F. Engholm, "African Elections in Kenya, March 1957" in W. J. M. MacKenzie and Kenneth Robinson, eds., *Five Elections in Africa* (Oxford, 1960), pp. 429ff.

100. The five groups were the Kalenjin Political Alliance, the Masai United Front, the Kenya African People's Party (led by a Luhya, Masinde Muliro), the Coast African Political Union, and the Somali National Association. *Tanganyika Standard*, June 27, 1960.

Notes to Chapter IV

101. Quoted in Louis Lomax, *The Reluctant African* (New York, 1960), p. 79.

102. Letter in *The Economist*, September 8, 1962.

103. See *East African Standard*, September 26 and November 28, 1960; *ibid.*, February 14 and August 9, 1961.

104. *Ibid.*, December 21 and 23, 1961.

105. *Ibid.*, August 12, 21, and 25, 1962; *Daily Nation*, August 15 and 18, 1962.

106. As one Kanu official put it, "Ngei's African People's Party was the best thing that ever happened to Kanu." The Kamba returned to the Kanu fold a few months after the 1963 election.

107. George Bennett and Carl Rosberg, *The Kenyatta Election* (London, 1961), p. 188; Clyde Sanger and John Nottingham, "The Kenya General Election of 1963," *Journal of Modern African Studies*, 2: 1–40 (March 1964).

108. Godfrey Binaisa, interview, April 26, 1963; Oscar Kambona, interview, March 1, 1963; Tom Mboya quoted in *East African Standard*, September 26, 1958. This section is based both on interviews and the Pafmeca files.

109. *Uganda Argus*, September 23, 1958.

110. See Mwanza Minutes, Second Day (September 17, 1958), Pafmeca files.

111. Interviews with Jeremiah Bakempenja, March 9, 1963; T. A. K. Msonge, March 2, 1963.

112. "Summary of Pafmeca Accounts, 13/9/1958–31/8/1959" in Pafmeca files.

113. "Constitution of Pafmeca" (mimeographed, 1958).

114. Minutes of Moshi Meeting in Pafmeca files; also *Tanganyika Standard*, September 8, 1959.

115. Mboya won by 38 votes to 23. See *Uganda Argus*, October 22, 27, 1960; Democratic Party, *Weekly News Bulletin*, Nos. 21 and 22 (October 22 and November 5, 1960).

116. See correspondence between Getachew Mekasha and Mbiyu Koinange in Pafmeca files. The matter was probably also discussed at an unofficial meeting of several Pafmeca leaders in Dar es Salaam in October 1961.

117. *Pan-African Freedom Movement for East, Central and Southern Africa* (published by the Africa Department of the Foreign Office, Addis Ababa, for and on behalf of the PAFMECA Secretariat).

118. Tom Mboya, interview, July 29, 1963.
119. *Pan-African Freedom Movement*, pp. 81–82.
120. Letter, October 14, 1961, in Pafmeca files.
121. Mbiyu Koinange, interviews, January 29 and February 23, 1963.
122. Milton Obote, interview, April 30, 1963.
123. Interviews with Jeremiah Bakempenja, March 9, 1963; Grace Ibingira, April 29, 1963; Michael Kamaliza, March 1, 1963. It is interesting that Adoko Nekyon, who expressed Uganda's objections during the 1963 federal negotiations was not an old Pafmeca figure.

CHAPTER V: ECONOMIC INTEGRATION

1. A shortened version of this chapter was published in the *Journal of Modern African Studies*, vol. I, no. 4 (Cambridge University Press, 1963), under the title "East African Economic Integration."
2. *Nigerian Daily Times* quoted in *Uganda Argus*, July 13, 1961.
3. By economic integration I mean a process which increases division of labor among a group—in this case, a group of nations. This is similar to the definition given by Bela Balassa in *The Theory of Economic Integration* (London, 1962), i.e., the abolition of "discrimination between economic units belonging to different national states" (p. 1).
4. See *The Future of the East Africa High Commission Services* (London, 1961), Cmnd. 1433.
5. Zanzibar was not a member of EACSO, although she participated in certain services—primarily, Income Tax Collection, the Directorate of Civil Aviation, the Meteorological Department, and the Marine Fisheries Research Organisation. She applied for full membership in 1962, but her application had not been accepted by the time she was invited to join the Working Party on Federation in July 1963.
6. *Tanganyika Parliamentary Debates*, October 10, 1961.
7. EACSO, *Report of the Africanisation Commission* (Nairobi, 1963), p. 4. Expatriate here refers to a person who is not a citizen of an East African country. During the course of the year, however, Africanization became much more rapid.
8. Lord Hailey, *An African Survey. Revised 1956* (Oxford, 1957), p. 189.

9. Uganda, *Proceedings of the Legislative Council*, September 21, 1959.

10. See further in Chapter VI.

11. *Proceedings of the Central Legislative Assembly*, vol. I, no. 1.

12. *Tanganyika Parliamentary Debates*, October 10, 1961.

13. EACSO, *Annual Report, 1962* (Nairobi); East African Airways Corporation, *Report and Accounts, 1962* (Nairobi).

14. Similarly, the assets of the Desert Locust Survey were transferred to the new Desert Locust Control Organisation for East Africa, with headquarters in Ethiopia, under an arrangement negotiated early in 1962.

15. *East African Standard*, July 2, 1963; *Report of the Africanisation Commission*, p. 4; EACSO, *1963–64 Estimates* (Nairobi).

16. East African High Commission, *A Decade of Service* (Nairobi, 1958).

17. J. T. Simpson in *Uganda Argus*, April 1, 1960.

18. *Proceedings of the E. A. High Commission*, 29th Meeting, November 26, 1959.

19. *East Africa, Report of the Economic and Fiscal Commission* (London, 1961), Cmnd. 1279.

20. Britain provided another quarter; private foundations and the East African governments made up the rest. This contrasted with 1959–60 when territorial grants constituted seven-ninths of EACSO's revenue.

21. Uganda Protectorate, *Executive Council Minutes*, 109th Meeting, January 24, 1961.

22. Uganda, *Proceedings of the Legislative Council*, May 16, 1961; Kenya, *Legislative Council Debates*, May 16, and July 6, 1961.

23. Cmnd. 1279, p. 7; also quoted in International Bank for Reconstruction and Development, *The Economic Development of Uganda* (Baltimore, 1961), p. 68. Restrictions on the movement of certain agricultural goods were the most important deviations in East Africa in 1963. There were also restrictions on the re-export of certain Japanese goods from Kenya. In 1964 the East African leaders authorized a departure from the common market principle in the form of quotas between the East African countries.

24. J. Loynes in *Tanganyika Standard*, November 4, 1960; *The Present Monetary System and its Future* (Dar es Salaam, 1963); Interviews with Treasury officials, November 1963. Subsequently,

in the spring of 1964, Tanganyika hinted publicly that it might establish a separate currency.

25. Jacob Viner, *The Customs Union Issue* (New York, 1950), pp. 44 and 70. This kind of analysis was of limited value in East Africa since it assumed full employment of resources and comparisons were difficult because there had been no separate entities since 1927.

26. Cmnd. 1279, pp. 17 and 19; T. A. Kennedy, "The East African Customs Union: Some Features of its History and Operation," in *Makerere Journal*, no. 3 (1959), pp. 14ff.

27. P. K. Lomas, "The Report of the East Africa Economic and Fiscal Commission," *The East African Economics Review*, 8:17 (June 1961).

28. IBRD, *The Economic Development of Tanganyika* (Baltimore, 1960), p. 238; see also, Michael Safier, "Industrial Location and Economic Integration in East Africa," (University of East Africa Conference Paper, Nairobi, 1963).

29. Sir Frederick Crawford, *Association of Chambers of Commerce and Industry of Eastern Africa, 1961 (Kampala) Session* (Nairobi), p. 5.

30. Colony and Protectorate of Kenya and Uganda Protectorate, *Annual Trade Report, 1922;* Tanganyika Territory, *Tanganyika Trade Report, 1922; Tanganyika Statistical Abstract, 1938–51*, pp. 17 and 18; EACSO, *Economic and Statistical Review*, June 1963, Table D 19.

31. Ian Stewart, "Customs Union in East and Central Africa," *Scottish Journal of Political Economy*, February 1962.

32. A. J. Brown, "Economic Separatism versus a Common Market in Developing Countries," *Yorkshire Bulletin of Economic and Social Research*, May 1961, pp. 38ff; B. F. Massell, "Industrialization and Economic Union in Greater East Africa," *The East African Economics Review*, December 1962; see also articles by D. Walker and J. D. Nyhart in *The East African Economics Review*, vol. 6, nos. 1 and 2 (1959), concerning the limited industrial opportunities in Uganda alone.

33. C. P. Haddon-Cave, "Real Growth of the East African Territories, 1954–1960," *The East African Economics Review*, June 1961, and ensuing notes; P. K. Lomas, "Report of the E. A. Economic and Fiscal Commission."

34. *East African Standard*, May 18, 1960. See also, for instance, the speeches of K. A. Abedi, A. E. Obone, and J. M. Okae in the

Notes to Chapter V

CLA, May 1962, and Joseph Nyerere in May 1963. Subsequently, a Makerere economist published a paper that can be used to support the beliefs. See D. Ghai, "Territorial Distribution of Benefits and Costs of the East African Common Market," *The East African Economics Review* 11:29–40 (June 1964).

35. A. J. Brown, "Customs Union versus Economic Separatism in Developing Countries," *Yorkshire Bulletin*, November 1961, p. 88.

36. H. W. Ord, "East African Companies," *The East African Economics Review*, 7:47 (June 1960); B. F. Massell, "Economic Union and Industrial Development in East Africa" (University of East Africa Conference Paper, Nairobi, 1963).

37. *The Economic Development of Kenya*, p. 106.

38. Cmnd. 1279, p. 25.

39. *The Economic Development of Uganda*, pp. 73–74.

40. *The Economic Development of Tanganyika*, pp. 133–134. In effect this advice was belatedly followed in 1964.

41. "The Economic Implications of East African Federation," Report by a United Nations Technical Assistance Mission to the Government of Tanganyika, June 1962, pp. 16–17.

42. E.g., statement by Dr. H. Schellenberg of CIBA in *Tanganyika Standard*, May 19, 1961.

43. T. A. Kennedy writing in the *Uganda Argus*, March 9, 1961.

44. A. Etzioni, "The Dialectics of Supranational Unification," *American Political Science Review*, 56:933 (December 1962).

45. *East Africa and Rhodesia* (London), September 20, 1962; *East African Standard*, May 26, 1962.

46. Cmnd. 1279, p. 29.

47. *East African Standard*, April 25, 1963.

48. *Proceedings of the Central Legislative Assembly*, May 3, 1963; *Tanganyika Standard*, March 6, 1963.

49. A. W. Southall, "Population Movements in East Africa," in K. M. Barbour, ed., *Essays on African Population* (London, 1961), p. 173; see also "The Economic Implications of East African Federation" (see above, no. 41); Uganda Protectorate, *Enumeration of Employees, June 1961* (Entebbe, 1962); Tanganyika, *Annual Report of the Labour Division* (Dar es Salaam, 1962).

50. *East African Standard*, May 13, 1963.

51. *Uganda Argus*, April 10, 1963.

52. Tanganyika Information Service Press Release, January 17, 1962.

53. *Sunday News* (Dar es Salaam), May 21, 1961.

54. *Proceedings of the Central Legislative Assembly,* August 28, 1962.

55. *E. A. High Commission,* 31st Meeting, November 23, 1960.

56. Kenya, *Legislative Council Debates,* July 16, 1961.

57. Tanganyika Information Service Press Release, December 15, 1961.

58. EACSO, *Annual Report,* 1962.

59. *East African Standard,* May 3, 1963.

60. *Uganda Argus,* February 16, 1963; *Proceedings of the Central Legislative Assembly,* May 8, 1963.

61. This explanation is not incompatible with the fact that EACSO had few executive powers. Even gathering and disseminating information involves decisions. One Ugandan once complained to me about the way "Nairobi" drew up the mailing list.

62. Chief Establishment Officer, interview, July 1963; *Uganda Argus,* June 11, and November 4, 1963.

63. *Proceedings of the Central Legislative Assembly,* May 23, 1962.

64. Kenya wished to develop the Tana River plant, in any case, because it disagreed with the economic calculations on which the IBRD recommendation was based.

65. Kenya, *Legislative Council Debates,* June 15, 1961.

66. *Uganda Argus,* June 6, 1962; Uganda, *Proceedings of the National Assembly,* July 30, 1962.

67. Notes on UPC Second Annual Conference, August 1962, by courtesy of Dr. C. J. Gertzel.

68. A. L. Adu, interview, May 22, 1963.

69. *Proceedings of the Central Legislative Assembly,* April 6, 1960.

CHAPTER VI: THE FAILURE TO FEDERATE IN 1963

1. *East African Standard,* June 17, 1960; Martin Lowenkopf, "Political Parties in Uganda and Tanganyika," unpub. thesis, London University, 1961, p. 134.

Opinion in Buganda was such that when the Katikiro wished to bar the president of the Democratic Party, Matayo Mugwanya, from a seat in the Lukiko, he did it on the pretext that Mugwanya was a member of the Transport Advisory Council of the High Commission. *East African Standard*, December 31, 1956.

See Kirya's election manifesto in *Uganda Argus*, October 15, 1958; also Uganda Protectorate, *Proceedings of the Legislative Council*, September 23, 1955.

2. Julius Nyerere, interview, February 13, 1963; Mboya quoted in Edwin S. Munger, *African Field Reports 1952–61* (Capetown, 1961), p. 273.

3. *Uganda Argus*, December 13, 1958; January 2, 1959.

4. Uganda Protectorate, *Proceedings of the Legislative Council*, September 1959; Democratic Party, "Manifesto" (mimeographed, April 1960); *Uganda Argus*, May 30, 1959; The one exceptional note in 1959 was a little-noticed statement by Nyerere in London predicting that some day East Africa would federate. *Ibid.*, August 7, 1959.

5. Amir Jamal, interview, November 30, 1962.

6. Interview, March 1, 1963.

7. *Tanganyika Legislative Council* (Hansard), May 17, 1960.

8. Michael Kamaliza, interview, March 1, 1963; Jacob Namfua, interview, March 6, 1963. Race was also a factor since the High Commission was associated with Kenya and settlers.

9. *Tanganyika Standard*, July 4 and 7, 1960; *East African Standard*, July 7, 1960.

10. Rashidi Kawawa, interview, March 4, 1963; Michael Kamaliza, interview, March 1, 1963.

11. *Tanganyika Standard*, August 2 and 29, 1960.

12. *Ibid.*, November 29, 1960, April 6, May 30, and October 11, 1961.

13. Interview, March 1, 1963.

14. Namfua, interview, March 6, 1963.

15. *Sunday News* (Dar es Salaam), May 21, 1961; Interview, March 1, 1963.

16. Julius Nyerere, *East African Federation: (Freedom and Unity)*, (expanded conference text reprinted by Pafmeca, Dar es Salaam, 1960).

17. *Uganda Argus*, June 17, 1960; *Tanganyika Standard*, June 17 and 22, 1960; *East African Standard*, June 24, 1960.

18. *Tanganyika Standard*, July 27, 1960. Another unexpected source of criticism which appeared somewhat later was an article by

the "Kanu office" in Cairo published in the Afro-Asian Solidarity Movement journal, *Afro-Asian Bulletin,* 3:12–17 (July–August 1961).

19. *Kanu Manifesto* (Nairobi, 1960), p. 3; Julius Nyerere, interview, February 13, 1963; *East African Standard,* November 23 and 24, 1960; *Uganda Argus,* January 11, 12, and 13, 1961.

20. *Uganda Argus,* January 14, 1961.

21. Interview, February 13, 1963; *Tanganyika Standard,* December 20, 1961.

22. *Uganda Argus,* December 21, 1961, January 11 and 21, 1962.

23. *Ibid.,* February 7, 1962.

24. *Ibid.,* November 14, 1962.

25. *Ibid.,* December 6, 1962; Ronald Ngala, interview, July 16, 1963; Rashidi Kawawa, interview, March 4, 1963; *Tanganyika Standard,* February 8, 1963.

26. *Uganda Argus,* December 12, 1962, January 4, 1963.

27. *Ibid.,* February 9 and 14, May 7, 1963.

28. *East African Standard,* May 2, 1963; Milton Obote, interview, April 30, 1963.

29. Kenya, House of Representatives, *Official Report,* June 27, 1963.

30. *Uganda Argus,* July 3, 1963.

31. *East African Standard,* June 6, 1963. A year later Obote emphasized the independence rather than the federal aspect of the resolution while also maintaining that he was not against federation. *Uganda Argus,* June 27, 1964.

32. See Chapter VII.

33. *Reporter* (Nairobi), June 8, 1963.

34. *Uganda Nation,* June 11, 1963.

35. *Uganda Argus,* June 14, 1963. Obote was then in America.

36. *East African Standard,* June 15, 1963.

37. An Ethiopian observer also attended this meeting.

38. *East African Standard,* July 2, 1963; *Uganda Argus,* July 3, 1963.

39. Adoko Nekyon, Obote's cousin and the politician who earlier handled the negative side of Obote's relations with Buganda, was appointed head of the Uganda delegation to the Working Party during the Kampala session. Nsilo Swai replaced Amir Jamal for Tanganyika at the Nairobi session.

40. Uganda Parliamentary Debates (Hansard), July 12, 1963; *East African Standard,* July 22 and 23, 1963.

41. *East African Standard,* July 23 and August 3, 1963; *Uganda Nation,* July 25, 1963.

42. *Uganda Argus,* August 13, 1963; *Uganda Nation,* August 21, 1963.

43. *East African Standard,* August 19, 1963; *Uganda Argus,* August 20 and 21, 1963.

44. *East African Standard,* September 14, 1963.

45. Obote pleaded ill health but this did not prevent him from seeing politicians in Kampala.

46. *East African Standard,* September 20, 1963.

47. Julius Nyerere, interview, February 13, 1963; *East African Standard,* September 24, 1963. By May 1964, Nyerere was willing to accept the idea of a two-nation federation proposed by a meeting of Kenya and Tanganyika back-benchers on the grounds that some sacrifice of sovereignty would be better for Pan-Africanism than none. Kenyatta reproached the Kenyans for the idea of leaving Uganda out, maintaining his hope of a workable compromise. *Reporter* (Nairobi), May 22, 1964.

48. Grace Ibingira, interview, October 31, 1963.

49. The press had speculated that the choice of Sir Geoffrey de Freitas as High Commissioner to Kenya meant that he would also be High Commissioner to the federation. *East African Standard,* October 11, 1963.

50. *Uganda Nation,* October 18, 21, and 24, 1963.

51. *Uganda Argus,* October 25, 26, and 30, 1963.

52. *Uganda Parliamentary Debates (Hansard),* November 4, 1963.

53. This section is based on interviews granted, on condition of anonymity, by Working Party members and others participating in the 1963 negotiations. Readers will have to trust my judgment of the reliability of sources. Sources which are less reliable are indicated as such in the text.

54. *Sunday Nation* (Nairobi), August 25, September 22, 1963; *Uganda Argus,* October 7, 1963.

55. "The Economic Implications of East African Federation: Report by a United Nations Technical Assistance Mission to the Government of Tanganyika" (1962), p. 7.

56. Kenya, House of Representatives, *Official Report*, November 27, 1963.

57. See also Obote's statement in *Uganda Argus*, October 26, 1963, and Kambona's disclosure of differences in *ibid.*, June 3, 1964. Nekyon was using the Addis Charter to justify Uganda's retaining its U.N. seat.

58. In mid-summer, Dr. Martin Aliker reported that Uganda was lagging with only 150 students in North America compared to 1200 for Kenya and 365 for Tanganyika, and 103 students in Eastern Europe compared with 200 Tanganyikans and 500 Kenyans. *Uganda Argus*, July 31, 1963.

59. This has been tested. See T. M. Mills, "Power Relations in Three Person Groups," *American Sociological Review,* 18:351–357 (1953).

60. Michael Lofchie, "Party Conflict in Zanzibar," *Journal of Modern African Studies,* 1:185–207 (1963); *Report of a Commission of Inquiry into Disturbances in Zanzibar during June 1961,* Col. No. 353 (London, 1961), pp. 2–8. I am indebted to Michael Lofchie for help on Zanzibar.

61. Keith Kyle, "Gideon's Voices," "How it Happened," *The Spectator* (London), February 7 and 14, 1964, pp. 175, 202. *Reporter* (Nairobi), May 8, 1964.

62. Interviews: Othman Shariff, Aboud Jumbe and Jamal Ramadhan, February 18, 1963.

63. Muhammed Shamte, interview, November 18, 1963; A. A. Baalawy, interview, November 19, 1963.

64. *Uganda Argus*, August 1 and October 28, 1963; *Uganda Parliamentary Debates* (Hansard), September 27, 1963.

65. *Uganda Parliamentary Debates* (*Hansard*), July 12, 1963. See speeches by Paul Muwanga and Joseph Kiwanuka.

66. *Uganda Argus*, July 3, 1963. Similarly, Nekyon stated in reply to criticism in Parliament that federation was within the objectives of Addis Ababa. *Uganda Parliamentary Debates* (*Hansard*), July 12, 1963.

67. *Uganda Argus*, October 8 and 11, 1963. Yet Pafmeca's chairman, Kenneth Kaunda, endorsed East African federation as a "very good beginning of African unity" and denied that Northern Rhodesia wished to join at the beginning.

68. Why did not the Arab government in Zanzibar similarly seize upon the convenient Ghanaian interpretation to reconcile reluctance to federate with public commitment to Pan-Africanism? Said one former Zanzibar cabinet minister, "We could not say that. It is too obviously hypocritical. No one would believe us."

69. Ernst Haas and Allen Whiting, *The Dynamics of International Relations* (New York, 1956), p. 45; Kenneth Thompson, *Political Realism and the Crisis of World Politics* (Princeton, 1960), p. 37. Another notion of national interest that defines it according to community consensus is even more difficult to apply in Africa because of the problems of what "community consensus" means in states with three quarters of the population illiterate and with weak group structure.

70. *Tanganyika Standard,* December 10, 1962; *Kenya Weekly News,* May 17, 1963; *Uganda Argus,* October 9, 1963.

71. *Tanganyika Standard,* January 28, 1963; *East African Standard,* October 8, 1963.

72. *East African Standard,* June 21, 1963.

73. *Uganda Argus,* October 19, 1963; *Uganda Nation,* March 21, 1963.

74. *Uganda Argus,* August 29, 1960; interview, April 30, 1963; Grace Ibingira, interview, April 29, 1963.

75. See Victor D. DuBois, "Mali and Senegal and the Dakar-Niger Railroad," American Universities Field Staff Reports, West Africa Series, vol. VI, no. 4 (June 1963), pp. 1–10; Anthony M. O'Connor, "Rail Transport in the Economic Geography of Uganda," unpub. diss., Cambridge University, 1963, p. 321.

76. This is true despite a contrary statement by George Magezi that Uganda was prepared in the case of isolation. *Uganda Argus,* December 20, 1962.

77. These included a food gift for the Congo Army, harassment of Sudanese refugees in Uganda, and deportation of Rwanda's exiled Owami.

78. *East African Standard,* September 27, 1962; George Weeks, "The Armies of Africa," *Africa Report* (January 1964), pp. 7, 19.

79. *Uganda Argus,* October 9, 1963.

80. David Apter, *The Political Kingdom in Uganda* (Princeton, 1961), p. 309; J. S. Nye, "Attitudes of Makerere Students towards

East African Federation," *Proceedings of the East African Institute* (Kampala, 1963).

81. B. K. Kirya, interview, December 20, 1962; Dr. E. M. Muwazi, interview, November 19, 1962.

82. See *Uganda Argus,* July 3 and 22 and August 22, 1963; Ali Kisekka, interview, March 29, 1963; *Uganda Argus* and *Uganda Nation,* June 11, 1963.

83. Kenya, *Legislative Council Debates,* June 15, 1961.

84. Kenya, House of Representatives, *Official Report,* June 27, 1963.

85. See ECA, "The Economic Implications of East African Federation."

86. See A. L. Adu, "Staffing and Training the Federal Civil Service," University of East Africa Conference Paper, November 1963.

87. *East African Standard,* December 4, 1963.

88. Nor were Tanganyikan leaders acting from apprehension of instability in their army. They were caught by surprise by the mutiny of January 1964.

89. Interviews with Bryceson, February 6, 1963; Brown, February 28, 1963.

90. Interviews with the author except as otherwise noted.

91. *East African Standard,* June 7, 1963.

92. *Ibid.,* October 18, 1963.

93. *Uganda Argus,* September 28, 1963.

94. Nyerere, *East African Federation.*

CHAPTER VII: THE REJECTION OF ASSOCIATION WITH THE EEC

1. It was Nyerere's opinion in February 1963 that the EEC problem had been the only crisis in East African unity. Interview, February 13, 1963.

2. For example, Hartz relies on a long time period to show the impact of the liberal tradition in America rather than showing how it affected decisions in shorter time periods. Louis Hartz, *The Liberal Tradition in America* (New York, 1955).

3. *Tanganyika Standard,* August 4, 1962.

4. *East African Standard* August 29, 1962.

5. *Uganda Argus,* September 26, 1960.

6. *Tanganyika Standard,* November 25, 1961.

7. *East Africa and Rhodesia,* September 20, 1962.

8. *East African Standard,* September 20, 1962; *The Economist,* September 22, 1962.

9. *East African Standard,* September 19, 1962; for a very readable account, see Nora Beloff, *The General Says No* (London, 1963).

10. *The African Worker vs. European Common Market* (Accra, 1962); Vella Pillay, "Africa and the Common Market," *Spearhead* (Dar es Salaam), March 1962, p. 8.

11. See Gottfried Haberler, *International Trade and Economic Development* (Cairo, 1959).

12. *The Times* (London), November 24, 1962.

13. Jo W. Saxe, "The Problem of the Associated States" in R. R. Bowie and Theodore Geiger, *The European Economic Community and the United States,* prepared for the Joint Economic Committee, Congress of the United States, 87th Cong. 2nd. sess., (Washington, 1961), p. 54.

14. Vernon McKay, *Africa in World Politics* (New York, 1963), pp. 134–139.

15. EACSO, *Proceedings of the Central Legislative Assembly,* August 30, 1962.

16. Publishing Services of the European Communities, *Treaty Establishing the European Economic Community and Connected Documents,* Article 131.

17. *Convention of Association between the European Economic Community and the African and Malagasy States Associated with that Community,* Protocol 1, Article 4.

18. Saxe, "The Problem of the Associated States" (see n. 13 above), p. 57; *The Spectator* (London), October 12, 1962.

19. *Africa Digest,* 10:110 (December 1962); Saxe, *ibid.,* p. 56.

20. *The Economist* (London), July 27, 1963.

21. See Ali Mazrui, "African Attitudes to the European Economic Community," *International Affairs,* 39:24–36 (January 1963).

22. E. A. High Commission, 26th Meeting, March 24, 1958; 31st Meeting, November 23, 1960.

23. *Uganda Argus,* January 28, 1960.

24. Julius Nyerere, interview, February 13, 1963.

25. *Tanganyika Standard,* May 25, 1962.

26. Milton Obote, interview, April 30, 1963.

27. Tanganyika Information Services Press Release, September 2, 1962; information was bound to be only partial because the draft Convention of Association was still subject to further negotiation.

28. *Daily Nation,* September 7, 1962.

29. Obote promised a White Paper and a National Assembly decision upon his return. He later publicly justified his contrary decision by claiming that Britain wanted an immediate reply, though in private he has claimed that he was already opposed to association before he left but wanted to withold his opinion until he spoke to the West Africans (particularly Nigerians) and found out the details of association in London. *Uganda Argus,* August 29 and 30, 1962, September 27, 1962; Milton Obote, interview, April 30, 1963. In Uganda, at a final meeting of four ministers and three civil servants at the end of August, Obote did not object to a discussion of the possibility of a choice of even closer association on terms similar to those given to Greece.

30. *East African Standard,* September 8, 1962.

31. *Tanganyika Standard,* September 10, 1962.

32. *East Africa and Rhodesia* (London), September 20, 1962.

33. *The Times* (London), September 14, 1962.

34. *East African Standard,* September 14, 1962.

35. *Uganda Argus,* September 16 and 18, 1962; *East African Standard,* September 15 and 17, 1962.

36. *Uganda Argus,* September 18, 1962.

37. *Ibid.,* September 27, 1962.

38. *Africa Digest,* 10:111 (December 1962). Muliro's statement was slightly inaccurate. The figure "three-fourths" properly referred to trade done with countries affected by Britain's decision to join the EEC.

39. The Economist Intelligence Unit, *Three-Monthly Economic Review: East Africa,* No. 40 (December 1962), p. 4.

40. EACSO, *Proceedings of the Central Legislative Assembly,* August 30, 1962.

41. EACSO, *Economic and Statistical Review,* December 1962, Table D 3.

42. *Ibid.,* Table D 10.

43. *Reporter* (Nairobi), September 29, 1962; *Weekly News: Uganda,* September 28, 1962.

44. Sir Jock Campbell, "The West Indies: Can They Stand Alone?" *International Affairs*, 39:343 (July 1963).

45. *East African Standard*, December 7, 1962.

46. The Economist Intelligence Unit (see n. 39 above); and private conversations.

47. *The Economist* (London), March 2, 1962; Sir Wilfred Havelock, "Two Common Markets," *Weekly News* (Nakuru), April 19, 1963, p. 9.

48. *Tanganyika Standard*, June 21, 1963.

49. *East African Standard*, November 26, 1963.

50. *Ibid.*, December 7, 1962.

CHAPTER VIII: PAN-AFRICANISM AND AFRICAN INTEGRATION

1. Hans Gerth and C. W. Mills, eds. *From Max Weber* (New York, 1946), pp. 63–64.

2. United Nations Economic Commission for Africa, "Approaches to African Economic Integration" (mimeographed, May 1963).

3. See Claude S. Phillips Jr., "Nigeria and Pan-Africanism," *Ibadan*, October 1962, pp. 8–11.

4. Clyde Sanger, "Toward Unity in Africa," *Foreign Affairs*, 42: 275 (January 1964).

5. Amitai Etzioni, "European Unification: A Strategy of Change," *World Politics*, 16:50 (October 1963).

6. For example, see Nyerere's views in *East African and Rhodesia*, December 7, 1961, p. 7.

7. See Mboya in *East African Standard*, December 12, 1963; Rashidi Kawawa in *ibid.*, December 30, 1963.

8. D. K. Chisiza, *Africa—What Lies Ahead* (New York, 1962), p. 13.

9. K. C. Wheare, *Federal Government*, 3rd ed. (London, 1953), p. 37; see also Amatai Etzioni, "A Paradigm for the Study of Political Unification," *World Politics*, 15:61 (October 1962).

10. Chanan Singh, interview, July 20, 1963.

11. As we saw in Chapter I, both Padmore and the first All African Peoples' Conference considered regional federation the most likely means to African unity.

12. Mathias Ngobi quoted in *Uganda Argus*, November 28, 1963.

13. Deutsch refers to this as a "pluralistic security community" in

constrast to an "amalgamated security community." Karl Deutsch et al., *Political Community and the North Atlantic Area* (Princeton, 1957).

14. Quoted in Gerald Howson, "A Visit with Dr. Okpara," *Africa Report,* November 1962, p. 26.

15. Concessions were made to Uganda on financial arrangements, agriculture, and higher education, but not on capital, citizenship, labor, or the strength of the presidency in relation to the upper house. *Uganda Argus,* June 27, 1964.

Index

Index

CLA (Central Legislative Assembly), 85, 94, 131, 132, 134, 135–136, 163, 165, 182, 223, 230

Classes, social, 46, 71

Closer union movement, (1920's), 57, 88–93

Cohen, Sir Andrew, 104, 106

Cold War, 117, 194, 215, 216, 234, 246

Colonial Paper No. 191: 93, 96, 97

Colonial Paper No. 210: 94, 97, 277, n. 27

Colonialism: impact of, 8, 13; African views of, 34–35, 47–48, 215, 241; and Buganda, 50–51; and integration, 84–94

Commercial and Industrial Coordination Committee, 134–135, 152, 157

Committee for Economic Coordination, 165, 166

Common Man: and leaders, 27, 37; movement (Uganda), 109

Common Market: defined, 141; East African, 131, 138–160, 203, 207, 223, 224, 230, 284, n. 23; location of industry in, 155–158

Communications, 57–61, 66–69, 75–80, 83, 136–137; Committee, 135

Community: defined, 6, 84; small, 38; and tribe, 44; and communications, 60; and power structure, 84

Congo (Leopoldville), 19, 124, 168, 169, 201, 219

Constitutions: territorial, 129; proposed federal, 186, 190–191, 193, 297, n. 15; Kenya, 187; Uganda, 202

Convention of Associations, 87

Corfield Report, 114

Currency Board, East African, 141–142

Customs union, 141–142

de Gaulle, Charles, 19

Decision-makers: motives of, 5, 207–210, 240–242

Decision-making: traditional, 38; EACSO, 134–135, 166–167, 168, 287, n. 61; and federation, 183–184, 189–191; EEC association, 220–230; and groups, 229

Defense, 137, 161; pact, 183, 201; Ugandan, 201; and integration, 246

Delamere, Lord, 57, 89

Democracy: and Pan-Africanism, 37

Democratic Party (Uganda), 22, 107–109; and federation, 176, 180

Deutsch, Karl, 28

Development, economic, 71–73; and integration, 20, 25, 61; planning, 153–155; and national interests, 199; and federation, 205

Diallo, Abdoulaye, 125

Disintegration, 275, n. 58. *See also* Spillback

EACSO (East African Common Services Organization): 14–15, 119, 126, 130–138, 177, 245; Authority, 131, 182, 223, 228; bureaucracy, 132–133, 136, 137, 138, 164–167; ministerial committees, 134–135; Secretary-General, 132, 135, 136, 170; Budget, 136–138; revenue, 284, n. 20; Economic Advisor, 155; and federation, 208; and EEC, 220, 222

East Africa Protectorate, 86–87

East African Airways, 136–137, 160–161

East African Association, 112

East African Federation, 104, 122, 125, 126, 246; early attempts at, 84, 88–91; Nairobi declaration of intent, 3, 4, 189, 209, 242, 246, 265, n. 2; 1963 attempt, 175–210, 246–251; Nkrumah's view of, 16; and KAU, 115; and public opinion, 26–27, 175–176; and regionalism, 41; decision to federate, 57–58, 183–184; negotiations, 183–188; role of Pan-Africanism,

Index

causation, 51–55, 209–210, 211–212, 239–242; defined, 25, 29–30; and facts, 44, 239–242; Pan-Africanism as, 48–51; and interest groups, 52–54, 177–179, 247; and national interest, 195, 203, 204, 207, 209–210, 246–251

Imperialism, 47–50

Income per capita, 72; within Uganda, 103; Kenya, 204

Independence: and cooperation, 139, 140, 169; and federation, 181, 184

Industrial Council, 156, 166

Industrial licensing, 94, 155–157

Industry, 72–73, 145–148; and integration, 18, 20, 243; location of, 155–158, 192, 200, 203, 205

Integration, vii, 151, 169–171; levels, 248; theories of, 17–20, 25–28, 249–251; European theory, 18; African, 243–251; and ideology, 25–28; social, defined, 60; social and political, 60, 83; political, defined, 84; and national-building, 85–86; Tanganyikan, 102; Ugandan, 110. *See also* Economic Integration

Jamal, Amir, 184

Japan, 152–153

Johnston, Sir Harry, 86, 88

Joint Select Committee on Closer Union, 57, 70, 91

Kabaka (of Buganda), 51, 104–106, 185, 187; and federation, 189, 202

Kadu (Kenya African Democratic Union), 47, 95, 111, 115–116, 228; and federation, 180, 204

Kahama, George, 39, 156, 224, 230, 238

Kakonge, John, 182, 184, 191

Kalema, William, 109

Kalubya, Serwano, 68

Kamaliza, Michael, 128, 178, 179

Kamba, the, 112, 117, 118

Kambona, Oscar, 37, 47, 100, 119, 133, 177, 180, 184, 186, 208

Kanu (Kenya African National Union), 47, 95, 110–111, 115–119, 120–121, 129, 282, n. 106; and federation, 180, 188, 204; and EEC, 228

Kariuki, Josiah, 114

KAU (Kenya African Union), 97, 113, 115, 227, n. 37, 281, n. 92

Kaunda, Kenneth, 126, 196, 291, n. 67

Kavirondo Taxpayers' Welfare Association, 112

Kawawa, Rashidi, 37, 46, 151, 178, 182, 183, 199, 208, 213, 223–227, 237, 238, 240, 242

Kenya, viii; geography, 61–62; population, 63–66; language, 68–69; groups in, 22–24; cabinet, 33; Northern Frontier District, 45, 183, 204; education, 63, 80–82, 291, n. 58; economy, 73, 143–149; urbanization, 74; communications, 76, 77–80; nationalist movement, 110–119; construction, 129; and economic cooperation, 138–140, 151–170; and federation, 180, 189, 191–193, 203–204, 208; national interest, 203–204; and EEC, 212, 220–230, 239–240

Kenya African Study Union. *See* KAU

Kenya Federation of Labor (KFL), 24, 189

Kenya National Party, 115

Kenyatta, Jomo, 31, 95, 97, 113–114, 116, 117, 134; view of history, 35; African unity, 40; and federation, 183, 187, 188, 190, 208, 290, n. 47

Khamisi, Francis, 96–97, 123

Kiano, Julius, 41, 43–44, 168

Kibaki, Mwai, 41, 211, 217, 230, 232, 240

Kikuyu, the, 44, 63, 69, 99, 103, 111, 112, 113–115, 116–118, 129

Kikuyu Association, 111

Kikuyu Central Association, 95, 112–113

Index

Index

Publications Written under the Auspices of the
Center for International Affairs
Harvard University

Created in 1958, the Center for International Affairs fosters advanced study of basic world problems by scholars from various disciplines and senior officials from many countries. The research at the Center focuses on economic and social development, the management of force in the modern world, and the evolving roles of Western Europe and the Communist bloc. The published results appear here in the order in which they have been issued. The research programs are supervised by Professors Robert R. Bowie (Director of the Center), Hollis B. Chenery, Samuel P. Huntington, Alex Inkeles, Henry A. Kissinger, Edward S. Mason, Thomas C. Schelling, and Raymond Vernon.

Books

The Soviet Bloc, by Zbigniew K. Brzezinski (jointly with the Russian Research Center), 1960. Harvard University Press.

The Necessity for Choice, by Henry A. Kissinger, 1961. Harper & Bros.

Strategy and Arms Control, by Thomas C. Schelling and Morton H. Halperin, 1961. Twentieth Century Fund.

Rift and Revolt in Hungary, by Ferenc A. Váli, 1961. Harvard University Press.

United States Manufacturing Investment in Brazil, by Lincoln Gordon and Engelbert L. Grommers, 1962. Harvard Business School.

The Economy of Cyprus, by A. J. Meyer, with Simos Vassiliou (jointly with the Center for Middle Eastern Studies), 1962. Harvard University Press.

Entrepreneurs of Lebanon, by Yusif A. Sayigh (jointly with the Center for Middle Eastern Studies), 1962. Harvard University Press.

Communist China 1955–1959: Policy Documents with Analysis, with a Foreword by Robert R. Bowie and John K. Fairbank (jointly with the East Asian Research Center), 1962. Harvard University Press.

In Search of France, by Stanley Hoffmann, Charles P. Kindleberger, Laurence Wylie, Jesse R. Pitts, Jean-Baptiste Duroselle, and François Goguel, 1963. Harvard University Press.

Somali Nationalism, by Saadia Touval, 1963. Harvard University Press.

The Dilemma of Mexico's Development, by Raymond Vernon, 1963. Harvard University Press.

Limited War in the Nuclear Age, by Morton H. Halperin, 1963. John Wiley & Sons.

The Arms Debate, by Robert A. Levine, 1963. Harvard University Press.

Africans on the Land, by Montague Yudelman, 1964. Harvard University Press.

Counterinsurgency Warfare, by David Galula, 1964. Frederick A. Praeger, Inc.

People and Policy in the Middle East, by Max Weston Thornburg, 1964. W. W. Norton & Co.

Shaping the Future, by Robert R. Bowie, 1964. Columbia University Press.

Foreign Aid and Foreign Policy, by Edward S. Mason (jointly with the Council on Foreign Relations, 1964. Harper & Row.

Public Policy and Private Enterprise in Mexico, by M. S. Wionczek, D. H. Shelton, C. P. Blair, and R. Izquierdo, ed. Raymond Vernon, 1964. Harvard University Press.

How Nations Negotiate, by Fred Charles Iklé, 1964. Harper & Row.

China and the Bomb, by Morton H. Halperin (jointly with the East Asian Research Center), 1965. Frederick A. Praeger, Inc.

Democracy in Germany, by Fritz Erler (Jodidi Lectures), 1965. Harvard University Press.

The Troubled Partnership, by Henry A. Kissinger (jointly with the Council on Foreign Relations), 1965. McGraw-Hill Book Co.

The Rise of Nationalism in Central Africa, by Robert I. Rotberg, 1965. Harvard University Press.

Communist China and Arms Control, by Morton H. Halperin and Dwight H. Perkins (jointly with the East Asian Research Center), 1965. Frederick A. Praeger, Inc.

Pan-Africanism and East African Integration, by Joseph S. Nye, Jr., 1965. Harvard University Press.

Occasional Papers, Published by the
Center for International Affairs

1. *A Plan for Planning: The Need for a Better Method of Assisting Underdeveloped Countries on Their Economic Policies,* by Gustav F. Papanek, 1961.

2. *The Flow of Resources from Rich to Poor,* by Alan D. Neale, 1961.

3. *Limited War: An Essay on the Development of the Theory and an Annotated Bibliography,* by Morton H. Halperin, 1962.

4. *Reflections on the Failure of the First West Indian Federation,* by Hugh W. Springer, 1962.

5. *On the Interaction of Opposing Forces under Possible Arms Agreements,* by Glenn A. Kent, 1963.

6. *Europe's Northern Cap and the Soviet Union,* by Nils Örvik, 1963.

7. *Civil Administration in the Punjab: An Analysis of a State Government in India,* by E. N. Mangat Rai, 1963.

8. *On the Appropriate Size of a Development Program,* by Edward S. Mason, 1964.

9. *Self-Determination Revisited in the Era of Decolonization,* by Rupert Emerson, 1964.

10. *The Planning and Execution of Economic Development in Southeast Asia,* by Clair Wilcox, 1965.

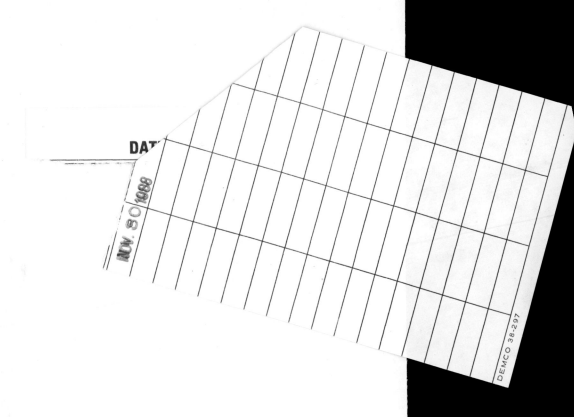